Encircled

Stories of Mennonite Women

by Ruth Unrau

Faith and Life Press
Newton, Kansas

Copyright © 1986 by Faith and Life Press, Newton, Kansas 67114
Printed in the United States of America
Library of Congress Number 86-80403
International Standard Book Number 0-87303-114-8

This publication may not be reproduced, stored in a retrieval system, or transmitted in whole or in part, in any form by any means, electronic, mechanical, photocopying, recording, or otherwise without prior written permission of Faith and Life Press.

Photo sources: Mennonite Library and Archives, North Newton, Kansas, pp. 16, 42, 72, 136, 206, 214, 234, 256; Huldah Stauffer, p. 8; Naomi Lehman, Berne, Indiana, p. 28; MLA and Florence Diller, Bluffton, Ohio, p. 34; Lubin Jantzen, Newton, Kansas, p. 54; Muriel Thiessen Stackley, Newton, Kansas, and Helen Coon, Deer Creek, Oklahoma, p. 62; John Gundy, Normal, Illinois, p. 84; Carl Smucker, Bluffton, Ohio, p. 94; MLA and Vernelle Waltner, North Newton, Kansas, p. 102; Lavera Hill, p. 116; *The Mennonite*, Newton, Kansas, pp. 116, 262; Clare Anne Hefflebower, Reedley, California, p. 126; Christine Purves, Bluffton, Ohio, p. 148; Evangeline Hiebert, North Newton, Kansas, p. 164; Richard Pannabecker, Bluffton, Ohio, p. 176; Robert Kreider, North Newton, Kansas, p. 186; Florence Fluck, Quakertown, Pennsylvania, p. 196; *Daily Intelligencer*, Doylestown, Pennsylvania, p. 196; Alice Loewen, North Newton, Kansas, p. 226; Margarethe Rempel, Leamington, Ontario, p. 244; Marie Janzen, Newton, Kansas, and MLA, p. 262; Hans E. Epp, Filadelfia, Paraguay, p. 274; Anna Ens, Winnipeg, p. 284; Howard Raid, Bluffton, Ohio, p. 298; Helen Friesen, Butterfield, Minnesota, p. 308; MLA and Esther Wenger, Newton, Kansas, p. 318; Lydia Penner, Amsterdam, p. 324; Rachel Kreider, Goshen, Indiana, p. 330.

Design by John Hiebert

Printing by Mennonite Press, Inc.

As for us, we have this large crowd of witnesses around us. So then, let us rid ourselves of everything that gets in the way, and of the sin which holds on to us so tightly, and let us run with determination the race that lies before us. Let us keep our eyes fixed on Jesus on whom our faith depends from beginning to end. He did not give up because of the cross! On the contrary, because of the joy that was waiting for him, he thought nothing of the disgrace of dying on the cross, and he is now seated at the right side of God's throne..

Hebrews 12:1-2, Today's English Version

Contents

The Writer's Journal 1

1. A Hardy Indiana Pioneer
   Verena Sprunger Lehman (1828—1913)
   by Naomi Lehman 9
2. Sister for the Household
   Hillegonda Cornelia van der Smissen (1848—1949) 15
3. With Open Arms for Children
   Magdalena Neuenschwander Sprunger (1855—1931)
   by Naomi Lehman 27
4. Grand Lady of Bluffton College
   Emelie Siemens Hamm Mosiman (1863—1953) 33
5. Helper in the Cheyenne Cause
   Bertha Elise Kinsinger Petter (1872—1967) 43
6. Knowing the Power of Prayer
   Anna Wiebe Jantzen (1875—1939) 55
7. Evangelist in Chicago
   Katharine Kroeker Wiens (1878—1946)
   by Helen Neufeld Coon 61
8. Builder of a Healing Community
   Frieda Marie Kaufman (1883—1944) 73
9. Generous by Nature
   Clara Louise Strubhar Gundy (1885—1979) 85

10. Trusting During Hard Times
    Mary Jane Stauffer Ebersole Smucker (1886—1971) 95
11. She Remembered Missions
    Susanna Theresa Nickel Schroeder (1888—1966) 101
12. Always Curious About the World
    M'Della Moon (1890—1963)............................115
13. Intrepid Traveler and Teacher
    Emma Mary Ruth (1891—1965) 125
14. Her Father's Daughter
    Elva Agnes Krehbiel Leisy (1891—1982).................135
15. Her Faith Could Smile
    Martha Lena Baumgartner Habegger (1892—1983) 149
16. Bonding White and Hopi People
    Polingaysi Qoyawayma (Elizabeth Q. White) (1892—   ) ..163
17. Prayer—Her Most Important Work
    Sylvia Tschantz Pannabecker (1893—1979) 177
18. Keeper of the Network
    Stella Rosella Shoemaker Kreider (1893—1977)
    by Robert Kreider 185
19. Gifts Given to God
    Florence White Fluck (1894—   )
    by Mary Lou Cummings 195
20. Making Art Respectable
    Lena Waltner (1895—   ) 205
21. To India with Love
    Christena Harder Duerksen (1896—1984) 213
22. Letting the Children Sing
    Ruth Krehbiel Jacobs (1897—1960) 227
23. Scholar of Life and the Human Spirit
    Honora Elizabeth Becker (1899—1982) 235
24. Shattered but Not Destroyed
    Margarethe Willms Rempel (1901—   ) 243
25. Saying Yes to Need
    Caroline Banwar Theodore (1901—1952).................255
26. Serving Where Needed
    Wilhelmina Kuyf (1901—1967).........................261
27. Strong Woman in the Chaco
    Katharina Ratzlaff Epp (1902—1984) 275
28. Singing the Lord's Song in Foreign Lands
    Anna Enns Epp (1902—1958) 285

29. Her Husband's Partner
    Pauline Krehbiel Raid (1907—1984).....................299
30. Breaking Through Her Prison of Pain
    Amanda Dahlenburg Friesen (1909—1982)
    by Helen Friesen..307
31. Reader of the Cheyenne Scriptures
    Julia Yellow Horse Shoulderblade (1913—1973)...........317
32. Finding New Forms for Christian Witness
    Margreet Stubbe (1926—   )
    by Lydia Penner 325
33. The Modern Victorian
    Sara Kathryn Kreider Hartzler (1943—1982)..............331

Index..341

The Writers 351

The Writer's Journal

I am asked by the Commission on Education of the General Conference Mennonite Church to collect the stories of thirty women who have made a significant contribution to the community and the church. I am given a long list of names. The women to be included in the collection are no longer living.

This book is to be a sequel to *Full Circle*, a collection of women's stories published in 1978. It is to be partially funded by a grant from the Schowalter Foundation.

I find a desk in the library, turn to the typewritten manuscript *Remembering* by Elva Krehbiel Leisy and immediately I become involved in the families, communities, and churches in which she lived. I go enthusiastically from Elva to Bertha to Christena, immersed in church history from the women's perspective. Church history from the women's perspective is not, however, the focus of this book. Here we are simply telling short stories of women of the church.

Following the leads

That was the way it started. This is not to say there were no low points. I looked through the thirteen archival boxes of correspondence and diaries of one of the women wishing that she had written about more than weather and funerals.

I followed all the leads in footnotes of already published material.

Often the story of a wife was found between the lines of the story of her husband.

A kind Providence allowed me to stumble upon information. While looking for Willa, I came across Caroline. While looking at the *Mennonite Women's Calendar*, I came across Verena, a minister's wife who had pounded a nail into her husband's wine barrel.

I ignored some of the guidelines. Not every woman belonged to the General Conference Mennonite Church. Margreet, the Dutch pastor, has no label because Dutch Mennonites are not divided into conferences. A few of the women are still living, although most of these have retired.

When possible, these articulate women speak for themselves.

Those women who wrote down their stories have let us examine what it was like to grow up in Berne, Indiana, in the mid-1800s; in Mountain Lake, Minnesota, in the early 1900s; in Russia, during the Revolution.

The stories are arranged chronologically. Note that Margarethe in Russia, Caroline in India, and Willa in Pennsylvania were born in the same year, within three months of each other, but with little in common except their Christian faith.

Ministers' wives

Not surprisingly, more than half, twenty of the women, were wives of ministers. By tradition, the minister's wife was expected to create a home to which her husband could retreat from the tension of his duties. She was also expected to be the spiritual leader of the women of the congregation, a model in dress and deportment, and the mother of ministers and of ministers' wives.

The church recognized her gifts of cooking, sewing, home management, nursing, and childhood education. It never asked if she had gifts for or interest in questions of doctrine or in the administration of a church. She was often told that as she counseled her husband she had immense power behind the scenes.

Did these ministers' wives ever yearn to preach or to be ordained? I found no written record that they did. I found no record of ordination of a woman in the General Conference Mennonite Church between that of Ann Allebach in 1911 and of the several who were ordained in the 1970s.

Missionary women

But some women found an alternative to being ordained for preaching in the local church: ordination for the mission field.

The nineteenth-century missionary, as commonly thought of during that period, was a man in a black suit preaching to awestruck natives. But more than half of those missionaries were women who complemented the man's preaching with their own work. Mennonite women were not criticized for ambitions to share in the work of their husbands, as women were in some other denominations. And single women found places on the mission field doing the same tasks as the male missionaries: teaching, preaching when needed, and healing.

Isabella Thoburn, led to India by one of God's coincidences, said:

> We have found sickness and poverty to relieve, widows to protect, advice to be given in every possible difficulty or emergency, teachers and Bible women to be trained, houses to be built, cattle to be bought, gardens to be planted, and accounts to be kept and rendered. We have found use for every faculty, natural and acquired, that we possessed, and have coveted all that we lacked.[1]

What woman, single or married, restless with unused abilities, could not be stirred by such a challenge? Many of the women who yearned for foreign fields prayed their children into mission work. The mission field held more status and excitement, and more opportunity for reaching people with the gospel than teaching, nursing, or maid's work at home. No stereotype confined these missionary women. Some were colorful, brash, and committed. Some were quiet, unassuming, and committed.

Winifred Mathews says, "Perhaps no form of witness is more fruitful than that of the Christian home in the non-Christian world. . . . If [women missionaries] had not worked among the women while their husbands taught the men, the churches established as a result of the men's work would have lacked depth and permanence."[2]

Qualities in common

Do women have to be ministers' wives or missionaries to have their stories told? Obviously not. These were all church women who found the basis for their faith in the faith of their parents and grandparents. Many of them had moving experiences of conversion and baptism. The church offered an outlet for their energies and a worthy focus for their commitment.

These women had a number of other common experiences. Many of them had to deal with grief. They wrote letters full of heartbreak back to their families in Russia or Indiana or Minnesota. They lost more children by disease than today's mothers, but their grief was no less intense for each child. They were touched by terror; they saw people killed; one of

---

1. Janet Wilson James, ed., *Women in American Religion* (Philadelphia: University of Pennsylvania Press, 1980), p. 177.
2. *Dauntless Women* (New York: Friendship Press, 1947), pp. 2-3.

them was raped. Fifteen of the twenty-three who were married became widows. Many were victims of the poverty of the Great Depression. But tragedy was only a part, not all, of life. Each of them was determined to survive, and their accounts are remarkably free of bitterness. Almost all of them were pioneers in some sense of the word as they blazed trails for others to follow.

Surprisingly, in the midst of tragedy and poverty, most of them display a sense of humor: Sister Frieda as she watches her staff starch the janitor's handkerchiefs and Martha as she contemplates her old age. To quote Frederick Buechner, "[Laughter] comes from as deep a place as tears come from, and in a way it comes from the same place."

The women's network

In their memoirs, these women often expressed appreciation for their teachers and pastors. Most often, they were part of a women's network. They had grandmothers, mothers, aunts, sisters, and friends from whom they learned to handle the tragedies and celebrations of living. (Sometimes bit players were just as interesting as the principals in these dramas. Sara Cornelia, mother of Hillegonda, deserves her own story.)

The married women in this book usually had large families. However, we cannot call them full-time mothers. They had egg and milk and garden businesses. As wives of ministers, they kept the equivalent of hotels as they entertained church guests and visiting churchmen. Some of them were midwives. These women never complained that they had no one to talk to but their children. Neighbors visited and customers came by. Nor did they feel their children were neglected when left with aunts and grandparents. A number of women said they were raised by older sisters.

They found their roles less sharply defined from those of their husbands than those their granddaughters were to experience. On the farm, husband and wife were often partners. "I liked to help with the harvest," Clara said. Even in family businesses, the wife often helped out. These women understood the woman in Proverbs who had business sense, was a good manager, was openhanded to the poor and needy. They did not, for the most part, think in terms of having a career outside the home; but quite a number found outlets for their creative energies. We may have thought of Mennonite women being even more quiet in the land than Mennonite men. But here we find Sylvia and Wilhelmina in the middle of China overrun by Communists, Clara co-directing a retirement home, and Bertha conducting funerals on an Indian reservation.

A few differences

There are differences among these women. There is disparity of education, some terminating even before grade eight, but at least one receiving a doctorate. They all seem to have had intellectual curiosity. Elva was the only Mennonite woman who could be called a peace activist in her generation, writing a chapter in her father's book with a particularly telling argument for women's involvement in the peace movement; but most of them were quiet pacifists. A few plunged into unconventional careers compared to those of their sisters: M'Della into the man's world of science, Lena into art. They were even different in their regard for womanly tasks: note Willa's aversion to cooking and liberated Sister Frieda's fondness for it.

Most of these women lived in an era when the line of authority was firmly established from God to the husband to the wife. Most of these women felt nourished and cherished by their husbands and fathers. However, we should not assume that all church women enjoyed a benign paternalism. There was a dark side to this authoritarianism. One church leader said:

> When Father died, I realized how Mother had suffered under that [patriarchal] system. She had kept her suffering to herself all the years of her marriage. But once she could trust herself to talk about it, she told how she tried to keep abreast of financial transactions that were never shared; how she sought to influence decisions without appearing to do so . . . how she did not even tell father about [five spontaneous abortions] because he might be angry. I knew then that she had suffered much more than we ever realized. Actually they both suffered. They were caught in a structure under which neither was really free.[3]

Saints on pedestals

Some women come to us through the mists of history firmly established on pedestals. Others, still in living memory, are not so well placed, but had special gifts that invite our admiration in spite of their human flaws. We often find the latter group more helpful to us in finding our way.

The women we read about are usually more saintly than the ones we talk about. I was to hear more than once: "Let me tell you something amusing about my aunt. But of course you can't print it." One of my missionary friends said, tongue in cheek, "The missionaries of the past

---

3. Diana Brandt, ed., *Being Brothers and Sisters* (Newton, Kansas: Faith and Life Press, 1984), p. viii.

were more saintly than the ones we know today." Children often hesitate to name the faults of their mothers, or perhaps with the passing of time, they forget the flaws.

Frederick Buechner, in explaining the meaning of the communion of saints, proposes that those who have gone before are saints "in the sense that through them something of the power and richness of life itself not only touched us once long ago, but continues to touch us."[4]

Women writing history

Why a book about General Conference Mennonite women? We acknowledge that women influence society. We hear often that behind every successful man is a woman of influence. So who were these women who stood in the shadow of our church leaders? Do we subscribe to the cliché that women can adequately express themselves through their husbands? Here we are giving women the opportunity to express themselves in their own voices.

We need history books written by women. Up to now, men have written history to meet their own needs and to satisfy their own curiosities. They have defined what women's roles in the church should be. However, we need to see the world from the woman's point of view. She was there when the church divided. She was there when a conference had its first meeting. While they prepared food for the church leaders, women listened and made judgments. Would that more of them had written down their observations.

Herta Funk asked in the Foreword of *Full Circle*, "What has history so far said about women, about women of faith, or about Mennonite women?" We should hear from many more of them. Let daughters (and sons) write their mothers' stories, and let daughters write their own stories. Shirley Abbott says: "One of those attitudes—to me a beatitude—is the conviction that the past matters, that history weighs on us and refuses to be forgotten by us, and that the worst poverty women—or men—can suffer is to be bereft of their past."[5]

In gratitude

Finally, I want to acknowledge my debts. The largest are owed to the Mennonite Library and Archives, North Newton, Kansas, and the Mennonite Historical Library, Bluffton, Ohio. David Haury, Laurie Wolfe, Harvey Hiebert, Delbert Gratz, and their staffs pointed me in the right

---

4. *The Sacred Journey* (New York: Harper and Row, 1982), p. 22.
5. *Womenfolks* (New York: Ticknor and Fields, 1983), p. 210.

directions. Rosemary Moyer found photographs. Rachel Waltner Goossen, especially, and many others, read chapters and made suggestions. And thanks to all the relatives and friends of these women who gave information and pictures. I often heard the statement, "She was such a wonderful woman." (I even considered naming this book Wonderful Women.)

I owe a debt to these women. Each taught me something, and not just about the church. They translated statistics into people. Frank Epp tells us in *Mennonites in Canada, 1920-1940* that 20,201 people moved from Russia to Canada between 1923 and 1930. The story of his mother who emigrated in 1924 gave substance to that bit of information. The love of these women for the church was obvious. Their love for people as individuals was far reaching. Such women!

Finally, I thank the other women writers and the token man who contributed to the collection. Their names appear with their stories.

RUTH UNRAU

Verena Lehman: Some years she knitted the the sewing society's entire assignment of stockings, always red, for the Indians.

1.
A Hardy Indiana Pioneer

Verena Sprunger Lehman
1828—1913

by Naomi Lehman

Verena Sprunger was born into a devout Swiss Mennonite home on the Muensterberg in Switzerland on November 1, 1828. Her long life was to be one of strenuous pioneering, deprivation, and often loneliness.

But she had spunk. She once killed a deer for food, walked ten miles to fetch a precious jug of molasses, and in the interests of temperance, hammered a nail in her husband's wine barrel.

Even as a child, she learned that life was not easy. The children had to take an active part in raising crops on the stony soil of the mountainside and learn various crafts and trades in the home to make ends meet. Mennonites were forbidden by the government to live close to cities or to farm the better land in the valleys. They were considered dangerous, a threat to the stability of the Swiss government. For years, their nonresistant position, refusal to baptize their infants, and noncooperation with the state church had brought them harassment and persecution.

Honeymoon in the Swiss mountains

When Verena was fifteen, her mother died, leaving her father Abraham with five children. Verena, as the oldest daughter, was responsible for taking charge of the home. In 1846, at age eighteen, she married Peter S. Lehman, a young school teacher. The young couple moved into a "honeymoon cottage" at the foot of a mountain on a piece of ground owned by her father. It was, however, not an ideal place to live, as often in winter they never saw the sun for weeks and for long periods never saw another person. They felt isolated and lonely indeed.

In July 1848, her husband Peter was chosen by lot for the ministry. For a long time he resisted the call, but then, after affirmation by another minister, decided to accept this as a call from God. The couple was able to leave their depressing home and move to a more attractive place.

We can only speculate about Verena's life as a minister's wife in Switzerland. Perhaps she needed to help more with the raising of crops than with pastoral duties and to encourage and support her husband who sometimes suffered from anxiety and depression. Two little girls had been born to them by 1850.

Coming to the wilds of Indiana

In the meantime her father, Abraham, had remarried, and his wife gave birth to Samuel F. Sprunger who was later to become a minister in Berne, Indiana, and a leader of the General Conference Mennonite Church. Abraham's second wife died in 1850. He then turned his eyes toward America, a country that allowed freedom of worship and offered more economic opportunities.

In March 1852, with his entire family, including daughter Verena and her husband and two small daughters, he sailed to America along with about twenty other families from the Muensterberg. The dangerous forty-day ocean voyage and the long, hard journey inland must have tested the courage and optimism of the immigrants.

On arriving in Adams County, Indiana, near the present town of Berne, the Lehmans bought 160 acres of land, only twenty of which had been cleared. Peter said, "Indiana was so wild—one has to see to believe it . . . . There were two tiny log cabins, very poor. One would have pitied chickens if they did not have a warmer house in winter. I said we could not live long in such a hut, that soon I would make a better one—but we were in this house for several years."[1]

The young mother struggled against many odds during those years. Peter became ill with malaria the first fall and was unable to work for a long time. The next year, he was chosen by lot to be an elder, but later that year became ill with dropsy. He wrote in his autobiography, "What a life in that miserable little hut. And what a winter for my dear wife caring for me night and day with two children. And on top of that, she gave birth to little Rachel on November 10, 1853."

1. *Chronik der Familie Lehmann*, p. 12.

Howling wolves in the timber land

Verena often spoke about her early experiences, and one of her younger daughters, Dina Lehman Welty, wrote those memories down.

> Sister Anna was only four years old, and Marianna two, when they moved here. Mother often told us of the wolves in the timber land. Since it was necessary for her to help Father clear the land, they had to lock the two little girls inside the cabin as they feared that the wolves might devour them even though she and Father were only a short distance away. Some nights they got very little sleep because of the constant howling of the wolves. . . .
>
> At one time little Anna's hand was badly bitten by a rat when she tried to pick up a piece of bread that she had dropped. The rat reached through a large crack in the floor. The hand got very sore and inflamed and they feared that she might lose it, but it finally healed.[2]

Of the birth of Rachel, Dina wrote, "Mother often said that Rachel entered the world in almost as poor conditions as Christ did. The day before Rachel's arrival, Mother made a small box from clapboards (long hand-hewn shingles) that had been left when the cabin was built. This was the bed for the baby when it arrived."

About the time when Verena began to have hopes of a better dwelling, Peter fell and broke his right leg while helping a neighbor build his house. Again he was "chained" to his bed for several weeks. About five years after their arrival in Adams County, the new log cabin was finally built, and although Verena was happy, her joy was dimmed somewhat by the difficult time she had had with a severe siege of malaria. It seems that even her strong constitution finally gave way to the plague which haunted the pioneers. Her husband said, "That Mama is lame in her limbs is no wonder. Many could not have endured what she suffered through."

The Civil War brought problems and sorrow into the small Mennonite colony. Both Peter and Verena were staunch believers in the Anabaptist doctrine of nonresistance, but a few of the flock were not. Other disagreements developed in the church and the fellowship and unity of the congregation were seriously disrupted.

Pioneers again in Missouri

In 1868, Peter sold his land near Berne, even the timber that was ready for building a new house. Vowing never to return to Berne to live, he and his

---

2. Bonnie Lehman Sprunger has a copy of Dina's recollections.

family, with as many other relatives and friends as could be convinced, moved to Hickory County in southwestern Missouri to begin a new Mennonite church there. At that time, Verena's brother, twenty-year-old Samuel F. Sprunger, was called to serve the Berne church as one of its ministers.

By this time, Verena and Peter's two oldest children were married. Their youngest child was three-month-old Emma. The trip was not an easy one for mothers and babies. They traveled about forty miles by horse-drawn wagon to Fort Wayne and then by train to Missouri, taking with them as many of their possessions as possible. It is believed that there was not one word of complaint from Verena all through this ordeal. She gave birth to one more daughter in Missouri. She was a grandmother many times over.

Again the Lehmans were pioneers in a new land. Daughter Dina wrote, "The place that Father bought had a one-room cabin and loft, with an unfinished board shell, lean-to kitchen which had no foundation nor was it plastered. The log cabin had a foundation but the lean-to was only on stilts and had a porous roof."

Shingling by the sign of the moon

Verena was a wonderful gardener. Her vegetable and herb gardens were beautiful year after year. She grew many varieties of medicinal herbs and knew what each one was good for. The attic hung full of them and many years passed by without the family's need of a doctor. She always planted in the right sign of the moon.

When they built a new barn in Missouri, everything had to be hand-hewn; the shingles were all made from one tree. As Peter started to shingle the barn, Verena cautioned him to wait a day or two for the right sign of the moon, warning him that shingles would warp and turn up if he nailed them that day. This amused Peter but did not stop him. After he had finished one side of the roof and started the second side, the moon was in the right cycle. To Peter's chagrin, the shingles on the first side did indeed curve up while those on the other side remained flat. The shingles were all made from the same tree and Peter could find no reason for the phenomenon.

In spite of hard work, the little colony did not thrive. The nearest market for their produce was sixty miles away; crops failed due to drought and insects. One by one the families moved back to Indiana or elsewhere. The Hickory County church, known as the Elkton congregation, was never more than thirty members. Too small and too far away from a sister congregation, by 1890 it was down to eighteen members and was discontinued.[3]

Red stockings for the Indians

At last, in 1893, Peter and Verena themselves moved back to Berne, purchased a home in town and retired there. In 1896, they observed their fiftieth wedding anniversary and their children and grandchildren surprised them with an impressive celebration.[4]

Peter died suddenly in February 1899 from a severe stroke. Verena moved to the country to live for fourteen more years with one of her daughters. As always, she made good use of her time. Reading the Bible or Spurgeon's sermons, knitting for the Indians of Arizona and Oklahoma, and raising house plants were her chief delights.

Some years she knitted the *Naehverein*'s entire assignment of stockings, always red, for the Indians. She was sure they liked red best. A granddaughter who is now in her nineties, recalls that grandmother would wash them, hang them on a line on the porch to dry, perhaps thirty to forty pairs at a time, then press them. During her last illness in 1913, she was able to finish only one of a pair of the red socks. It was found in her knitting basket after her death.

Verena loved flowers and had many house plants, starting them in empty tin cans decorated with wallpaper scraps. She showed her thrift and ingenuity by using cooked oatmeal scrapings for her glue.

A woman of spirit

One might conclude that Verena's life and experiences were similar to those of many other pioneer women. In some aspects, that is true, but Verena had spirit and determination not found in some of her peers.

She was in the forefront of those who believed in temperance, even abstinence from alcoholic drinks. Living in a time when every household made its own wine and always kept a keg ready for use, she found her position difficult. But once she hammered a nail into the Lehman wine barrel. After most of the wine had seeped out, she told her husband that the keg was leaking.

Whoever could have guessed that once, when she came unexpectedly upon a deer caught by the horns in a bush, her hands could do what they did. The struggling deer looked at her in fright. She looked back at it.

---

3. Samuel F. Pannabecker, *Faith in Ferment* (Newton, Kansas: Faith and Life Press, 1968), pp. 88 and 198.
4. *Chronik*, p. 16.

"Meat for the table," she thought, and drove a knife into the neck of the captive animal.

In her later years, Verena broke a hip which was never set properly. It gave her much pain for the remainder of her life. A special chair was prepared for her which made her more comfortable at home. However, she never missed a communion service in her church even though the hard benches caused her much pain.

A singing family

Music meant much to her. In the early church in Berne, when her husband was pastor, singing was simple, but Verena loved harmony. She taught her eight children to sing parts, and in Missouri they were known far and wide as a singing family. The English folk for miles around came to hear them. When their one son, Japhet, left home, one of the girls learned to sing tenor. Verena even tried her hand at arranging hymns. At her funeral in 1913, her more than forty grandchildren sang a hymn she had arranged.

Verena Sprunger Lehman has been gone for more than seventy years. What is the legacy she left? One of her granddaughters, Martha Gilliom Sprunger, wrote these words in 1938:

> Do not think that the only heroines are those whose names are blazoned in headlines across the pages of our daily papers or whose praises are sung from the housetops. Greater heroines than these are found in obscure places, whose names do not appear in the limelight of publicity, but are hidden from the public eye, properly evaluated and truly known only by those who know them best. Such a one was Mother Lehman.[5]

---

5. Quoted in Eva F. Sprunger, *The First Hundred Years* (Berne, Indiana: Berne Mennonite Church, 1938), p. 195.

2.
Sister for the Household

Hillegonda Cornelia van der Smissen 1848—1949

To tell Sister Hillegonda's story is to tell a family story. She grew up with a strong sense of history, and she considered her service to that family as her lifework. As it happened, that service was the prelude to her service to another family, the sisterhood of Bethel Deaconess Hospital in Newton, Kansas.

Roots in the sixteenth century

The van der Smissens have been described as a "patrician family of Brussels" in the sixteenth century. When the bloody Duke Alba killed 18,000 Protestants and Anabaptists and seized their property, Gysbert van der Smissen was an alderman in Brussels with a large estate in Flanders. In 1568, his family fled to Haarlem, Holland, where they became bakers. While most European countries persecuted religious dissenters, Holland offered them a place of safety.

Frederick III, Duke of Gottorf, let the Mennonites build a town on the islands between the river Treene and the river Eider on condition that they build dikes to keep the flood out of the river Treene. They were promised religious liberty there.[1] By 1623, they had built the dikes and Friedrichstadt, a city that was friendly, unusually clean, and beautifully land-

---

1. In 1680, Friedrichstadt, a Dutch colony, was the only city in Denmark open to Catholics, Jews, Mennonites, and Remonstrants.

Hillegonda van der Smissen: She found her other family in the sisterhood of the Bethel Deaconess Hospital.

scaped, with pleasant places along the canals for drinking afternoon coffee.

In the early years, many Mennonites came to Friedrichstadt to take refuge there. The Mennonite church and parsonage were built in 1627 on the middle canal.[2] In this beautiful city, Hillegonda spent a "joyful, happy, blessed childhood and early youth." Here and especially in the German city of Altona, members of the van der Smissen family lived for 300 years.

A pretty and pious grandmother

Hillegonda's grandparents were Jakob and Wilhelmine Weihe van der Smissen. During the Napoleonic wars, Wilhelmine's parents in Westphalia were forced to give lodging to soldiers of the French army who had invaded that part of Germany. The troops were most demanding. Wilhelmine, to help her parents, went to Altona to earn money. There Hinrich van der Smissen gave her a job. Even those earnings were not enough; her parents sent word that they were in dire need. Wilhelmine sold her hair, and to cover her embarrassment, made herself a little widow's cap. Hinrich's brother Jakob visited and asked about the little widow, and Hinrich told him the story. Jakob was attracted to her and eventually they became engaged.

"Grandfather got a pretty, unusually efficient, pious wife," Hillegonda said.

Hillegonda's father, Carl Justus, was born in 1811 near Altona but grew up in Friedrichstadt where his father was the pastor of the Mennonite congregation. He was sent by an uncle to Basel and later to the University of Erlangen to study. The Friedrichstadt church called him to be their minister in 1837.

Earlier, Carl Justus had told his uncle Gilbert that he loved his second cousin, Sara Cornelia van der Smissen, who was also the niece of his uncle's wife. The uncle, without telling Carl, found it convenient to ask Sara Cornelia to marry Carl, and she consented. Uncle Gilbert sent his nephew the travel fare, telling him to come quickly to celebrate his engagement.

Hillegonda's mother Sara Cornelia, born in 1814, was the seventh of eleven children. As was usual in this Altona Mennonite community, she received her education from a governess and a tutor. For family celebrations, the children gave little concerts of classical music with their friends. In winter, the family lived in the city, but in summer they moved to a

---

2. Sister Hillegonda, *Sketches from My Life* (Newton, Kansas: Bethel Deaconess Hospital, c.1935), p. 6. Unless otherwise noted, the information comes from this autobiography.

beautiful country home. Unfortunately, because of heavy losses suffered in the war, the fine properties had to be sold.

Fleeing on a powder wagon

Mother Sara Cornelia grew up speaking the Dutch language, but it was replaced by German when she was grown. Up to her eighteenth year, she used all her time for her education and then spent a year with a pious Quaker family in England, where she heard Elisabeth Fry, renowned for her ministry to prisoners. Before her marriage, Sara Cornelia went to live with relatives to learn housekeeping. She and Carl Justus were married in 1837 and moved to Friedrichstadt.

By 1850, Sara Cornelia and Carl Justus were the parents of four daughters and one son, including Hillegonda, born June 30, 1848. Another son had died.

The year 1850 was a tragic time. The son and a daughter died of quinsy (tonsillitis), and that fall the city was bombarded by the Schleswig-Holsteiners. The family fled from Friedrichstadt on a powder wagon to a neighboring city and then to Altona.

Carl Justus returned to his congregation in Friedrichstadt to find that the church and the parsonage had escaped serious damage. When the family came back in the spring, they discovered that the parsonage, although undamaged, had been looted of everything, even the silver chimes from the organ.

After the war, two boys were born, but the youngest died in early youth. The surviving children were Elisabeth, Wilhelmine, Hillegonda, and Carl Heinrich. The children took catechism from their father with the other children of the congregation. (Her brother noted that Hillegonda was the best of the pupils.)

Sara Cornelia had a significant role in ministering to the community. She went with her husband on pastoral visits, helped with a sewing school for girls, and started a mission society for the children. She seems also to have run a small mental health facility. "Two melancholy ladies, who one after another asked to be taken into the family, and who by God's help under father's pastoral care were healed, she served with infinite patience, showing her unselfish love," said Hillegonda.

God led them to Wadsworth

The parents celebrated their silver wedding anniversary in Friedrichstadt. In 1866, the congregation built a large parsonage so that the pastor could have a comfortable home for his old age. However, in 1867 he received a call to serve as director and teacher of the first Mennonite school in

America, which was to be built in Wadsworth, Ohio. Carl Justus refused immediately. At fifty-seven he felt that he was too old to commence something entirely new. Sara Cornelia thought it was a call from the Lord but said nothing.

When a second, more insistent call came, it could not be refused. Elisabeth Horny, the oldest daughter, and Carl, who was studying at Weilburg, remained behind.

"O such pain! Many of our loved ones stood on land waving, weeping .... Only mother did not shed a tear, but was glad that the Lord led us His ways."

They arrived in Pennsylvania in the cold of December. As they visited the congregations, Carl Justus preached twenty-one times in three weeks. Sara Cornelia, who had said at the farewell on leaving Friedrichstadt, "The only thing that is hard for me with this change is that I will not hear my husband preach as often," must have felt satiated.

Sara Cornelia adapted well, feeling the kindness of the people, but Hillegonda and Wilhelmine, nineteen and twenty-six years old, wept into their pillows for homesickness. They were also hungry; having been seasick on the boat and then often riding in sleighs in the cold, they were always famished. Except for the sweet potatoes, the girls enjoyed all of the strange food.

They sang often. At one time they were to visit a highly-esteemed minister who was not enthusiastic about the new school. The road was long, and to pass the time, the girls sang in two-part harmony. As the sleigh approached the home, the hymn reechoed from the hills. The old minister's heart melted. He visited Wadsworth the following summer and later sent his son. "The son was rather wild, but God was gracious while he was in school and he was thoroughly converted."

The Christian Education Institution of the Mennonite Denomination, the imposing name given to the Wadsworth school, was the first Mennonite school in North America.[3] It opened in 1868, during the depression that followed the Civil War, carrying a debt with interest that had to be paid. The debt was to plague the school during its short eleven-year life.

Miracle and the inner voice

The students often enjoyed picnics in the Hunsburger woodland and the making of maple sugar in the spring. Hillegonda remembered a rat hunt in the stable and a fine sleigh ride, along with the comment of a student, "I don't know which is more fun, a sleighing party or a rat hunt."

---

3. Anna Kreider Juhnke, "The Wadsworth School," *Mennonite Life*, April 1959, p. 66.

Hillegonda and Wilhelmine organized and taught a Sunday school in the school building. "We hear that our Sunday school pupils said: 'The college girls (that is what they called us) talk very nice to us; it is only a pity that we do not understand so much of what they say.' " But they soon learned to comprehend each others' German dialects.

Because the Wadsworth school was centrally located among the Mennonite congregations, the van der Smissens had as their guests many of the conference ministers and leaders who came to the school for meetings. The girls helped with the homely duties of hospitality, such as warming bricks for cold beds and then visiting around the stove with their guests.

In 1876, her inner voice said to her: "Pray for the brethren in the Territory," which she did quietly as she worked. The voice persisted and she went into her bedroom to pray for several hours until she felt her prayer was answered. Later she learned that A. E. Funk and his companions had been lost in a snowstorm on the Oklahoma prairie.

They had committed their lives to God and were resigned to freezing to death. Suddenly they saw a light in a window and found haven in a store. The miracle was that the owner had gone to the store to get something for his wife and had lit a candle for only a few minutes. Hillegonda discovered that this happened the same evening that she had prayed for them. "I did not say anything, but only thanked my heavenly Father. I adored Him because He wanted the prayers of His child before He would help."

Lessons from a failed frontier school

Sara Cornelia filled in when the school needed a German teacher, and also taught German, music, and French to pupils from the town. In 1876, young ladies were admitted, either because the board understood the importance of education for women or because women students could help with the financing. Hillegonda and Wilhelmine taught drawing, painting, and fine needlework.[4] Even though every measure was taken to raise money, the school had to be sold in 1878 because of the debt. Of the Wadsworth school's death, Hillegonda said:

> Now after fifty years one does not see anything of the school . . . . Those who have studied there, some of whom were of great blessing, have finished their course. To those still living, the evening of life has come. Soon there will be no one who remembers the Mennonite seminary of Wadsworth, Ohio. But thanks be to God! it was there not in vain; the blessing can still be felt, and is still exerting an influence.

4. Juhnke, p. 68.

Lack of money had not been the only problem of the Wadsworth school. The well educated, aristocratic van der Smissen had brought to the school a high level of religious and missionary zeal. As administrator and teacher, van der Smissen had trouble imposing his European culture onto the Mennonite pioneer community. Dissension arose between the theological head, van der Smissen, and the principal, Risser. Even with personnel changes, the school could not overcome its problems.

Church leaders agreed with Hillegonda, however, that the Wadsworth school had been a worthwhile enterprise. It had introduced a trained ministry for the churches and provided many outstanding leaders. "Moreover, the van der Smissens had shown the American frontier Mennonites that higher education could go hand in hand with humility and evangelical zeal."[5]

Back to the dear old homeland

Where were the van der Smissens to go after the school closed? Carl van der Smissen had finished his studies in Germany and was serving the Salem congregation near Hayesville, Ohio. With Hillegonda, the parents moved into a house near their son. Her father, now sixty-eight, could keep busy as secretary for the mission board and as editor of *News from the Heathen World*. When Carl was called to a larger congregation, her father took over the Salem church. The family often had boarders, young Mennonites from the academy in Hayesville.

In 1885, the van der Smissen parents and Hillegonda went to visit "the dear old homeland." After their return, Carl Justus and Sara Cornelia celebrated their fiftieth wedding anniversary.

After her father died in 1890, Hillegonda and her mother rented a house in Summerfield where Carl and his wife were living. Hillegonda felt they had been called by God to be there to help at the time of the death of Carl's wife in 1892. When he married again, he and his family moved next door. Sara Cornelia enjoyed the grandchildren, giving piano lessons to the eldest daughter.

When her mother died in 1901, Hillegonda felt that her lifework was done. "I had the beautiful, blessed duty to be the support of my dear parents in their declining years." She was fifty-three years old, and she felt she might soon follow them, as her health was weak.

But Hillegonda forgot about her health when her sister Elisabeth asked her to come to Germany for a year. She made the trip and visited with many relatives. In Hamburg, she was surprised to find that the large

5. Juhnke, p. 69.

Hamburg-Altona church was sparsely filled compared to the crowded Summerfield church.

Finding a model for deaconess work

In her travelogue for the *Bundesbote*, she wrote of the many churches she visited and the sermons of church leaders that she listened to. Hillegonda was much interested in the mission societies. She was asked to speak about the American Mennonite mission among the Indians in Oklahoma and the newly-formed mission in India. In Holland, she wrote of the work of the Baptist-minded (Mennonite) churches, their homes for single women, widows, and orphans; their method of teaching catechism and classes for children.

The deaconess home at Kaiserswerth on the Rhine was of particular interest to Hillegonda. Two hundred sisters lived there, and from there 900 others went out to work in different countries. She was impressed by the extent of the facilities: educational buildings, seminary for lady teachers, houses for the leading pastors and the Sisters, the book concern, farm and stables, hospitals for both mental and physical illness, and an orphan home. She must have thought of this model some years later when Sister Frieda asked her to join the sisterhood at the Bethel Deaconess Hospital.

Christmas was spent with her sister Elisabeth Horny at Scheuern. Elisabeth and her husband were for thirty years the superintendents of an institute for 300 mentally retarded persons. The residents in the home were being taught with a progressive curriculum. From Scheuern, Hillegonda did considerable traveling to visit acquaintances or to do sightseeing in Germany and Switzerland, often with a niece or relative but sometimes alone.

"But of all the pretty things which I saw in North and South, to me nothing was more beautiful than the little town where I was born, lovely Friedrichstadt," where the cows had to be milked three times a day because they gave so much milk, where the storks walked along the canals, "the larks rose jubilantly heavenward, the lambs played lively; everything as it was when I was a child, and yet, how different!"

Caring for the Haury children

She visited the little church where her grandfather and father had preached, and the cemetery. "O, how many graves of relatives and acquaintances have I visited on this trip!" When she left in June, she counted 200 visits that she had made and 2,000 miles that she had traveled.

She had not intended to return in June, but rather had planned to stay for a year. At no extra cost she could have spent a pleasant summer visiting with relatives and friends. However, she was asked by Dr. S. S. Haury in Newton, Kansas, to come care for his children while he and his wife studied in Europe for a year. They knew she was in Europe but thought she might be back in July.

> This caused me great trouble; to give up the summer in Europe seemed almost too much of a sacrifice. On the other hand, my dear mother did not need me any more; if the Lord had a task for me, would entrust the children to me, would it be right, for my pleasure's sake, to say no? With much prayer and many tears, I became willing to bring the sacrifice and to return in June.

So she went to Kansas to visit first with her sister Wilhelmine Schwake who was superintendent of the Bethesda Hospital at Goessel, and then to Newton to the Haurys. Mrs. Haury gave Hillegonda her Sunday school class to teach, and Hillegonda accepted the responsibility as an act of kindness. She found work also with the mission society and the young people's class.

When Haurys returned a year later, Hillegonda was free to travel again, using the gift that Dr. Haury had given her. (She hesitated to accept it, thinking she should oblige him for friendship's sake since he had been a student of her father.) Accompanied by her nine-year-old niece, Hillegonda Cornelia, she visited in Colorado, Oregon, and California. After a visit to the Oklahoma mission fields, she returned to Summerfield.

A call from Sister Frieda

Hillegonda had been away from her own home for two years and was glad to be back, but she missed her mother sorely. One or two of her brother's children came for dinner every day and Hilda or Frieda stayed for the night. She helped them with their studies or their fancy work and they all sang together. Frieda Andreas remembers the love and enjoyment given at those times.[6]

During the summer of 1904, she had over one hundred guests, many of whom came for the St. Louis World's Fair. One of her guests during this period was Frieda Kaufman on her way to Cincinnati for deaconess training. Hillegonda bought a house for herself that was large enough to entertain her mission society and children's classes. An inherited income, careful living, and her garden made it possible for her to live comfortably. She thought she would be spending the evening of her life in Summerfield.

Then in 1909, when she was sixty, a request came from Sister Frieda of the newly organized Bethel Deaconess Home and Hospital in Newton

---

6. Interview with Frieda Andreas, North Newton, Kansas, February 1984.

to come as sister for the household. Just try it for six months, Sister Frieda suggested. Hillegonda accepted the call, leaving Summerfield in January 1909.

"It came as a surprise to me when I received a call to help in the work. Sister Frieda knew that I was interested in deaconess service and that I had visited a number of deaconess institutions on my two previous trips to Europe . . . . With a rather timid heart, I began my work in 1909."[7]

"I found the new assignment so very different from my little household, at first I was glad that I had my home yet; but when the six months were passed, I could cheerfully go home and dissolve my household." On September 16, 1909, she received the deaconess garb and was consecrated.[8]

As writer and poet

To her work as deaconess, she brought a special feeling for family. Her duties at the hospital were in housekeeping, but she also had opportunities to offer spiritual sustenance to the ill. She helped with the training of the new deaconesses and taught Bible lessons to the sisters on Saturday evening. During vacations, she attended conferences or visited relatives and friends.

Sister Hillegonda and her mother had started mission societies wherever they lived. In 1892, Sister Hillegonda was the chairperson of the first meeting of the women's societies at the Middle District Conference at Pulaski, Iowa. In 1899, she presented a paper to the women's meeting entitled, "The Rise and Progress of Mission Sewing Societies Among the Mennonites."[9] Sometime after 1927, she wrote a thirty-two-page book that grew out of her interest in mission societies in Europe and America. *The History of our Missionary Societies* was published by the Literature Committee of the Women's Home and Foreign Missionary Association. Written in German, it was well organized and factual.

Sister Hillegonda was also a poet, composing for many special occasions. The workers in the home and hospital enjoyed her reading and storytelling during quilting hours, canning time, or social gatherings. Her Bible teaching continued, not only for the deaconesses, but also for a large class of older women at Newton's First Mennonite Church. At another time, she had a Sunday school class for young girls.

The editor of the hospital magazine was touched by her prayer life.

---

7. "Sister Hillegonda van der Smissen," *In the Service of the King*, March 1942, p. 7.
8. *In the Service of the King*, June 1943, p. 4.
9. Samuel F. Pannabecker, *Faith in Ferment* (Newton, Kansas: Faith and Life Press, 1968), p. 107.

"We saw her on her knees praying for needy ones, for missionaries, for friends, and for those who had spoken hastily or unkindly. We shall never forget those folded hands, that radiant face, and those fervent prayers in rhyme or prose, but always coming from a heart filled with the love of God."[10]

Blessings to those around her

Her nature had still another facet. At the Christmas Eve party in the dining hall, after each student had unwrapped her gift from the sisters, amidst the laughter and talk, a loud voice shouted, "Children, children, come help me!" And there was Sister Hillegonda in the doorway. The eighty-year-old woman was dressed in a huge overcoat and hat and carried a heavy bag. She was the Santa Claus bringing in the letters and packages that had accumulated over several weeks.[11]

When she was eighty and in poor health, the sisters relieved her of her housekeeping duties; but they let her bake the Christmas cookies.

Wilhelmine Schwake, her sister, came to live at the Bethel Home and died there in 1930 at nearly ninety. Her brother Carl and his wife Elizabeth came to live at the Bethel Home in 1932. Elizabeth died two years later. From then on, Carl and Sister Hillegonda kept each other company. They took daily walks. Anna Entz, for many years a friend to the residents of the home, reported that a woman who did not know the van der Smissens watched them walk past her house every day and was touched by the love they had for each other. "They are a blessing to me. Just to see them makes me blessed," she said.

Sister Hillegonda was a blessing to other people. When Wilhelmina Kuyf stopped on her way to China in 1936, she wrote to her parents: "This sister is alert, cheerful, wide-awake, and humorous, much more so than I had thought possible at eighty-eight. It was fine too to have her remark that she would pray for me, for one gets the feeling that she is thoroughly, completely consecrated."[12]

Sister Hillegonda died September 29, 1949, aged 101. Her brother followed her in less than a year at age ninety-nine.

Old age in itself may be an achievement, but Sister Hillegonda is remembered for more than longevity. She came from a well-educated, cultured family that included a large number of "working women." While

---

10. *In the Service of the King*, October-November 1949, p. 3.
11. Katie Funk Wiebe, *Our Lamps Were Lit* (Newton, Kansas: Bethel Deaconess Hospital School of Nursing, 1978), p. 64.
12. From the Wilhelmina Kuyf Collection, Box 130-1, Folder 1.

they shared a sense of family pride, they fulfilled their responsibilities with humility and love for those they served.

Sister Hillegonda had had an excellent preparation for her almost twenty years of deaconess work.

> Her ten years of service in the school at Wadsworth, her subsequent adjustments while still a young woman to various communities in America, her bright mind, her great interest throughout her life in all phases of church work, and two extended return trips to Europe where she visited Holland, Germany, and Switzerland had given her a broad outlook on life.[13]

Sister Hillegonda had observed and learned from her parents a way of thanksgiving for every blessing. The written record of her life is one of thanksgiving and praise.

---

13. *In the Service of the King*, June 1943, p. 4.

3.
With Open Arms for Children

Magdalena Neuenschwander Sprunger
1855—1931

by Naomi Lehman

When Magdalena Neuenschwander Sprunger was forty-five years old, she heard that a foster child was being mistreated by the father of the family. Neighbors feared that the child would die of the severe abuse that she was receiving.

Maddy, as she was known in the community, went with her daughter to visit the family. She found the little girl, Jennie, sitting on the floor playing with a few nuts. Maddy asked if she could take the child. She learned that the father had adoption papers and probably was interested in Jennie for the work she could do.

Looking at the papers, Maddy cleverly argued, "These are not legal because they were made on a Sunday." The man responded angrily that they might as well take the child. He predicted that they would have nothing but trouble with her since she was not strong physically and had a hearing problem.

And so Jennie came to share the love of a home which had nurtured four children from Maddy's husband's two former wives, two of his stepchildren, her own eight, and various foster children. Jennie was to be a great help to her in her old age.

By covered wagon to Berne

Magdalena Neuenschwander was born into the pioneer family of Abraham and Catherine Zurflueh Neuenschwander on February 18, 1855. She

Magdalena Sprunger: For a time, her chief duty on Sunday morning was to get her many children ready for church.

spent her early years in Putnam County, Ohio, where the Neuenschwanders had settled along with the large group of Swiss immigrants from the Jura area who left their home in 1852 to find a new life in America. While many of the immigrants moved on to Adams County, Indiana, that first year, the Neuenschwanders chose to remain in Putnam County near Pandora for fourteen years.

Soon after her mother's death in 1866, the family moved by covered wagon to Berne, Indiana. Maddy and her older sister Katherine helped look after the needs of the family of seven children. When the four girls needed undershirts, Maddy and Katie took the diapers no longer needed by the youngest brother, cut them up, and sewed them by hand as they had seen their mother do.

Soon Maddy was old enough to "work out" to supplement the family income. She did housework in an Amish home for about two years. Later, she was courted by a young man with whom she attended a wedding celebration. She was shocked when he became intoxicated. Drinking was common at weddings and social events at that time. But Maddy would have none of that and the romance ended then and there.

Abraham's third wife

When she was about sixteen she began to work in the Abraham A. Sprunger home. Mr. Sprunger had been married to Anna Sprunger (half sister of the well-known minister, S. F. Sprunger) and they had one son, Levi, after which Anna died. Abraham married again, this time to a young widow with two small children. Together they had three more children. This mother died in 1872, a year after Maddy had come to work in that home.

Maddy felt she should leave, but Abraham begged her to remain as the children loved her very much. Soon he was attracted to her and they were married in 1873 when Maddy was only eighteen. Thus, she became responsible for the care of six children besides all the work which fell to a pioneer woman in the 1870s. She and Abraham had eight more children.

In the early 1930s, Maddy's oldest son, Albert N. Sprunger, wrote an article about pioneer home life in the Berne community and the growth of the Mennonite church there. His writing reflects the childhood experiences of his parents and also of their life together.[1]

> Let us take a look for a little while at the homes often of one room only. It was a kitchen, dining room, bedroom, parlor, washroom,

---

1. *Berne Witness*, January 29, 1934.

and workshop all in one. It held rude and homemade furniture, and doors without locks, wooden levers with latch-strings being used to open and close them.

To maintain even that much it often became necessary to work almost day and night, men working hard at daytime cutting timber, clearing land, and in the evening and night hammering away at the weaver's lathe; the women sitting at spinning wheel until eleven, twelve, and one o'clock at night, and walking four and five miles to bring in such work and again to deliver it, all this for the measly sum of five cents a pound for the wool spun into yarn, to make ends meet.

This period [the 1870s] might well be called the walking age for it was nothing out of the ordinary for parents to walk six, eight, or even ten miles to church, carrying their babies every step of the way. . . . It is this kind of stock that makes a church grow.

[A later time] might well be called the horse and buggy days. Top buggies, spring wagons, two- and three-seated, loaded to capacity, pulled by horses coming at a full trot from all directions, all on their way to church until the number of these vehicles would run as high as 75 to 100 all quartered in the long rows of stalls, and tied to the hitching racks around the church.

The church was the center of the religious and social life for the Sprunger family. Maddy had little responsibility in the church, her chief duty being to get the many children ready to attend the services. Because the Sprungers lived only about one and one-half miles from Berne, they often provided Sunday dinner for families who were prevented by distance from going to their own homes between the morning worship and the afternoon Sunday school.

Tiny girl folded in her apron

Even with all the work she had, Maddy still had time for the Women's Missionary Society, or *Naehverein*. She was faithful in attendance and served for thirty-eight years on its purchasing and cutting committee, the group in charge of the quilting bees.

She was also supportive of her husband who was in the earliest group of Sunday school teachers and who also served as trustee and church treasurer for about fifteen years.

Her most fulfilling role was probably in her home where she found many opportunities for loving service. She opened her home to various foster children for either short or long periods of time.

First came Bert, whose father begged the Sprungers to take his motherless son. Later, a little handicapped girl was taken in. She was lame and needed to be carried around, but the children all loved her. Still later, another family lost their mother and asked if the Sprungers would take Bertha, remarking that no one could handle her. Abraham said, "We'll try." She caused no problems and only once did Maddy have to punish her. When a diphtheria epidemic hit the community, Bertha became very ill and died in Maddy's arms.

One day Maddy went to visit a sick mother who pleaded with her to take her ailing baby home with her. So Maddy wrapped little brown-eyed Lydia in her apron and took her home. Her daughters asked, "Mam, what do you have in your apron?" She opened it up and there was the tiny girl whom they nursed back to health. The family was very sad when later she was taken back to her own home.

Illness and death entered the Sprunger family when typhoid struck in 1888 and four of the children became ill and eleven-year-old Alina died. Another, Ferdinand, died of polio. These were not easy times.

Not only did Maddy take foster children into her home, she also welcomed adults with needs. In about 1870, when Dr. Dan Neuenschwander came to Berne and wished to set up practice, he asked the Sprungers if he could have a room in their country home. His wish was granted, and according to foster-daughter Jennie Miller, he remained several years. When a patient from the Bluffton, Ohio, community came to Berne with her sister, they had no place to stay during treatment. As might be expected, Maddy found room for them for about two months. Jennie tells us there were eighteen persons around the table during that time.

While the family lived on the farm, Abraham loaned money at various times to several young men so that they could come from Switzerland to America. He then employed them as hired hands and of course they ate with the already large family. It must be added that Abraham also hired local girls to help with the housework. Maddy's own daughters helped as well.

Midwife at the birth of seventy-five

Maddy always had a beautiful and productive garden in the summer, and the Sprungers raised their own beef, pork, and chicken. An adequate supply of food always seemed to be available. Maddy was known to be an excellent cook. She baked breads, cakes, and pastry to perfection. The dinner bell rang exactly on time, and it was said that the neighbors could set their clocks by the bell. Maddy was an efficient woman, and her household ran smoothly.

This remarkable woman had another gift. She was midwife at the birth of at least seventy-five babies. Neighbors called on her many times. She also delivered a number of her early grandchildren. Her neighbors, J. W. and Emma Ruth Kliewer, called her to help with their newborn babies. Kliewer was pastor of the Berne Mennonite Church and later became president of Bethel College.

The Sprungers moved to town in 1903. Abraham died in 1906, and Maddy was to be a widow for twenty-five years. Maddy might then have had an easier life, but that was not her way. Around 1915, she gave a home to her old uncle, Abraham Zurflueh, and took care of him. By this time most of her own children were married.

Was there to be no end to the foster children Maddy cared for? In about 1920 a young mother died in Berne, leaving four young sons. Maddy opened her heart and home to the youngest, not yet two. He lived with her until her death.

Dr. Neuenschwander, whom the Sprungers had befriended, left Berne but returned some years later, not so much as a physician for the body, but rather for the soul. He had become a minister in the Reformed Church. When the Sprungers moved to town, he was a neighbor and frequently visited the home. Jennie remembers that in Maddy's later years, she and the doctor often engaged in spiritual and theological discussions.

Maddy died of a heart attack in 1931. Her friend, Dr. Neuenschwander, shared in the memorial service. At the time of her death, she had fifty-two grandchildren and fifty-seven great-grandchildren, all of whom share the legacy of Maddy's love.

The words of Proverbs 31 describe Maddy's life: She sets about her work vigorously; her arms are strong for her tasks. . . . She opens her arms to the poor and extends her hands to the needy. . . . Her children arise and call her blessed, her husband also, and he praises her.

4.
Grand Lady of Bluffton College

Emelie Siemens Hamm Mosiman
1863—1953

To the students of Bluffton College, Emelie Hamm Mosiman was "the most unforgettable character I ever met."[1] To historians, she was known as the "Mother of Bluffton College." To some of the Swiss Mennonites in the Bluffton community she was "The Proud Prussian." To her relatives she was "Tante Mila." And to most others she was a warm, gracious, and generous woman who expected the young people she taught to develop those same traits.[2]

Emelie Hamm was born February 3, 1863, in Marienburg, East Prussia, the daughter of Peter and Emily Siemens Hamm, the fourth of five children. Her father was a town official and businessman; and when the family came to Nebraska in 1875, Mr. Hamm entered the lumber business in Beatrice. During their second winter in Nebraska, the parents were asphyxiated by the fumes of a coal heating stove.[3]

The younger children had to choose between remaining in Nebraska with relatives or returning to Danzig to make their home with the grandparents. Emelie made five trips to Germany in the next few years, but

---

1. "Bluffton College Loses Its 'Grand Old Lady,'" *The Bluffton News*, December 17, 1953, p. 1.
2. This biography includes the reminiscences of Minnie Beidler, Lena Moser, Sylvia Pannabecker, Mary Holtkamp, Florence Diller, Sue Sprunger, Howard Raid, Muriel Thiessen Stackley, Edna Ramseyer Kaufman, Sally Lehman, Donovan Smucker, Christine Purves, and Marjorie Ruth; and Beatrice Church records.
3. *The Bluffton News.*

Emelie Mosiman: She would sail majestically into church wearing those beautiful flowered hats.

finally decided to live in Beatrice with the other family members.[4] She was baptized in the Beatrice Mennonite Church in 1879.

Emelie graduated from the Hoehere Toechter Schule in Danzig. Sometime before 1900, she attended the University of Chicago.[5] Her education and her excellent German background enabled her to teach German for ten years in the Nebraska schools.

The Queen Victoria of Beatrice

Even in Beatrice she had earned something of a reputation for her tall, stately carriage. As a child, a niece remembers that she would "sail majestically into church, my idea of Queen Victoria, wearing those *beautiful* flowered hats."

Firmly established in Beatrice in her middle forties, looked upon by the community as "the grand old maid," Emelie found her life changing dramatically in 1908 when Dr. Samuel K. Mosiman came to Beatrice for a General Conference meeting.

Dr. Mosiman, with his farm background, had delayed his education until H. J. Krehbiel, the minister of the Trenton, Ohio, church, encouraged him to prepare for a life in Christian service. Samuel had worked in the Oklahoma mission, married H. J. Krehbiel's sister, and won a $2,000 scholarship for further study in Germany in the field of biblical languages, Hebrew, Aramaic, Greek, Syrian, and Arabic. His wife died at sea in 1905 while the couple was crossing to Halle Wittenberg University where he was to study. Returning in 1907 with his doctorate, Dr. Mosiman had been called to teach at Central Mennonite College, and then he was asked to become president the next year of that school which was to become Bluffton College.

What a husband shouldn't be

When he came to Beatrice, the housing committee assigned him to the home of William Hamm, where Emelie was living. Emelie and Samuel were married the following year, August 12, 1909.

A number of her friends reported that Emelie Hamm had said that there were three kinds of men she would not marry (but when the list is completed, there are more than three): she would not marry a preacher, a widower, a man shorter than herself, a man younger than herself, or one with a beard. She would tell this story on herself, and then she would

---

4. E. G. Kaufman, compiler, "Samuel K. Mosiman," *General Conference Mennonite Pioneers* (North Newton, Kansas: Bethel College), 1973, pp. 181-189; material from Herbert W. Berky.

5. *God's Love in Action* (First Mennonite Church and Mennonite Church of Beatrice, Nebraska, 1978), p. 43.

laugh and say that when Samuel asked her to marry him, she forgot all about these resolutions.

Dr. Mosiman had just been chosen president of Bluffton College. Someone had asked him if he had been hired to give the college a decent burial, but he had no intention of doing that. He told Emelie that he needed help in saving the school. "The Lord spoke to me. I felt that God was asking me if I could do that," she told Lena Moser. Another report has her saying, "God pushed me." At any rate, it was more than *just* a love match.

And so the Prussian married the Schweitzer. "With the charm of culture and an intriguing sparkle, she assumed an almost perfect complement to her serious, solid, homespun husband. Together they became a team with a single purpose."[6] Together they set their goals for Bluffton College, hoping to unite a divided constituency and to raise enough money to assure the school's survival. Neither of these aims was ever fully realized, but the Mosimans gave the college their best efforts. The junior college enrollment was at eleven when they took it over. It became a four-year college in 1913, and by 1925 had increased to nearly four hundred students with a growing campus.

Bible teacher for college women

Emelie took her position as president's wife seriously. She told one of her students that her husband had noticed that she was not as vivacious as she had been when he first knew her, and her response was that she felt that now that she was a college president's wife, she should display more dignity. (From this point on, we will refer to Emelie as Mrs. Mosiman, as befits her dignity.) The Mosimans always appeared in public impeccably dressed, Dr. Mosiman in swallow-tailed coat and striped trousers for official occasions.

Mrs. Mosiman knew her German. Two of her students were granted Rhodes scholarships to study in Germany.[7] She also knew her Bible. As a devoted member of First Mennonite Church, she contributed her talents as Bible teacher. For thirty years, she taught the Women's Bible class, the class for college women. She was able to adapt the lessons to the needs of her class. Her gift of teaching Bible was remembered by many of her students, and they visited her class when they returned to their alma mater. Sylvia Tschantz Pannabecker especially appreciated her Bible courses where she shared her life and hard struggle for a complete commitment to the Lord.

6. Kaufman, p. 184.
7. *The Bluffton News*.

Mrs. Mosiman also took an interest in other departments of the college. She encouraged Elizabeth Baehr, the home economics teacher, to help her students to learn more about life away from the farm. Elizabeth, at her advice, had the grocer order vegetables out of season from Lima so that she could teach her students how to prepare them.

Perhaps because of her Sunday school class, she was always a bit late for church. For many church members, the memory of Mrs. Mosiman, in Bluffton as well as in Beatrice, is her entry into church, proceeding erectly down the aisle to the second row from the front, settling down in her seat, and pausing to pray. Then she nodded politely to the other worshipers before getting ready for the service.

Children, and perhaps the less pious adults, studied the design of her hats, for they were magnificent. Mrs. Mosiman followed the service carefully and nodded her flowered head when she agreed with the minister. After the service, she enjoyed visiting with the congregation.

During their first years in the church, the common cup was used for communion. Because a number of the men chewed tobacco, Mrs. Mosiman brought a white linen napkin to wipe the edge of the cup before she drank. The church leaders must have observed this fastidious gesture, for within a few years a communion set with individual cups was purchased.

Open heart and open house

Her faith in God was abundant. When she needed money, she prayed for it, and often she received exactly what she asked for. She herself was a generous person. When she had money, she gave it, without troubling to save for a rainy day. Lena Moser recalls that Mrs. Mosiman put her last dollar in the offering plate one Sunday, knowing that somehow her own needs would be cared for.

The brick house at 210 West Grove Street in Bluffton became an open house for students and friends from every part of the world. Sylvia Pannabecker wrote, "On the first week of school, Mrs. Mosiman invited all the girls to her home for tea. We were a small group then, and found the occasion an opportunity to learn to know everyone. I always had a warm spot in my heart for her because she did that."[8]

As a social arbiter, Mrs. Mosiman, the Prussian, was well qualified. Howard Raid, a Bluffton neighbor, remembered her as a "tall, erect, stately lady, with very exact manners. When she greeted you she would bow just a bit and smile. She was always interested in who you were and

---

8. Sylvia Pannabecker in a letter to Sue Sprunger, May 1978.

where you had been raised. She entertained people with more 'class' and generally was rather forward for a woman of her day."

A long crusade for culture

Mrs. Mosiman cultivated a "strong affinity for correctness. She presided over the social life of the campus. Concerned about some of the rustic manners of the students, she began a long crusade for culture."[9] She insisted that these students, many of them just off their mid-West farms, learn the fine points of etiquette, not only because she wanted them to be polished and gracious adults, but because she wanted them to represent the college at its best. She started with their need for tender loving care.

In addition to frequent teas, talks in chapel, and her presence in the dining hall, she tried to teach the students by way of the *Witmarsum*, the campus newspaper:

> Think again: to rush into the dining hall and sit down to eat without any pause is not only lack of worship but utter disregard of good manners and highly recognized social customs.[10]

One of the rules that Martha Habegger remembered was "Don't eat the lettuce leaf under the salad. You can never be a successful person if you are so gauche as to eat the salad's lettuce leaf."[11]

Mrs. Mosiman thought it was her duty to help students grow up, and she did not hesitate to speak out on this subject. Another lesson she tried to instill was gratitude. "Never forget to say thank you," she said. "If you come from Bluffton College and don't know enough to say thanks, it will reflect badly on the college."

Baking was an important facet of her entertaining. She had special cookie recipes that she never gave away. But those cookies were also available to the neighbor children who came by. Each child received one cookie per visit. She did not like housekeeping particularly, but she enjoyed entertaining. As a collector, she favored fine china and lace, treasures handed down in the family, which she often gave away to her friends. A number of people still treasure a cup and saucer from Mrs. Mosiman. She also collected and gave away paintings, some of which were considered very good.

Mrs. Mosiman had a certain reputation as a matchmaker. "She was a great promoter of matches between the campus men and women. When she invited Martha Habegger to a party, she said, 'Bring your male friend

---

9. Von Hardesty, *The Narrative of Bluffton College* (Bluffton College, 1974), p. 13.
10. Hardesty, p. 13.
11. In a letter from Christine Purves, May 1984.

to the party, I am *infiting* him, too.' Mrs. Mosiman turned away and then whipped back to Martha coyly, 'You do *haf* a male friend, do you not?' "

General opinion is that she was the one who introduced the May Day celebration with the intricacies of winding ribbons around the Maypole to the Bluffton campus.

A good team for the college

The Mosimans were devoted to each other. But she seemed to keep reminding herself and others that one of the foremost reasons for marrying him was to help the college. She put her generous abilities to this task.

Lloyd L. Ramseyer, a later president of the college, said, "[Dr. Mosiman] was not a man who enjoyed going out to ask people for money. He said that he sometimes walked around the block several times trying to steel himself for an interview with a possible contributor."[12]

She gave him courage. As a team and separately, they went to the churches and to private homes to inform the congregations about Christian education in general and Bluffton College in particular. "They were welcomed with greater and greater fervor."[13] Emelie spoke well before a group, and she was invited to speak to community as well as college organizations. It was Mrs. Mosiman who raised the money for the first dormitory, the Ladies' Hall, receiving $1,000 each from two women friends, and then enough from speaking in churches to make the $4,800 for the purchase of the property. The Mosimans made a good team, she forthright and aristocratic, saying what she thought, he calm and common.

"She didn't always see eye to eye or agree with Dr. Mosiman, but he listened to her. Oh, but she sure told us sometimes," Lena Moser said.

Send us students

On Saturday evenings, she and Dr. Mosiman dressed up and walked up and down Main Street, visiting with the people. They were soliciting for money and students. The subject of student solicitation was close to her heart.

Christine Purves heard her speak up at a church women's meeting. The women had talked and talked about what to give Bluffton College: teaspoons for afternoon coffees? a new chair for the library? "Mrs. Mosiman finally could hold still no longer and stood, erect as always, 'If you want to help Bluffton College, want to *gif* the College *somesing, gif* us your children! Send us students!' "

12. From a tape of a speech; Mennonite Library and Archives, North Newton, Kansas.
13. Kaufman, p. 185.

The Mosimans gave generously themselves. They donated their home and their personal library to the college, and their name is on the music hall. Besides giving to Bluffton College, she later made gifts to the Memorial Home and to Mennonite Biblical Seminary. In 1926, Mrs. Mosiman received an inheritance from her brother. She and Dr. Mosiman took a trip to Europe and the Near East, then gave the remainder of the money to the college.[14]

Mrs. Mosiman was always thoughtful of the faculty. She encouraged them when they were working on advanced degrees. She supported literary and cultural life on campus, seeking out lecturers, attending all college functions as long as she was able to go.

The college president and his wife at one time had a little three-seated car. He sat in front to drive, and she, being fashionably ample, spread out in the back. But most people remember his $900 Ford. The owner of the local Ford garage said that Dr. Mosiman came to him on one occasion asking for "rings, pins, valves, and bearings." When asked what he was going to do with all those parts, he said that he was taking Emelie to visit her folks in Nebraska and that he was going to rebuild the motor while she visited with her family.[15]

On such trips, Mrs. Mosiman was the navigator. In those times, maps were not as precise as today. On one trip, the blue book she was following was so useless that in a fit of irritation she threw it out the car window.[16]

As a German, Mrs. Mosiman felt some antagonism from townspeople during World War II. She belonged to a number of prestigious clubs in Bluffton, and a few of the members made pointed references to Hitler that were intended to hurt her.

Her friends agree that she could be somewhat overbearing. One of her defenders felt that she was really a kind person but was not able to communicate with people on their level. "In her last years, she became quite blunt and outspoken and her peers did not admire her as did the generation of students under her like Martha Habegger and me," Sylvia Pannabecker wrote.

Caught by controversy and hard times

There was some opposition to the Mosiman regime from the church community, particularly from the Swiss. In bringing in Dr. Mosiman, an outsider from Trenton, the college offended the local Swiss who were in power. It might have been that one of the pastors had strongly wished to

---

14. *Bluffton News.*
15. Howard Raid.
16. A memory from Edna Ramseyer Kaufman.

become president of the college. For her part, Mrs. Mosiman, with a love of High German, was irritated by what she regarded as the illiterate use of German in the local pulpits.

During the 1920s, a strong attack, headed by the Berne pastor, was made on the leaders of the school for their theological doctrines. Dr. Mosiman, instead of giving superficial answers to a questionnaire, gave detailed discussions that tried to explain his stance on theological issues.

He had inherited the fundamentalism-modernism controversy and was criticized for preaching a social gospel that he insisted grew out of love of God. His lectures were somewhat heavy for young farm students, but they had faith in the Mosimans and the Mosimans had faith in God. Before each financial drive, Dr. Mosiman called for a prayer service. His greatness lay in the way he met problems and controversy. In all his endeavors and vicissitudes, Mrs. Mosiman gave him her unfailing support.

The real obstacle to success was financial. "From 1922 to 1939, the college never had a balanced budget."[17] The Mosimans built the college to a respectable size with the needed facilities. Continuous borrowing was necessary to meet expenses. When the crash of 1929 wiped out its paper assets, the college was in debt by $250,000. Whispers of unwise spending and misappropriation forced Dr. Mosiman's resignation in 1935. By the time of his death in 1940, he had worked out a plan for payment of the debts so that the college could survive.[18]

After her husband's death, Mrs. Mosiman continued to be active in the community and to support the college. Lena Moser was one of her closest friends, and Mrs. Mosiman relied on her and her husband Ezra for getting around. To them she was "Tante Mila."

Her last weeks were spent in the hospital where she remained cheerful, quoting Scripture verses and psalms that she had memorized. "Mrs. Mosiman lived a very close life to the Heavenly Father. She often said, 'When I am lonesome or disturbed I talk to my Heavenly Father who helps and comforts me,'" Lena Moser wrote in her tribute. Mrs. Mosiman died December 15, 1953.

Even in her last days she treated visitors as the gracious lady she was. She welcomed them and inquired about their activities. And she always said thank you or *danke schoen* for whatever they did for her.

17. Ramseyer.
18. Hardesty, p. 16.

Bertha Petter: She married in 1911 and spent the rest of her life assisting her husband and promoting his work.

5.
Helper in the Cheyenne Cause

Bertha Elise Kinsinger Petter
1872—1967

In an age when women's roles were limited to mothering, nursing, and school teaching, many women sublimated their unusual energies and talents to unabashedly promote the careers of their husbands. Bertha Kinsinger Petter was one of those women.

As the first single woman in her denomination to become a Mennonite missionary, the first Mennonite woman to earn a college degree, and probably the first white woman to learn the Cheyenne language, she could have made a place for herself on her own credits.

Born December 21, 1872, to Joseph and Helen Kennel Kinsinger, Bertha grew up in Butler County, Ohio, as a member of the Trenton Mennonite Church. She was of Swiss-German ancestry. She recalled a pleasant and wholesome childhood with her sisters Julia and Ida, and an enjoyable experience in the district school.[1] After passing the county teachers' examination, she began teaching before she was eighteen. She attended Wittenberg College at Springfield, Ohio, graduating *cum laude* in 1896.[2]

To the Asian or to the American Indians?

Wittenberg was a Lutheran college with a strong religious and missionary

---

1. From the records of the Trenton Mennonite Historical Committee furnished by Hazel Neubrander.
2. Lois Barrett, *The Vision and the Reality* (Newton, Kansas: Faith and Life Press, 1983), p. 28.

emphasis. As a Student Volunteer, she signed a pledge, "It is my purpose, God willing, to become a foreign missionary." The Lutheran Board asked her to go to their field in South India the following fall, but she made way for another volunteer who was ready to go.

Her cousin, S. K. Mosiman, urged her to stay with the Mennonites and work among the American Indians. "My family were definitely opposed to my going to the Indians. Knowing it was of the Lord, I have never known a shadow of turning back."[3]

The mission board sent her to Cantonment, Oklahoma, in 1896 to teach Indian children. Her friend Agnes Williams, whom she recruited from Moody Bible Institute, became her co-worker. This Indian territory, not yet a state, must have been a shocking environment for the two women from Ohio. Together they preached, taught, and conducted funerals, having charge of the Clinton mission field for two years when no men were available for these duties.

After four years, the board assigned her as an assistant to Rodolphe Petter, who had undertaken the task of learning the Cheyenne language and writing its first dictionary and grammar. "At the same time, I took up the study of the language with intense interest and close application. The study of Cheyenne provided not a single dull moment. I tackled it as I had tackled calculus at college. It was fascinating and satisfying." Her alma mater granted her a master's degree in 1910 in recognition of her studies in a difficult Indian language.

When, in 1910, Mr. Petter's wife Marie died of tuberculosis, Bertha continued to help him in his work and with his children. In November 1911, they were married. The remainder of her life was to be spent assisting him and promoting his work.

In the world of the Cheyenne language

Rodolphe Charles Petter was born at Vevey, Switzerland, in 1865, to French-speaking parents. His mother's ancestors were Huguenot and Waldensian. This background gave him an appreciation for the Mennonite faith of Samuel Gerber, whom he met while he was in the medical corps, fulfilling his required military training.

When he met S. F. Sprunger who was visiting in the Jura Mountains, he was encouraged to consider working among the American Indians. After six years of study at the Basel Missionary Institute, he was ordained. He married Samuel Gerber's sister, Marie, and they sailed for America.

---

3. January 21, 1948, letter in Petter correspondence, File 1940-1949. Unless otherwise indicated, the information comes from the Petter files in the Mennonite Library and Archives, North Newton, Kansas.

The General Conference Mennonite Mission Board assigned them to Cantonment, Oklahoma, in 1891. The Petters had two children, Valdo and Olga, at the time of Marie's death.

Petter was a brilliant linguist and took up the study of Cheyenne with enthusiasm. The missionaries before him had not taken seriously the need to know the language, or perhaps they felt it was too difficult, and for the most part relied on interpreters or the use of English. Petter was the first to put the Cheyenne language into writing.

His outstanding achievements during the fifty-six years he worked with the mission included a Cheyenne dictionary and grammar, a translation of Bunyan's *Pilgrim's Progress*, portions of the Old Testament, the entire New Testament, and sixty Cheyenne hymns. He became internationally known as an ethnologist. Cheyenne is not only a spoken language, but also one of signing, pictures, and ceremonial forms, all of which must be learned to truly understand the people.[4]

Bertha entered into this world of language with energy and enthusiasm. She did not translate, but she was her husband's mainstay in proofreading and correcting. When the New Testament was finished, Petter reread it, four Cheyenne Indians read it separately, and an Indian woman representing the average reader of the tribe read it. Finally Bertha read it before it was printed.[5]

Loss of a son in Lame Deer

The Mennonite mission field in Montana had been opened by G. A. and Anna Linscheid. In 1916, the Petters were transferred to Lame Deer, Montana. One of the reasons for moving was that here Petter did not suffer from the hay fever that plagued him in Oklahoma.

Their knowledge of Cheyenne gave the Petters a ready welcome in Lame Deer where he continued his work with translations as well as pastoring the church. In 1923, Bethel College awarded him the Bachelor of Theology degree and later the Doctor of Divinity in recognition of his work.

In 1935, with the financial help of Sister Frieda Kaufman, the Petters traveled to Switzerland for a five-month visit to his old home. The trip began tragically, for soon after they left, his son Valdo died.

Valdo had been brought up to join in his father's work with the Cheyennes. He knew the language well. He and his wife Laura Rohrman

---

4. Rodolphe Petter, *Reminiscences of Past Years in Mission Service Among the Cheyenne* (no publisher or date), pp. 47-48.

5. "And Now the Message of Christ Is in the Cheyenne," *The Billings Gazette*, January 26, 1947, p. 1. The clipping is in the MLA.

Petter worked at the Ashland station, twenty-one miles east of Lame Deer. At his death in 1935, not only did the Petters grieve for the loss of a son, but for the loss of the only person capable of carrying on their work as they had envisioned it.

In 1935, at the age of seventy, Petter retired from the active ministry, devoting himself to corrections and additions to his grammar and revising his many sermons for the benefit of the other missionaries. Mission board policy insisted that missionaries retire from their fields at age sixty-five, but Petter resisted all efforts to remove him from Lame Deer.

The couple made another trip to Europe in 1939. Petter had developed heart trouble in 1938, which eventually caused his death in January 1947. He was buried in the Lame Deer cemetery.

Mixed feelings about Cheyenne religion and culture

Not all of the relationships between the missionaries and the Indians were friendly. The non-Christians tried to intimidate the Christians, circulating petitions that were sent to Washington, D. C., in an effort to have the Mennonite missionaries removed from the reservation. There were forty-two Christians when the Petters arrived, and they reported adding 200 more, but, during the course of the years, some died and the indifferent ones left, some joined the peyote cult (the independent Indian church), and some were enticed to the "Romish" church. The numbers faithful to the Mennonite mission were often discouragingly small.

Bertha with her husband had mixed feelings about Cheyenne religion and culture. On the one hand, the missionaries rejected all things "pagan." On the other, they were involved in learning the language and preserving the culture. The Petters gathered a large collection of Indian artifacts: war bonnets, medicine bags, charms, and ceremonial clothing. Petter had great respect for the customs and legends of the older Indians, and was concerned that the younger generation would grow up knowing nothing of Cheyenne lore and mythology.[6]

But to save the Indians' souls, they knew they must destroy the pagan practices. Bertha shared her husband's disheartening feeling that his beloved Cheyennes had no sense of sin. Some of the ceremonial dances were evil. Wives were given to the medicine men for the night, resulting in pregnancy and strife in families.

When an Indian Christian protested to Washington about the immoral practices included in the dance ceremonies, Washington responded by

---

6. Margaret Dietzel, "Rodolphe Petter: A 'Called' Linguist," research manuscript, May 1971, p. 34, MLA.

declaring such practices unlawful. The Petters won that battle in 1919, but they lost it in 1930 when the new administration adopted the policy that the Indians' own religion was just as valid as the white man's religion. The Petters were confused and appalled by the government's change of policy.

The Petters always used Scripture as the basis for their definition of sin, and the Indians would counter that "our God told us another way!" They could not understand the Petters' teaching that there is only one way. "Such an attitude was absolutely foreign to the Indians who were ready to see something good in all ways."[7]

Bertha as missionary

Because of her husband's frequent absences, Bertha was active in the missionary duties to the church. Her husband knew that he could depend on her to see that the work went on while he was off to his apple ranch at Kettle Falls, Washington, 850 miles away, or to other mission outposts. She spent much of her time with Indian Christians, directing their reading of Cheyenne Scriptures, teaching Bible lessons, and helping the lay leaders prepare sermons. Mr. Petter's philosophy was that it was better to teach the Indian leaders to read Cheyenne and to have them carry on the work of the church than to bring in new missionaries who would first have to learn the language.[8]

Peyote worship was a threat to the Indian Christian church. The Native American Church, or the peyote cult, was organized in 1918. The cult spread from Oklahoma to Montana. The services included a mixture of Christian and traditional practices, one being the eating of peyote, derived from cactus, for its hallucinating power. The use of peyote was part of the communion sacrament, along with Bible reading and prayer, feasting, drums and dancing. Of course, the Petters could not condone it.[9]

Bertha's diaries indicate that she was an avid radio listener. Whenever she could, she tuned in to the Saturday afternoon opera. "Beethoven's opera *Fidelio* was especially fine. Kirsten Flagstad was Lenore. I sent for the libretto." An accomplished pianist, she sometimes presented piano concerts of classical music in the Lame Deer church. She deplored the trend toward gospel music.

Her diaries record funerals, car trouble, and weather. Intense cold and heat had an effect on the mission program, as did car trouble, when the roads were impassable and the tires thin. But the funerals were the most draining. She sometimes conducted them when Petter was away.

7. Dietzel, pp. 24-30, from an interview with Mrs. Alfred Habegger.
8. Dietzel, p. 20, quoting from a letter from Petter to Bertha.
9. Dietzel, p. 29.

Her writing reveals a genuine love for her Indian co-workers. She was, however, High German imbued with European culture. A fellow missionary could not remember that she ever invited Indians to her table; they were fed on the back porch with a simpler set of dishes. The Valdo Petters, a generation removed from such reserve, were closer to the Indians in social relationships. After Petter's retirement in 1935, Bertha continued to protect him in his work and did not let the Indians disturb him. She was still active in running the mission.

On January 6, 1947, Mr. Petter died while fixing some breakfast for himself. "I arranged him, phoned to Busby [to the Habeggers] and waited in agony for the car to come. Hustle, bustle, phoning. Olga replied by phone. On January 11, the Cheyenne service was in the a.m. and English service in afternoon."

The Indian and missionary community gathered round, and her work went on with much the same routine as before. The next fifteen years were full, but eventually a struggle developed between the mission board executive secretaries and the aging missionary woman who knew the time had come to turn over her tasks but could not bring herself to do so.

The strings in her harp

Much of the controversy centered around her husband's lifework. Earlier, someone on the mission board had written that "Mrs. Petter harps on the language." The correspondence confirms this statement. However, the problem of the use of the Cheyenne language was only one of several strings on Mrs. Petter's harp, but it was played as the dominant chord. In a February 1940 letter, her husband responded for her that "she harps on the vehicle of the Gospel as every faithful minister harps every Sunday on the Gospel itself."

The Petters recognized that the problem was how to provide for the future when no one was prepared to take their place. Even in his own Montana field, Petter had been deeply hurt at being bypassed as a language teacher because the other missionaries thought he made language study too difficult. Only a few Indians, including Julia Shoulderblade, were good readers.

Bertha wrote to the mission board, "Alas, after almost fifty years, there is but one other [missionary] on the field in Oklahoma or in Montana who is building on the foundation so well laid. . . . SAD BEYOND WORDS!"

Later she wrote, "Will then the extensive work of the senior missionary be relegated to museum and library shelves? Surely God had not meant it so." This was her worst fear: that the lifework of her husband would be set aside.

Along with this fear was the hurt that came with her perception that Petter's work was not properly recognized by his church. She complained that her husband's articles were not being printed in the church papers. She pointed out that two pages of the conference yearbook had been devoted to two churchmen, while only a mere paragraph was devoted to the outstanding accomplishments of Missionary Petter.

The matter of their salary was further evidence to them of the board's lack of consideration. "If the pastor of the Berne church has a salary of $2,000 per annum with the fine parsonage included, why not a missionary of Mr. Petter's attainments? . . . Now do not interpret this as even a trace of jealousy, we are simply thinking of *fairness*."

Furthermore, foreign missionaries were given more time at conferences and for speaking tours. The Petters felt keenly that overseas missionaries had more prestige. At a conference in 1920, they seemed to have been overlooked when housing assignments were made and they were given a room off the grounds. "We are human enough to contrast this [room] with the comfort we had enjoyed in Washington, D. C., where one of the foremost scientists of the Smithsonian Institute showed us every courtesy and honor in their power."

To this letter, the Petters received a reassuring answer from the board that they too had been disappointed with the arrangements at the conference, for they had requested time for Mr. Petter on the program. Unfortunately, when an invitation was extended to the Petters to tour the churches, they replied that they could not possibly leave their work.

Disobeying board instructions

The Petters did not always follow board directives: "We found it advisable to disobey the instructions of the Board that Mr. Petter 'translate only in spare time.' Neither did Mr. Petter take up the direction of the work on the Muddy Creek as was advised. Neither did Valdo take the care of Birney with Frank [a Cheyenne church worker] because that was out of the question."

They gave advice to the mission board about its policies: it had expanded too much for such a small denomination, and now they, the missionaries, had to suffer for it. Agnes Williams, Bertha's bosom friend, had not accepted God's call to Lame Deer, feeling a different call, "going her own way, as so many so-called faithful people did."

Bertha was right, of course, or at least sometimes right. Language study *is* important for missionaries. But Petter had developed such a complicated system that it was difficult to learn the "pure" language. By then its daily use was disappearing; it would become the second language of the younger people as they learned English in school. The Petters were probably right about his lack of recognition. It was difficult for the average rural family to understand what this brilliant scholar had accomplished, and it was only among his professional peers that he was honored. Lacking tact and tolerance, the Petters were irritatingly right about some board decisions.

She felt she had a right to stay

The last string on her harp was reserved for the tune of retirement, a refrain that began as early as 1930 when Mr. Petter was sixty-five, and ended in November 1967. The mission board must have become thoroughly tired of it.

The place at Kettle Falls had probably been considered at one time as a retirement home, but already by 1933 the plan for the Grand Coulee Dam put the farm eighty feet under water and spoiled Petter's little bit of Switzerland. So the Petters had continued living in the mission house until his death.

Then Bertha looked at a log house that Agnes Williams had built during her short term in Montana. She persisted in a plan to have it restored as a place for her retirement. She felt she had a right to stay in the field because she was the only one with a thorough knowledge of the language. She considered herself part of the mission team at Lame Deer.

The date for her retirement was 1947, at age seventy-five. She began disposing of her husband's books and artifacts and sent a pickup truck load to the Kauffman Museum at Bethel College. That removal was a wrenching experience for her. As the Indian helpers carried his desk and his papers through the door, "We worked with intensity of feeling and few words. There was no levity in the whole procedure. It seemed as though we were carrying the body of my husband out of the home and from my side a second time."

To Mennonite World Conference at eighty

Bertha still kept busy. She and volunteers prepared Petter's dictionary for a mimeographed reprinting and there was considerable correspondence about that, particularly when the selling price the press put on it was "ridiculously low." The Library of Congress had asked for his entire collection of books and papers, but she was persuaded to leave them to the Mennonite Library and Archives. Another task was to see to the microfilming of the dictionary.

In 1952, when she was almost eighty, she attended the Mennonite World Conference at Basel, traveling alone. She negotiated with a number of women to come live with her as companion and housekeeper, but they all disappointed her. She had special gratitude for Alfred and Barbara Habegger from the Busby station for the help they gave her.

One of her self-imposed tasks was to improve the cemetery on the rocky hillside where her husband was buried. She wrote in her Christmas letter of 1954: "I had great satisfaction in sponsoring the moving of a fence, the construction of a cattle guard, the grading of a driveway. . . . also the planting, irrigating, and cultivating of 200 spruce and Chinese elm treelets."

Along with these activities she continued her contact with the Cheyenne, interceding with articulate letters to various Indian agencies on behalf of Indian friends in trouble, teaching a Sunday school class in Cheyenne, and helping some of them with their reading.

In 1960, Andrew Shelly of the mission board received a letter from the owner of a store in Lame Deer saying that although Mrs. Petter had made a great contribution to the community, it was now time for the mission board to step in to remove her for her own health, that she should not be living alone. "Frankly, we feel that it is psychologically impossible for Mrs. Petter to sever her Lame Deer ties without help."[10]

Escaping Newton's web

Finally, Bertha agreed with Shelly that she would go to Newton, live at the Bethel Home for the Aged, and work on her husband's life story at the Mennonite Library. She agreed to stay for the summer, although the mission board considered the move to be permanent. Dates were set and a farewell planned, but Bertha kept insisting that she was needed at Lame Deer to encourage the use of the valuable translations.

"Indians weep on my shoulder," she wrote. " 'Don't go. Do your writing here.' " Finally, Shelly sent Barbara Habegger, who had retired from the field in 1958, to accompany her to Newton on the train. He wrote a sympathetic, tactful, but firm letter outlining the plans.

There was a little party upon her arrival at the Bethel Home, and she seemed to adapt graciously to her surroundings. She settled into her room at the Home and made daily trips to the library, taking her lunch and a cot to rest on.

She wrote back to Lame Deer about how unhappy she was at the Home. She felt the Lord's leading to go back to Lame Deer where, as the

10. Board of Missions, Box 19, 1960, MLA.

only white woman in the world who understood Cheyenne, she could be useful. Her grandson Valdo was to be married, and she begged the board to let her go back for the wedding. Reluctantly, they allowed her to go, but Shelly had her sign a promise to return in two weeks.

Back in Lame Deer, she wrote, "Praise the Lord. The fly has escaped the spider web." She asked that the board disregard her promise to be back in two weeks, since she had decided to stay in Lame Deer until her doctor advised her to go to a home. She kept finding reasons for staying: her responsibility for the cemetery, visits from friends, funerals of Indians.

Finally, the missionaries at Lame Deer came to her defense. They wrote saying her attitude had changed, that the world did not revolve around her as it had before she left for Newton, that she went out of her way not to give additional work. "So let it go for the time being," since she was now content to live alone, and the Indians seemed to be standing by her and looking after her to some degree.

The mission board decided that she might as well abide in peace in her log house at Lame Deer. She lived frugally, writing occasionally, asking the board to find someone to live with her, resenting inquiries about her financial status.

In December 1963, she made the decision to enter a new retirement home in Billings, Montana. She died on November 7, 1967, lucid to the last, and was buried beside her husband in the Lame Deer cemetery.

Committed to the Word and to her husband

What should be said about this remarkable woman?

As the first General Conference Mennonite woman to receive a college degree, Bertha could probably have had a career that would have brought her prominence even in church circles. She could have become a respected teacher or, if she had waited until after 1900, a missionary to India or China. Or she could, as she said, have joined the Lutherans and enjoyed the prominence to which her scholastic attainments entitled her.

But she became a single missionary in a field that was not given much prestige, and then at age thirty-nine married a man whose academic achievements overshadowed hers. She had to depend on his accomplishments to make her own life significant. A woman endowed with more grace could have risen above the oblivion or drowned herself in it.

Rodolphe Petter's work was extraordinary and deserving of recognition. He became *the* authority on the Cheyenne language.[11] He could not have done it as well without such a qualified helpmate as Bertha, who was able to assume the main burden of missionary work.

What he accomplished was priceless research to which scholars would refer. His associates on the mission field found it less useful. As Bertha feared, the body of work is now sitting on library shelves useful to scholars but of little use to church workers in the Cheyenne fields. The Cheyenne language is little used in the churches in Lame Deer.

Still, Rodolphe Petter had the approval of the mission board to pursue his language studies and Bertha was assigned to him as a helper in that study. She did well what she was assigned to do. She felt she was called by God to do this work, and she did it with utmost commitment to the language, her husband, the Cheyennes, and the Word.

It may be easier for some of us to understand and love a woman who is human enough to feel and express hurt than to understand one who is too saintly to talk back.

---

11. For an exposure to the written body of work that he developed, see *Memoirs of the American Anthropological Association*, Vol. I, Part 6, "Sketch of Cheyenne Grammar," September 1907, pp. 443-478.

Anna Jantzen: The young bachelor couldn't help but notice the pretty, blue-eyed young woman in her long flowing skirts as she rode sidesaddle.

6.
Knowing the Power of Prayer

Anna Wiebe Jantzen
1875—1939

When the two younger Jantzen sons returned home from the Summit Grammar School, they expected their mother to be in the kitchen, ready to hand out freshly toasted *zwieback* or a piece of coffee cake. But there were days when they did not find her there. Nor would she be sewing in the bedroom nor was she across the yard at their Grandma Jantzen's house.

If that was not the day for the sewing society at a neighbor's house, the only other place they might expect to find her was in the *Grosse Stube*, the parlor. The shades would be pulled and she would be kneeling in prayer at one of the large chairs. The children learned to respect her quiet time there.[1]

Anna Jantzen had many concerns and responsibilities as the mother of a growing family and the wife of a busy pastor-farmer. She had early in life learned to renew her strength in communion with the Lord Jesus, her helper and friend.

At home on the Volga River

Anna, second child in a family of eleven, was born on March 18, 1875, to Aron J. and Maria Fieguth Wiebe. Theirs was a middle-class German

---

1. This material comes from "We Remember Mama," reminiscences by Aron and Kathryn Jantzen, compiled in 1984, and from interviews with Mathilda and Lubin Jantzen and Helene Janzen.

Mennonite home in Lysanderhoeh, one of several prosperous villages near Saratov on the Volga River in East Russia.

Her father, born at Altenau, West Prussia, in 1845, had migrated to East Russia with other Mennonites who shared his strong convictions against militarism. A man of many abilities, he was a farmer, a minister in the local church, and a doctor of homeopathic medicine.

Anna enjoyed her childhood, but she learned early to be useful. Although Russian peasants worked on the farm and in the home, Anna's help was needed to manage the home, since her mother was often not well. Anna, as the oldest daughter, had much of the care for the smaller children. She also went with her father on his visits to patients and learned some nursing skills. She became an excellent cook and frequently prepared meals for guests. Like every good housekeeper, she learned to knit, crochet, and embroider; a trained seamstress taught her to sew.

Although she had little formal schooling, her education was not neglected. She learned to read and write, as well as memorize poems and Scripture. In this Christian home, Anna developed a strong faith in Christ, a deep love for the Word of God, and the value of prayer. She felt close to her large family. By the time she was fourteen, she had experienced with her parents the loss of five small brothers and sisters.

Learning to live with pain

When she was twelve, Anna fell while skating on the Volga River, fracturing several vertebrae in her spine. Her father treated her to the best of his ability, but the illness of her mother claimed the family attention at the time. Travel to a bone specialist was out of the question. By the time she was taken for medical treatment, the damage could not be corrected. During her lifetime she gradually became more and more stooped. Another of her handicaps was her loss of hearing which became worse as she grew older.

When Anna was sixteen, her mother died of cancer. Her death was a great shock to the family. Anna, with the help of her older brother Gerhard, assumed responsibility for the younger children, Jacob, Henry, and Katherine as well as two-year-old Maria. Anna shared her father's deep grief and did her best to take the place of her mother. Eighteen months later her father married his wife's sister, Johanna Bergmann, a widow. Her son John joined the family and became brother as well as cousin to Anna.

To Nebraska and California

Anna's father felt a foreboding of coming events, making him uneasy about remaining in Russia. In 1894 the two older sons, Gerhard Wiebe and John Bergmann, who were nearing the age of conscription, emigrated to America. In the spring of 1896, the rest of the family left Russia to make a home in America.

For a short time, Aron and Johanna and their seven children stayed in the Mennonite community at Beatrice, Nebraska. In 1897, they followed a group of Mennonites led by Elder Jacob Hege and Jacob Claassen to San Luis Obispo County, California. Anna's oldest brother Gerhard stayed behind to raise his family in the Beatrice area.

The new country was one of beautiful hills, valleys, and woods, but it demanded a great deal of physical effort of its pioneers. The Wiebe family applied the industry and frugality that they had learned so well in Russia. In the fall of 1897, the community organized as a congregation, led by Jacob Hege as elder and Aron Wiebe as assistant minister.

As the community grew, the families felt the need for their own school and a Christian teacher. They wrote back to Beatrice, Nebraska, asking Daniel Jantzen to come. He responded that he was unable to move, but he recommended his brother Frank F. Jantzen. Frank had grown up on a farm near Hillsboro, Kansas, and had taught for five years in the area. He had graduated from the Bethel Academy in Newton in 1900 and then attended the college for a year. Frank went to California and began teaching in the small school in 1901.

Courted on horseback

The young bachelor soon became acquainted with members of the congregation and with Anna Wiebe. Anna was an excellent rider, and he couldn't help noticing the pretty, blue-eyed young woman in her long flowing skirt as she rode sidesaddle on her white mare, Beauty. He courted her on horseback, sometimes holding a white umbrella to keep the sun off her, to their neighbors' amusement.

They were married on January 15, 1903, by Reverend Hege, who used as his text Joshua 24:15, "But as for me and my house, we will serve the Lord." This was the text they were to apply literally as the motto for their years together. Frank was called to be assistant minister that same year. Because of his musical talent, he was often called on to lead the singing.

After their marriage, even with the more general use of the horse and buggy, the young minister and his wife would arrive at church on horseback each with a child in arms.

Life in rural California was utterly different from that in East Russia. Here there were no servants. Living in a small, simple house, with her husband occupied with farm, school, and church, Anna accepted most of the responsibility of caring for the children and maintaining the home. Her Russian experience was good preparation for managing her expanding household.

The family grew. Mary, Albert, Oswald, and Minna arrived during the first seven years. The community also grew, and as land became scarce, a number of families moved to the Willow Creek area. The Frank Jantzens moved to a fifty-acre farm with a few rickety buildings. They repaired a small shack and added a room to make a small house. The San Marcos church was moved to the new area with Anna's father and husband as ministers.

A community catastrophe

In 1910, tragedy struck the community. Five babies, all born in 1909, became ill with poliomyelitis. A short time before they came down with the disease, all five had been put to sleep on the same bed at a birthday party. Minna, then about seven months old, was not able to stand. Her cousin Edwin was left with a similar handicap. Fortunately, the three other children were less affected.

It soon became evident that both of Minna's legs were paralyzed and that she would not be able to walk. In their search for help for Minna, Anna and Frank were advised to take her to the Children's Hospital in San Francisco. Using muscle-tendon transplants and various surgical procedures done over several years, the weak legs were finally straightened. By the time she was eight, Minna was able to walk with crutches.

Aron's arrival in 1911 made five small children in the crowded quarters. When the Jantzen parents made plans to move to California and live nearby, Anna and Frank hurried to build a large two-story house. It was completed in 1912, and the elder Jantzens with their daughter Margaret moved into the old cottage.

Working as a pastor of a small congregation brought in little money. To maintain a growing family, the farmland had to be worked and made productive. Anna and Frank, with the help of their children, cleared the land, planted an orchard of fifty fruit trees, a vineyard, and fields of grain. Some of the fifty acres was left for grazing. The family maintained a large garden and raised chickens. Since Frank was occupied with tasks of school and church, Anna was left to supervise the children in the many tasks around the farm. Church friends came in to help when a new baby was born. Sometimes they had to hire help when the burden became too heavy.

The family was not yet complete. Richard was born in 1912, John in 1914, just before the outbreak of World War I. Lubin was born in 1916, and Anna in 1918. Ruth, born in 1921, was the last and tenth child, making a dozen around the table.

Calmness under stress

An almost disastrous fire alarmed the family in 1918. Mother Anna had put Baby Anna to sleep in the bedroom while she canned fruit in the kitchen. The rest of the family washed the Model T Ford, their first car and their pride and joy. (They were not the first family in the community to buy a car, and the children had been sensitive to the fact that they were being passed by on the way to church.)

On this occasion, Anna turned the flame low on the kerosene stove while she went outside. The fruit boiled over and caught fire. When Anna returned, she gave the alarm and then darted into the house through a side door to pick up little Anna from the bedroom. Outside with the baby in her arms, Anna collected the little ones around her, leading them away from the house into the middle of the yard. Frank and the older children put out the fire. Her family was impressed by their mother's calm control.

Educating the family

One by one, the ten children entered Summit Grammar School and then went on for further study. Few from the community attended high school at that time. A car pool was organized with another family to take the children to Templeton High School. Once the ice was broken and it was known that Grandpa Wiebe's grandchildren were risking the possibility of becoming modern, other families began sending their children to Templeton High School, making a bus route practical.

Completing high school was not enough for this family. Eventually nine of the children attended the Bible Institute of Los Angeles. The call to Christian service came to each child in a different way. Long before any of the family were aware of it, Aron Wiebe, Anna's father, had prayed that some of his children or grandchildren should serve the Lord in some needy part of the world.

Missionaries from India, China, and the American Indian fields had come to the Willow Creek Mennonite Church, and of course they would remain for the night and take their meals at the home of the pastor. The children knew that Anna spent much time in prayer for them, desiring that each learn to know God's will for his or her life. Anna's prayers supported Frank's sermons as he concentrated on the Lord's call to "go into all the world, and preach the gospel to every creature." An unusually high percentage of the young people from that church of 125 members went into full-time Christian service.

Anna was a fervent believer in prayer and in teaching her children to pray. Every evening at bedtime she gathered the younger ones around her; while she sat with the baby on her lap, the others knelt and each would pray, from the youngest to the oldest. She also encouraged each child to memorize Scripture portions and to read from the Bible in daily devotions. Anna also spent some time each day alone in prayer, and as the children scattered, she spent more time in intercessory prayer.

Acting out her faith

The parents also acted out their faith. After World War I, they sent food parcels to hungry relatives in Russia. Anna made new clothes to send. She wanted to include notes or money with the clothes, but the family had been told not to do so. Later they heard that those packages that had included money had been refused by the government, and she was glad she had followed instructions. When a family fleeing from Russia came to California, the Jantzens gave them food and furniture and helped them find housing.

One of Anna's friends, Helene Janzen, remembers her as one of the "quiet in the land." One of her daughters-in-law said that she never spoke unkindly of anyone. Anna was sensitive to the feelings of others. One son remembers being scolded for mimicking his grandfather's walk.

Anna died as she had lived, working industriously and thinking of the welfare of her family. Shortly after she had bid good-bye to two of her children and their families as they went overseas as missionaries, she suffered a stroke. She collapsed while tending her chores before going to church. Her last words were, "Just get yourselves ready to go to church. Don't worry about me." She died January 8, 1939.

Anna Wiebe Jantzen lived a full life, similar to that of many pioneering women in her community. Physical suffering was a constant companion to her work. She confided to her sister that she was never without a pain in her back.

Her children saw in her a mother who was an excellent homemaker, a servant to others, a quiet witness to the grace of God in frail human form. She may have looked to heaven for her reward, but she must have felt great peace in seeing her children fulfill her prayerful expectations. Six of her ten children became overseas missionaries and all took part in Christian service in their local congregations. Her children acknowledge that her prayers had a profound influence on them. Indeed, "her children rise up and call her blessed" (Prov. 31:28).

7.
Evangelist in Chicago

Katharine Kroeker Wiens
1878—1946

by Helen Neufeld Coon

Katharine Wiens quietly closed the door to her bedroom each day after the noon meal. Her children never knew what went on then, but they guessed that this was her time for prayer, Bible reading, pleading with God, and possibly resting. She needed a time to rest and momentarily forget the concerns of raising a family, visiting the parents of Sunday school children, helping to deliver babies, and trying to cope with the endless housework.

For missionaries Katharine and Abraham Wiens, the call to reach people for Christ came from the growing edges of the city of Chicago. Katharine needed to close the door briefly each day to the voices from the outside: peddlers, garbage men, and fighting ruffians. She also needed to close the door to the sound on the inside: her seven lively daughters giggling or quarreling.

Sounds of seven daughters

On one particular day, Katharine was startled from her quiet time by a thunderous crash in the kitchen. This time she did leave her solitude to find that the table legs and the legs of her four youngest daughters were tangled together. Instead of sitting around the table as ordinary children should, they had been sitting *on* it. Their wiggling had been too much for it.

Katharine Wiens: We all knew that God was first in her life, father second; and there was still plenty of love left for her seven daughters.

Remembering her own years of growing up, she knew that children should be spanked for such behavior, but Katharine refrained. And she wouldn't let her husband Abraham spank them either. She did not mind giving discipline or letting her husband lead, but she felt her role was one of bringing quietness, control, and comfort to the lives of the persons around her.

Katharine's own life, however, had seldom been peaceful and serene. The fourth child of Bernhard and Katharine Ott Kroeker, she was born December 12, 1878, near Henderson, Nebraska. Prior to her birth, her parents had suffered the loss of their second child who had died on the 1878 trip from South Russia to the United States. Later, Katharine grieved with them when they lost a daughter and a pair of twins. Katharine was left with six brothers and sisters, and later she would have two half brothers.

Pulling the plow

Katharine's father was an ordained Mennonite minister of the Peters' church which later grew into the Evangelical Mennonite Brethren. In addition, he was an evangelist, teacher, and farmer. He ministered to small groups of Mennonites who had settled in Colorado, Texas, and Nebraska. This work as a church leader was, in addition to the farm work, the means of supporting his family. Everyone worked. Even six-year-old Katharine, wearing boy's trousers, helped pull the plow.

In 1893, the family moved to Genoa, Colorado. But the lack of rain resulted in poor crops, and many of the families of the community moved away. In 1897, the Kroekers moved too, first to Katie, Texas, then to Richmond, where a group of Mennonites had opened up a settlement to grow cotton and sugar cane.

Her father taught his own children, and eventually the oldest daughters helped in teaching young students in a private school in their home. Students from a distance boarded in their home during the week.

About this time, Katharine learned to know Abraham F. Wiens. Born in 1868 at Schoenau, South Russia, he was the son of Abraham F. and Elizabeth Klassen Wiens. This thin, handsome young man, a recent arrival from Russia, caught Katharine's eye. She had other suitors, but it was Abraham who won her hand. His background included early education in the *Dorfschule* and four years of forest work in lieu of military training. Katharine and Abraham were married on May 29, 1898 and settled at Richmond. The family prospered financially in this settlement where houses were being built and crops of cotton and cane flourished. Their daughter Catherine was born in June 1899.

Changed by a wall of water

On September 8, 1900, their lives changed drastically. A severe hurricane and wall of water hit the Galveston, Texas, area, including the town of Richmond. The hurricane and tide which lasted in that part of the country from August 27 to September 8 resulted in the loss of some 5,000 lives.[1] Katharine and Abraham's home was entirely demolished. Abraham narrowly escaped being crushed by a falling stone, but he fell into a glass cupboard and cut his face badly. Katharine and the baby were unharmed.

The most tragic result of the storm was yet to come. Katharine's mother died from her injuries. Her husband wrote to the church paper describing the event:

> We found each other and were all alive but my dear wife said right away that she was hurt internally and that she would die. Daughter Sarah and I made her a bed and I sat beside her and we discussed serious matters as she was facing death. . . .
>
> Now I must tell you something of us that are left behind. I am about well again; I had a wound on my head and my back was injured. Sarah had an injured foot, Anna had both legs injured and Bernhard had suffered terribly with a bad knee and it looks like the leg will wither. Heinrich, the youngest had a broken leg below the knee and a sore arm. May the Lord give us grace not to lose courage in these afflictions that are very hard to bear.
>
> Our buildings were worth $500 and everything is gone. Of the furniture there is not one chair that is not broken, clothes are all blown away and my dear wife is dead. Pray for us.[2]

Abraham and Katharine helped her sister Sarah with the sad task of preparing their mother's body for burial. They washed her, put some dry grass in the coffin, and covered her with a sheet given them by the Thiessen neighbors who had the only dry linens available. The coffin had been built from boards of broken houses. Katharine Kroeker was one of four from the same Sunday school who were killed in the hurricane: two mothers and two girls.[3] Young Katharine and Abraham stayed in Texas long enough to help with the cleanup of the storm's devastation. In the meantime, in 1901, a second daughter, Elizabeth, was born.

The disaster helped the Wienses respond to a call they had both heard. As a result, they were the first couple to volunteer for Evangelical Menno-

---

1. "Disasters of the World," *The Encyclopedia Americana*, 1959 edition.
2. *Mennonitische Rundschau*, October 3, 1900, p. 4.
3. Sarah Kroeker, *Texas Hurricane of Sept. 8, 1900* (no publisher or date), pp. 5f.

nite Brethren mission work. In 1902, the young family headed for Inman, Kansas, where the couple spent the next four years studying in nearby McPherson College and Academy. Abraham received a diploma in Bible in 1906. Katharine, listed as Katy or Katie in the school records, was a student in the Bible department. Sometime during the period, she took a course in midwifery, which she was to practice in Chicago.

An argument with her husband

Abraham and Katharine had to choose where their call should take them. According to family members, a disagreement here resulted in the only severe argument the couple ever had.

In later years, when asked by one of her daughters if she had ever had a fight with her husband (the daughters sometimes argued with their father), Katharine replied that when they felt the call of God to Christian service, the possibility of being sent to a foreign country presented itself. Furloughs were rare in that era of missionary work, and Katharine worried about whom her two daughters would marry if they were sent to a place such as Africa or India. She didn't want them to marry men of another color, although Abraham didn't see much wrong with that.

The argument must have resulted in hurt feelings, and Katharine decided never to argue with him again. Whatever the reason, the Wienses accepted the request to enter mission work in Chicago. It was their daughters who later became foreign missionaries.

According to the oldest daughter Catherine, Abraham and Katharine were ordained in 1906 at Jansen, Nebraska. Catherine, aged seven, was impressed by that occasion: "I shall never forget that solemn day when the brethren of the church conference laid their hands on my father and mother and blessed them and gave them the privilege to go forth as workers in His vineyard."[4] There are other memories of a special service at Mountain Lake, Minnesota. The Wienses went to Chicago, that winter of 1906, staying first at the 26th Street Mission in order to get acquainted with city life.

The house above the tavern

Get acquainted they did! Their temporary home was above a tavern. Occupants of the lower floors would sometimes disturb the peace of the family, and sometimes they found drunks lying on their stairway. One evening, Father Wiens arrived home with a broken nose, the result of a well-placed punch.

    4. Catherine Neufeld, "Life and Passing of Rev. Abraham Wiens," typewritten manuscript furnished by Esther Neufeld Kressly.

In 1907, work was opened up at the Hoyne Avenue Mission at 33rd Street and Hoyne Avenue. During the panic of that year, the mission supplied many persons with food. A hall for services faced the street with living quarters in the rear. Daughter Catherine said:

> How well I remember the children throwing corks and peelings into the faces of the brave workers. The hall soon was crowded with children and grown-up people. The Sunday school needed all the rooms in the back for classes. Across the street was a noisy saloon, and as little children, we dreaded the place. Often at night we were awakened by a noisy, drunken brawl across the street.[5]

After about a year, the mission and family moved to the Mennonite Rescue Mission at 35th Street and Oakley Avenue. Here there was room for chickens and a flower and vegetable garden. A large barn with a rope swing inside afforded the girls some fun away from the rest of the world. By now, the older ones were attending school.

Another girl, and another

The fourth daughter Martha was born in 1907. Helene was born in 1909. Years later, Katharine confessed that Helene's appearance was a disappointment. She had hoped to have a son, not for herself, but for her husband, even though he had never in any way shown any disappointment as daughter followed daughter. Then, too, she wanted to raise preachers, and of course *men* became preachers.

Prior to the birth of this fifth child, she had prayed earnestly for a son. When, during her pregnancy, she became larger than usual, she was certain that God had answered her prayers. Nevertheless, Helene, all fourteen pounds of her arrived, and Katharine's faith in God was visibly shaken. She became ill, needing the services of a doctor, but gradually she recovered and carried on with renewed faith.[6]

The Sunday school thrived at the 35th Street location. Katharine visited the parents of the children who attended so that they also became interested in coming to the services. Katharine's sister, Sarah Kroeker, assisted in the work while she took courses in nursing.

In 1912, a property was purchased and a move was made one block over to 34th Street and Oakley Avenue. Here again services were held in a hall in the front and the Wiens family lived at the rear. In the attic,

---

5. John T. Neufeld and Jacob C. Fast, compilers, *The Family of Abraham and Elizabeth Klassen Wiens*, 1970, p. 3.
6. From a questionnaire filled out by Helene Wiens Dick, furnished by Mary Lou Cummings.

temporary curtained-off rooms were fixed as bedrooms for the five girls. When the hall proved too small for the Sunday school, the building was remodeled. Then the family of seven lived in the basement. This work prospered until the Sunday school averaged over a hundred children, and remarkable conversions took place. Later, some of these members formed the nucleus of the Brighton Mennonite Church.

The seven little Wienses

In 1912 and 1914, Sarah and Esther joined the family, making seven daughters. Abraham pronounced the family now complete. Ella Baker, one of the young women who often spent evenings with the family, called them "Papa Wiens and Mamma Wiens and seven little Wienses and how they grew on *pluma moos* and *borscht*."[7]

Ella, as well as many others, often enjoyed the hospitality of the Wiens family. Sunday dinner and supper for many years was the time for company, those helping with the mission work as well as visitors. Several of these workers and visitors eventually became husbands of the Wiens daughters. Katharine's sister Sarah later went out under the Congo Inland Mission as one of its earliest missionaries. Visiting missionaries had a direct influence on the career choices of the daughters.

The family recalls that because of limited funds, Sunday was the only time butter appeared on the table. For a time, only one dollar a week was spent for milk, providing one quart a day for the whole family. Papa and Mamma Wiens got the cream off the top for their coffee and the rest was used in cereal and cooking. One week they didn't even have a dollar for the week's milk, but, according to daughter Helene, the milk was miraculously provided.

Another move

A difficult time in Katharine's life came in 1916 when "at the request of the conference"[8] (Evangelical Mennonite Brethren) another minister, more vigorous and dramatic, took up the work of the mission at 34th Street and Oakley. The Wienses were hurt by this action, but "the Conference gave them conditional permission to open another [mission]."[9] They might have returned to farming, but instead they took the little money they had to make a down payment on property at 42nd and Rockwell Street.

---

7. Mary Wiens Toews, *The True to Life Story of the Wiens Family* (no publisher or date), p. 12.
8. D. H. Epp, *A Historical Sketch of the Churches of the Evangelical Mennonite Brethren* (Rosthern, Saskatchewan), no date, p. 103.
9. Epp, p. 81.

"Weeks of prayer and fasting to God for His guidance preceded this endeavor," said Abraham.[10]

In 1917, the family went out into the streets and invited boys and girls to Sunday school. Twenty-seven came the first Sunday. The work grew and by the third Sunday, fifty-eight were present. Known then as the Mennonite Bible Mission, this group later became Grace Mennonite Church.

The strain of the work was too much for Abraham, however, and he became ill. For a time, services were suspended and the Wienses took time to rest before they opened the church again to the people of the neighborhood. Katharine did a good bit of visitation work, and there were about sixteen besides the family who attended the first Sunday it reopened. The work was continued under the Evangelical Mennonite Brethren Conference. "The Conference offered them no definite salary or support but decided that each of the conference churches send them one offering a year."[11] Unfortunately only occasional freewill offerings were received, usually from relatives of the family.

It took until 1921 for the first baptism to take place at the Mennonite Bible Mission. But the work grew until between 1926 and 1937 the average attendance was over one hundred. Sundays found Katharine at the church early to greet the people. Activities included morning and evening services on Sunday, Wednesday services, and sewing classes, with street meetings and Bible school during the summer.

"Grace Mennonite Church (then Mennonite Bible Mission) located at 4221 Rockwell Street was the work of the Abraham F. Wiens family, with emphasis on the family, for they all participated," is the way one historian summed up that chapter in their lives.[12]

Katharine, the storyteller

Katharine Wiens is remembered for her help in the sewing classes, her visiting, and especially her story telling. Her own children remember the gripping tales she told them in Low German as they gathered around in the evening while she darned socks. These stories were usually of dramatic answers to prayer that she had read earlier in a German paper from Russia.

Years later, summer Bible school students would recall her story

---

10. A. F. Wiens, "25 Years in Chicago Mission Work," 1931; handwritten manuscript furnished by Esther Neufeld Kressly.
11. Epp, p. 82.
12. Samuel F. Pannabecker, *Faith in Ferment* (Newton, Kansas, Faith and Life Press, 1968), p. 276.

telling. She would stand in front, her hands clasped over the closed book, and tell the stories in such detail that in retrospect her listeners would wonder if she had been reading the story. But the book had always been closed.

On days when Katharine did her visiting, she put a pot of soup on before she went out so that it would be ready for the family when she returned at five thirty. She was adept in managing money, time, and tasks, and she did have help from her daughters. They also helped greatly with the finances of the family as they became old enough to work outside the home.

Praying for bargains

Abraham, more verbal than Katharine, was the leader, and she supported him in this role. She also backed him in prayer. Once every two weeks, he went downtown to find bargains. While he was gone, she set up the ironing board and spent the day ironing and praying aloud. This supplemented her own quiet time and the morning family devotions led by her husband. He was often seen on his knees in the church sanctuary. Besides giving spiritual leadership to the family, he saw to it that they had occasions for fun, including a yearly outing to Lincoln Park on the Fourth of July, with a boat ride on Lake Michigan.[13]

Katharine's work was often that of a servant: midwifery in the early years, caring for the newborn, keeping children of sick mothers in her home, and even cleaning the heads of children with lice. Daughter Helene said, "We all knew God was first in her life, father second; and there was still plenty of love left for her seven daughters."

Music was important to the family. Often the girls heard their mother starting the day with "My Lord, What a Morning." A piano and music lessons were usually a part of their lives even when finances were limited. Quartets, solos, choir leading, piano and pump organ playing were all part of the family's contribution to the services and street meetings. Other times, the girls sang just for the fun of it, sitting in the large box swing in the yard. During a storm, the family, sitting in a circle, used singing as therapy. On Sunday afternoons, they gathered around the piano with any of the assorted guests, some of whom might be suitors. Katharine and Abraham sang duets, even singing at the farewell for daughter Elizabeth when she left with her husband for missionary work in India.

---

13. Interview with Martha Wiens Ewert.

Summer German classes

Education was also important to the family. During a few summers, they held their own personal German classes around the kitchen table. Although a number of the daughters had to leave high school to find employment, all seven attended Moody Bible Institute. Four of the girls graduated from there, and four received bachelor's degrees and two received master's degrees, three of these from seminaries.

The Rockwell Street location, their fifth home in Chicago, became their last. After several remodelings, it became an attractive home and mission which Katharine shared with Abraham until his death in 1937. After leading the morning service and teaching a Bible class, he was on his way to a men's meeting when he died of a heart attack. Together Katharine and Abraham had served Christ in the city for about thirty years.

Into all the world

What became of the "seven little Wienses"?

Catherine followed in the footsteps of her mother, teaching, and then marrying John T. Neufeld. Together they carried on the Chicago mission work.[14] John also served as business manager of the Mennonite Biblical Seminary in Chicago for ten years.

Elizabeth and John Thiessen were missionaries in India for years. Later he served as executive secretary of the General Conference Board of Missions.

Mary and Henry Toews worked with the Congo Inland Mission. He later served as pastor and hospital chaplain in the United States. She was a writer and a teacher.

Martha and August Ewert became missionaries to China and later he served as business manager of Grace Bible Institute. Martha has always been active in music and Christian education.

Helene and George Dick entered home mission work in Lima, Ohio, followed by other pastoral and voluntary service assignments. She worked as a teacher and a licensed practical nurse.

Music, the care of her mother, office work, and advanced studies filled the life of Sarah Wiens. She graduated from Mennonite Biblical Seminary in 1950 in the first class to have women graduates.

Esther, the youngest, taught at a number of private Christian schools for twenty years and then married George P. Janzen, Sr., a farmer. In

---

14. More about this era is told in *The House at the Back of the Lot* by Helen C. Coon (Newton, Kansas: Faith and Life Press, 1982).

1959, she was the first woman elected to the Board of Missions of the General Conference Mennonite Church.

General Conference support

In 1939, the General Conference Mennonite Church began to support the work of the Mennonite Bible Mission and later bought the property. The church, now known as the Grace Community Church, is part of the the Central District Conference of the General Conference. After a fire in 1977, an attractive building was erected on a corner location.

Katharine continued living at Rockwell Street after Abraham's death, helping Catherine and John Neufeld carry on the work of the mission-church. Quilting, story telling, and hospitality continued. Several of the daughters helped to care for her in her later years. Diabetes took its toll and she died June 5, 1946.

It was fitting that at the fellowship meal following her funeral the relatives and friends gathered to sing the songs she loved. Katharine and Abraham are buried in the Fairmount Cemetery (now Willow Hills Memorial Park) near Chicago in the midst of the graves of many of the persons whom they helped lead to Christ.

Unknowingly, Katharine and Abraham left a legacy of suffering in the form of the inherited disorder of Huntington's disease. It is believed that Abraham passed it on. Sarah and Elizabeth died as a result of the mental and muscle deterioration that started at midlife.

Their greatest legacy, inherited by their children and grandchildren, was a missionary zeal for spreading the good news of Christ's love. Because of Katharine and Abraham's life together, the work of Christ continues at various places in the world.

Frieda Kaufman: At twenty-five, she began a lifetime of administration, a feat equaled by few other women.

8.
Builder of a Healing Community

Frieda Marie Kaufman
1883—1944

Sister Frieda Kaufman's formal career began when she became deaconess mother and sister-in-charge of Bethel Deaconess Hospital at the age of twenty-five. During the next thirty-six years, she earned a bookful of credits toward an honorary degree of Doctor of Humane Letters. And when she died, she had plans that were still in her head.

Yodeling from the mountain

Frieda was born on October 23, 1883, at Haagen, Baden, Germany, near the Black Forest and a few miles from the Swiss border. Her parents, John and Marie Egle Kaufman, had moved across the border from a farm near Basel. Frieda was the last of the nine children, six having died before she was born. Her family had expected her to be a boy, but they were only momentarily disappointed when she joined her much older sisters, Anna and Lisette.

Frieda attended the kindergarten in her village run by the Lutheran deaconesses and then attended public school. One of the pleasures of that time was yodeling. "One group of students would stand on a mountainside and sing to another group on a nearby mountain."[1]

During its last year in Germany, the family lived across the street from a group of nuns who allowed her to help with the kindergarten

---
1. Marilyn Bartel, "Sister Frieda Kaufman: Builder of Institutions and Lives," research paper, Bethel College, 1966, p. 24, in the Mennonite Library and Archives, North Newton, Kansas.

children. These kind women, Lutheran and Catholic, first stirred Frieda's enthusiasm for the vocation of deaconess.[2]

From Haagen to Halstead

The family emigrated to Halstead, Kansas, in 1892. Frieda was a vivacious child and made friends on the train and on the boat. She enjoyed visiting with everyone, even older women. Her friendship with the chief cook on the boat gained advantages for the entire family.

Two years after the move to Halstead, her mother died. At the age of eleven she found her stable home shattered. Her sisters married soon after and her father lived with her oldest sister. In her desolation, she turned to Christ's message of comfort and she was challenged by Christ's sacrifice. She professed her faith and received catechism instruction from Christian Krehbiel, her pastor at Halstead. She was baptized in June 1897.[3]

John Kaufman subscribed to three secular newspapers. From them, Frieda learned about the deaconess work of other denominations. She had no idea that someone was incubating the idea of a deaconess order within the Mennonite community.

David Goerz and the deaconess idea

As early as 1890, David Goerz had presented a paper advocating deaconess work to a meeting of the General Conference Mennonite Church. In 1898, the Goessel community built Bethesda Hospital but had no trained workers to operate it. Goerz kept studying the problem, reading all he could find on deaconess work. "His thoughts were not concerned with establishing professional nursing as a vocation among the Mennonites. He wanted young women to serve in varied labors of love under the auspices of and in connection with the church."[4]

When Frieda was sixteen, her father asked her to work for a short time for an older woman until her new helper came. Frieda did not like the idea of giving up her Christmas vacation, but she was an obedient daughter. From Mrs. Kramer, she learned what it meant to be a good housekeeper, but only in later years did she appreciate these lessons.

On the evening that Frieda was to leave, Mrs. Kramer had a stroke. Because the new housekeeper would not have anything to do with the nursing, Frieda stayed on. While she did not care much for housekeeping,

---

2. "The Bethel Deaconess Institutions," *In the Service of the King*, March 1942, p. 6. Much of the information is found in articles which continue from March through May 1943.

3. Alice Claassen, "Sister Frieda Kaufman," *Pioneers in Profile* (North Newton, Kansas: Bethel College, 1945), pp. 6f.

4. Katie Funk Wiebe, *Our Lamps Were Lit* (Newton, Kansas: Bethel Deaconess Hospital School of Nursing, 1978), pp. 2f.

she loved nursing. By chance, Goerz heard of her interest in nursing and deaconess work and asked her to come to see him.

He wanted to be sure that she would look upon the deaconess service as a life calling and that she did not want to become a professional nurse. Goerz was to leave soon for India with a shipment of grain, but he suggested that she enroll at Bethel College until she was old enough to enter deaconess training.

When Goerz returned from abroad in December 1900, he brought back a gift of $150, given by interested friends in Russia for his deaconess dream. In 1901, Frieda Kaufman was named a deaconess candidate.

A liberal education

Her two years at Bethel College gave her a high regard for history, literature, science, and art. Speaking in the metaphor of her time, she wrote, "But best of all, she had been led to the stream which flows from the throne of God and drank deeply of the soul satisfying water of life."[5]

Years later in speaking to the home economics graduates at the college, she regretted that she had not had courses in home economics.

> Had I known exactly what I needed for my later life, I would have chosen, beside Home Economics, a course in plumbing and steamfitting. I should have learned to read blue prints and memorized the terms which a carpenter uses in construction and building—and of course, I should have learned many, many other things! But absolutely nothing which I learned at school has ever been useless or empty ballast.[6]

In the fall of 1902, Frieda accompanied David Goerz and his daughter Katie on a trip east to visit training schools. He left Frieda in Summerfield, Illinois, while he went ahead to spy out the land. There she met Hillegonda van der Smissen whom she would invite to join the diaconate seven years later.

Goerz returned, impressed with the program of the Interdenominational Deaconess Home and Hospital in Cincinnati. Before he put her on the train to Cincinnati, he presented her with a Bible, a small ruler, and a sharpened blue pencil. He did not give her advice or preach a sermon. But she cherished the gifts and used them to the end of her life.

In Cincinnati, Frieda completed the regular two years of theory and practice in nursing. Goerz had arranged that she could be involved with

---

5. *In the Service of the King*, October 1942, p. 12.
6. Sister Frieda Kaufman Collection, Box 84-A3, MLA.

the furnishing and equipping of the new hospital. After basic training, most of what she learned was from observation. She spent the last few months at the Ohio Maternity Hospital.

Although there were few textbooks for nursing at this time, Frieda met a teacher who allowed her to copy her lectures, over three hundred pages of hand-written teaching notes, on the care of patients suffering from a variety of diseases. There was also an extensive section on complications of childbirth.[7] In the light of today's knowledge of medicine, some of the advice was good, some not, but it was the nursing bible of the time.

Not being one with narrow interests, Frieda enjoyed the cultural assets of Cincinnati and the social contacts she made with her patients. She met the leaders of her own denomination when she attended church services and conferences at Trenton, Ohio, and undoubtedly impressed upon them the merits of the deaconess cause.

Sister Frieda, Deaconess

Sister Frieda returned from Cincinnati in the fall of 1904 eager to begin work as a deaconess. Although the Bethel Deaconess Home and Hospital Society had been formed in 1903, its building had not yet been started.

Frieda needed nursing experience. She found that although she was ready to practice as a private nurse, few people were willing to pay for this service. Nursing was considered housework, and hired girls were paid in room and board and a small allowance. While waiting for calls, Frieda worked in the Bethesda Hospital at Goessel.

While there she received a letter from a family friend in Newton asking her to care for his wife when their baby came. When the call came two days before Christmas, Frieda hitched a ride with the mailman in his mule-drawn wagon. The trip in the bitter cold took five hours, and the baby arrived before the nurse. However, the doctor was so pleased with Frieda's aftercare that he recommended her to other patients.

Gradually the community came to accept her services for what they were worth. She was able to influence her patients toward better health care, dispelling superstition about illnesses. Sister Frieda could persuade the grandmothers that they should place clean pads on the labor bed, rather than dirty horse blankets to save washing; and that the pacifier of powdered toast and sugar in a wet rag was the cause of the baby's intestinal infection.[8]

---

7. Wiebe, p. 7.
8. *Lamps on the Prairie*, (Emporia, Kansas: Kansas State Nurses Association, 1942), p. 123.

Sister Superior of Sisterhood

The Deaconess Home and Hospital was dedicated on June 11, 1908, and the first three deaconesses were ordained on the same day. Sister Frieda, Sister Ida Epp, and Sister Catherine Voth moved into the hospital. Ten days later, the first patient was admitted. Two days later, the first baby was born there.[9] Bethel Deaconess Home and Hospital began its long service to the community, and Sister Frieda, at age twenty-five, began a lifetime of administration to be equaled by few women of any denomination.

The three sisters divided the work among themselves. As mentioned, Sister Frieda was sister-in-charge and deaconess mother. Sister Catherine was head of the operating room, supervisor of the floors, part-time instructor, and laboratory technician.[10] Sister Ida attended to housekeeping and nursing duties and later went to help out at the Mountain Lake hospital. In 1910, the Bethel Deaconess Home was provided by Mrs. Bernard Warkentin as living quarters for the sisters.

Along with patients, the hospital needed candidates to join the diaconate. A lifelong commitment was expected, for a "deaconess is a woman serving Christ and His church, who, free from all other duties desires to devote her time and efforts to the service of the Lord in ministering to suffering humanity."[11] Sixty-one women were to respond to the diaconate, some for a lifetime, some for shorter periods.[12]

In addition to her title as Sister Superior of Sisterhood, Sister Frieda was Director of Religious Life, meaning that she was the chaplain. Visiting with each patient twice a week, she asked about likes, dislikes, and hobbies; she read to them, prayed with them, and laughed with them.[13] She conducted Bible study with the sisters on Saturday evenings.

She was Director of Public Relations and in charge of personnel.

> We have never had a serious quarrel among our helpers. Of course, little things will happen. . . . Our first group of girls, three in number, did not like the first janitor and cold-starched his red and blue handkerchiefs so that they could actually stand alone if set across a corner, until at last the poor man reported his trouble and we came to his rescue.

---

9. "Deaconesses Serve BDH," *In the Service of the King*, June 1983, p. 3.
10. Sister Catherine was a trailblazer in her own right. Founder of the Kansas State Nurses Association, she was president of the State Board for the Examination and Registration of Nurses from 1916 until her death in 1926.
11. Wiebe, p. 3.
12. Wiebe, p. 75.
13. Claassen, p. 10.

She wrote also of a fine French cook, the best they had ever hired, who insisted that the most effective method for getting a really hot fire was to slap a pound of butter into the flames. Sister Frieda decided that she could not afford her.[14]

Another of her titles was Supervisor of the Sewing Room and Dry Goods.[15]

Unofficially, Sister Frieda was gardener and landscaper. She enjoyed getting into the garden herself, planting and weeding. She was a designer. A bassinet and dressing cabinet for the nursery was described in a two-page article in the July 1932 *American Journal of Nursing*.

Always there was a building program.

In 1912, she was asked to plan and raise money for a new building and a school of nursing for the Mountain Lake, Minnesota, Hospital. This was an involvement that lasted until 1930.

In 1913, an addition was built onto the Newton hospital.

In 1918, the Herman Suderman home was purchased to provide for more room for sisters in training.

In 1926, the Bethel Home for the Aged was dedicated.

In 1927, the ground floor of Serepta, the nurses' home and school of nursing, was finished. In 1938, the second floor and in 1942, the third floor was added. Her involvement here was a joint effort with Sister Catherine.

In 1929, an annex to the hospital was built.

In 1932, the hospital society accepted the gift of the Wilhelmina Warkentin home from the Warkentin family.

In 1939, another addition was made to the hospital to house the new clinic that Sister Frieda has persuaded the doctors was necessary.

In 1944, she was in the middle of plans for remodeling the third floor of the hospital and building a separate chapel when she died.

Sister Frieda was involved in all these projects, either raising money for them or drawing the plans, probably both. She had the ability to inspire people to give. She must have been one of the first Mennonite professional fund raisers, for Dr. R. S. Haury said that she knew the exact steps to take to organize a fund-raising campaign and she knew whom to ask to lead in such projects.[16]

---

14. *In the Service of the King*, June 1942, p. 4.
15. Bartel, p. 16. The titles come from the list of duties she retained when she handed over administrative duties to H. J. Andres in 1938.
16. Claassen, p. 10.

Building a home for the aged

In the case of the Bethel Home for the Aged, she had to educate the public for the need of a home. She felt that the elderly were often being neglected by their own families. H. J. Andres, the administrator who followed her, gives Sister Frieda credit for the total planning of the building and the operation of the institution. In preparation, she read about and visited other homes.[17]

Her friend, Anna Entz, said that it was for this project that Sister Frieda wished she had had a course in plumbing and carpentering. There was a story going around at the time that Sister Frieda had suspected that the roofers were not using the right nails, so she climbed up on the roof to find out.[18]

The Bethel Home was a model for its time. D. G. Hiebert wrote from Mountain Lake asking if he could study her plans. Sister Frieda gave him the liberty to copy them and also gave suggestions for changes and improvements.

Mother of the family

The sisterhood was a family. Sister Frieda assumed rightly that she was mother and older sister to the deaconesses. "How interesting a life like ours is, and what opportunities for study of natures and for giving us experiences, and I also hope, wisdom!" she wrote to sisters serving in another hospital. "Much love to each one of my dear family," she wrote while away for a much-needed rest. Her letters were spritely, encouraging, and uplifting. One can imagine the sisters drawing together to read aloud the letters she sent, and then going to their rooms to compose equally loving responses.

Celebrations were a part of their lives. Sister Frieda made an occasion out of a birthday, an anniversary, a dedication. "But on the twenty-fifth anniversary of the Bethel Deaconess Home and Hospital, she met her match," Anna Entz said. "It was a very hot day and the sisters in their black garb suffered. Sister Frieda promised them that she would never again on a hot day in June ask them to celebrate their twenty-fifth anniversary."

"Christmas was her favorite time for celebration," said Anna. "I remember that she always trimmed the tree with red apples and white candles." Christmas was an impressive occasion for the students, too, as they followed the ritual established early for the Christmas party, caroling

---
17. Claassen, p. 18.
18. Interview with Anna (Mrs. J. E.) Entz, March 1984.

in the town, and then on Christmas morning caroling in the halls of the hospital.

The student nurses loved her, but they were also somewhat in awe of her. One described her thus: "She was rather short and somewhat overweight. . . . Her countenance was always very pleasant, as if she always wore a smile." Another remembers her lighthearted laughter and her genuine sense of humor. The first hypodermic injection is rarely forgotten by students. "But it helped if the first needle was Sister Frieda's insulin shot, and she hollered like anyone else."[19]

"She had her office door open, so that as we nurses went to and from our rooms at the sisters' home, we received from her the sense of assurance that with the Lord's help, all was well."[20]

For many years, she or Sister Lena Mae Smith conducted morning devotions in the dining room.

> In the early gray dawn, the students rushed into their uniforms to gather at the breakfast table in the old hospital dining hall at 6:15. . . . No student was allowed to go on duty without breakfast; it was as unthinkable to Sister Frieda that a student leave for work without spiritual food.[21]

She could be tactful and diplomatic. Jessie Brown Gaeddert, a nursing student and later an instructor, wrote: "When I had turned in an article denouncing cooperation with the Red Cross because of their close alliance with the military during the war, she complimented me on the article and said she would keep it for future reference as she had plenty of articles at the moment."

Sister Frieda had a favorite quotation: "A fly should be swatted twice," and she tried to teach her students and co-workers that nothing should be done in a halfhearted manner.[22]

Sponsor of the stained glass windows

Sister Frieda worked with other institutions. She had a close tie with Bethel College and was asked to speak there on a number of occasions. She served on the Advisory Council and was listed as a member of the college faculty from 1937 as Associate in Deaconess Work. She was the first woman to be chosen by Bethel College for the honorary degree of Doctor of Humane Letters.

19. Wiebe, p. 81.
20. Wiebe, pp. 70f.
21. Wiebe, p. 58.
22. Bartel, p. 28.

She was a member of First Mennonite Church from the time of her ordination. She taught a Sunday school class and was the initiator of the teacher training class. Here, too, Sister Frieda was a builder, instrumental in planning the educational wing of the church, and responsible for the stained glass windows in the sanctuary.

When Wilhelmina Kuyf stopped in Newton on her way to the China mission field, she wrote home that First Mennonite was a perfect gem of a church. "When she was in Europe she made a thorough study of churches, cathedrals, etc. The congregation is conservative, yet their church building is most worshipful."[23]

Anna Entz said, "Our church was not ready for a Sister Frieda. Our *Brudershaft* did not want stained glass windows, but she insisted on them. A dignitary visiting from Germany recognized that Sister Frieda was an outstanding person, ahead of her time."

Saving money for Europe

Travel was her way of resting. Some of it was imposed on her when her health demanded it. The highlight of her travel was a trip to Europe in June 1934, one that had been long in the planning. She had been saving pennies and nickels to make $1,000. When she had saved $300, she decided that she was being selfish. She offered the money to missionary friends, but they refused it. When she had finally saved what she needed, a friend gave her another $1,000, so she gave the money she had saved to missions.[24]

She was ready to leave in 1927 when the death of Sister Catherine Voth changed her plans. Finally, seven years later with her two nieces, she was able to visit her homeland. She wrote a book about her travels, *Auf Wanderwegen*, that was considered highly entertaining.

She enjoyed handwork, knitting, and crocheting. On a trip to Yellowstone with J. E. and Anna Entz, she knit bed socks from the beginning to the end. She also enjoyed cooking and eating, which were her undoing. A diabetic, she was on a special diet during the last years. She would take her unappetizing tray to her office rather than eat with others.[25]

Sister Frieda was a prolific writer. *In the Service of the King* was begun in December 1941, and much of the material appears to have been written by her. She wrote articles for *The Mennonite* and other papers and poems for all the celebrative occasions, poems much appreciated by the recipient. Her speeches display an eloquent use of language. She was

23. Wilhelmina Kuyf Collection, April 1936; in the Mennonite Library and Archives.
24. Sister Frieda Kaufman Collection, MLA, Box 84-2A. Correspondence indicates that she gave a substantial gift to enable the Missionary Petters to go to Switzerland in 1935.
25. Claassen, p. 10.

master of the metaphor and used biblical analogies and illusions.

With all her virtues, no one ever accused her of being vain or proud. She prayed to be kept from pride. On the day after receiving the Doctor of Humane Letters, she was found scrubbing the floor of a hospital room. She sometimes felt a sense of sin that would move her to tears.[26]

Tasks left unfinished

Her last year was spent quietly. Death came August 7, 1944, as she was resting on her bed in the deaconess home. She died shortly after a heart attack. Thorough to the end, she left instructions for her funeral arrangements.

Some projects, however, remained unfinished. She had been overseeing the furnishing of the third floor of the hospital annex. And the chapel building was still only an idea. The Sister Frieda Chapel was completed in 1953 from memorial funds.

Sister Frieda must have worried about the future of her beloved deaconesses. She knew that only six had joined in the decade before her death, and there were to be only four who joined after 1944. After the war, although the school of nursing had its largest student body to date and received praise for its high standards, Sister Frieda's dream of an ongoing motherhouse for the deaconess movement became dimmer. The sisterhood did not grow.

In a paper in which she explained the difference between a deaconess and a Christian nurse, she said, "History reveals the fact that men must furnish the leadership and direct the work if the organized female diaconate shall prosper."

Did the Mennonite church need another David Goerz to hold up and give new emphasis to the opportunities for women in church service? In 1939, Sister Lena Mae asked, "Is the day for the deaconess work a day of the past?"[27] Sister Frieda had hoped through *In the Service of the King* to interest more young women in deaconess work.

Sadly for many, the day of the deaconess movement in the General Conference Mennonite Church was past. Even another David Goerz probably could not have revived it.[28] As more women entered college and became eligible for other respectable careers, they found different avenues of Christian service.

---

26. Claassen, p. 10.
27. Wiebe, p. 35.
28. Ernst Harder and Elmer Ediger envisioned Women in Church Vocations which was organized in 1956. Begun with enthusiasm, it was disbanded in 1961.

Sister Frieda met the need of her day with intelligence and audacity. She imparted a vision that sent women as nurses into the "uttermost parts" as well as back into their own communities; she gave a definition to the idea of vocation to women who had energy for which there was no market; she mixed bricks and mortar and lives together to make an institution. Perhaps these accomplishments are enough for one woman in one short lifetime. It is sad to see a good cause die, as has the deaconess movement, but the idea of Christian service for women that Sister Frieda advocated is still going strong.

Clara Gundy: The honeymoon was spent visiting relatives. And then they began farming on her parents' home place.

9.
Generous by Nature

Clara Louise Strubhar Gundy
1885—1979

When Clara Gundy was ninety years old, the administrators of the Meadows Home in central Illinois crowned her "Queen for a Day." At the close of the program of reminiscences, Hilda Troyer said, "People have looked at Clara Gundy and they have said, 'Clara Gundy, you are a saint!' "

Someone else said, in describing Clara, "She was the wife of a farmer who was also a minister, and then for many years they were in charge of the Meadows Home. But she was *more* than the wife of a farmer-minister-administrator and the mother of three children."

The whole of Clara Gundy's life does seem to be more than the sum of its parts.

Her life can be divided approximately into twenty-year units. Growing up in a close family of Strubhars and Guths (Clara was one of seven children), she married when she was almost nineteen. She and her husband farmed the Strubhar family homestead for twenty-two years before becoming administrators of the Meadows Home for another twenty-two years. Then came a twenty-year period of retirement in their own home in Meadows before Clara moved to the Meadows Home as a resident.[1]

---

1. *Reminiscences of Clara Gundy* is a seventeen-page manuscript contributed by her grandson, John Gundy, from which much of this material is taken; a copy is in the Mennonite Library and Archives, North Newton, Kansas, along with a letter from John Gundy and articles from the Meadows Home periodical.

Grandmother's bread

The Strubhar ancestors had come from Alsace-Lorraine. Grandfather Peter acquired enough land around Danvers, Illinois, to give each of his four boys 160 acres. When the boys married and took over the farms, the grandparents moved to Washington, Illinois, where they kept a few animals and ran a small store, selling farm produce. Clara's grandmother, Barbara Sweitzer Strubhar, had the reputation for making the "best bread," using whey as her secret ingredient, big round loaves that she sold for ten cents.

Clara was born January 28, 1885, the first child of Valentine and Katherine Guth Strubhar. When Clara wrote her memoirs at the age of ninety, she included many of the highlights of growing up among her many relatives. Christmas was celebrated with the four Strubhar families at the home of her grandmother. A special treat for the day was a platter of sliced, sweetened oranges. She also remembered a sloe tree (sour wild plums) in the yard from which they made jars of red sloe butter.

Grandmother Strubhar died when Clara was seventeen. Clara was impressed by both her generosity and her frugality. "Grandmother's gate was marked, and the tramps always stopped in to eat. She always fed them, even if she had to take some potatoes from the bucket for the chickens, but they were clean and they still tasted good." This woman mothered four of her grandchildren from two families when their mothers died.

Buying from J. C. Penney

Three of the four Strubhar brothers married Kates. Clara's mother was known as Faulty's Kate. The brothers exchanged help in threshing and butchering and other projects. Her father once went to Missouri with a group to look at some land that J. C. Penney had for sale—land that had belonged to Penney's parents.

Later, when it had been improved, Penney bought it back for sentimental reasons. When he visited with her family, Clara took note of his frugality. He drove a little old-time car and wore an old suit and hat. She also observed that he was concerned for the welfare of his tenants.

Clara had spoken only German before beginning her six years at Greenridge School. The Strubhar children walked the mile and a half across the fields with the neighbor children. These neighbors had "the best tasting cough syrup, and mornings if we had to wait till they got ready we surely had to cough and Mr. Hostettler would give us each a dose of syrup."

Clara's teachers as well as her friends wore their long dresses until they were threadbare. One remarkable teacher wore the same dress every day for two years.

The children played their own kind of ball, tearing a board off the adjoining fence when they needed a bat. "We could hit the ball easier with a wide board." In winter they walked on snowbanks for weeks at a time.

She attended the Washington town school for seventh and eighth grades, and thus ended her years of schooling. That was the year her parents built a new barn and added a half story to the house. Clara was needed at home to help cook for the carpenters.

When Valentine Strubhar was called to take charge of the East Washington country church in 1893, Clara and her sisters were made responsible for the chores and gardening on the farm. She enjoyed working outside more than in the house. One of her crops was salsify, the roots of which were cut into cubes, cooked and seasoned to taste like oysters.

Onions were used for medicinal purposes as well as for seasoning. Fried onions were put in a sack and placed on the chest to relieve a cold. "You could smell them a long time. Of course, not everyone could enjoy them, but they sure helped."

The family home was large and comfortable, heated by a hard-coal stove with opaque isinglass panes in the door so that the fire cast a welcome red glow over the room. A register in the ceiling of the living room warmed the upstairs. Clara found the register a good place to stand to read at night.

The pleasant life of her childhood was interrupted twice by tragedy. When Clara was seven, her six-year-old sister Ada died of spinal meningitis. A few years later, her five-year-old sister Lucy died of burns when her clothing ignited from the hot ashes of a trash fire.

When her parents rented out their farm and moved to town, Clara went with them.

Days when conferences inspired

When Clara was fourteen, the central Illinois church leaders met together with Joseph E. Stucky, "father" of the Central Conference of Mennonites from the mother church at Danvers, to talk of a convention or conference. This organization came to be known as the Stucky Church.

Clara knew well the first ministers: Joe King from the North Danvers church "could talk on any subject and the words just rolled out of his mouth." Uncle Peter Schantz "was a real preacher, not very well educated, but fundamental as all our preachers were." Lee Lantz at Congerville was a school teacher and an evangelist. And she thought of Andrew Vercler at Meadows as a fine man. Her father had the Washington church and "was more slow than some but he knew the Bible and taught it."

When some of their English neighbors began coming to Sunday school at the East Washington church, an English class was organized for them. The use of English caused a rift in the congregation and some of the members left to start the South Washington church, led by Mike Kinsinger. "But after Mike Kinsinger died, the church was finally sold and many of the members came back to our church. The sad thing about that was it split Mama's family [the John Guth family] and it took years to heal that wound."

She remembered the Sunday school convention of October 1902, held at the East Washington church where her father was the preacher. "We young members helped our mothers plan the dinner. I don't remember the menu, but it was like a picnic dinner, with chicken for the main thing."

The meetings grew larger each year, and they had to hold them in a tent. The owner of a steam engine was hired to heat water to make the coffee and cook the wieners. "Everybody loved the apple butter. It was bought, and much sweeter than the homemade."

At ninety, Clara had a great deal of nostalgia for those two-day conferences. "The speakers were all so good and now yet we old timers talk of the fine meetings we used to have." As a later conference goer with her minister husband, she regretted that so much time was taken up with conference business; reports on the Home, the hospital, and foreign mission work left less time for the good speakers.

Conference time was also a time for the young people to learn to know one another. "We had our conference at the [Rock Creek] fairground one year. Part of the time it rained so hard. A bunch of us young folks were sitting together and we couldn't hear the speakers when it rained, so we got pretty well acquainted . . . but we went every year, rain or shine."

Clara's moment of conversion came, however, not during a Mennonite conference but at a revival meeting held by the Salvation Army in the Methodist church in town. She was twelve at the time and later that year when revival meetings were held in her country church, she was baptized by her father. "I've tried to be a faithful Christian ever since, with the Lord's help."

George Gundy won the prize

The Gundy family was part of the church community. George was the middle child of the eleven children of Jacob and Lena Kinzinger Gundy. Clara mentions him first in her memoirs as a young man who won the prize for the best horse and rider at the Rock Creek Fair. He was competing against a man who had won it for the previous several years, "and were we ever proud."

They were married January 6, 1904, shortly before her nineteenth birthday. The material for her dress was purchased in Peoria. It was *peau de soie*, a silk with a ribbed texture. She kept a piece of it to the end of her life. The wedding was a small and rather sad occasion because Mr. King, the singing teacher who was staying with them, was desperately ill. He died two days after the wedding. When they learned of the situation, the boys who came to shivaree the newly married couple instead sang a hymn and departed quietly.

The honeymoon was spent visiting relatives around the community, and then they began farming the Strubhar home place, living in the house in which Clara had grown up. George traded his famous riding horse for a team of work horses, harness, and wagon, and thus entered the world of responsible adults. The Gundys and Kinzingers joined Clara's network of Strubhar and Guth relatives.

Their three boys, Gerdon in 1905, Ralph in 1910, and Donald in 1917, were born on the Strubhar family farm. Ralph must have been a particularly active child, for one of their friends called him "the destruction that wasteth the noonday," when he saw the gallon of cottage cheese that Ralph had scattered around the kitchen in an unguarded moment.

Life as a farmer's wife was filled with activity. She was busy with garden, house, and chores. Clara remembered incidents that grew to be in-family jokes. A city friend who was recuperating from illness stayed with them for a few weeks. Trying to be of help, he offered to bring in the cows one winter day and tie them in their stalls. He reported that he had got along all right but had had a little trouble with one of them. When Clara went out to milk in the shadowy barn, "I sat down on my stool and put the bucket under the gentleman cow. If he hadn't been so busy eating the feed, I don't know what would have happened to me."

A home at Meadows for the aged

In 1908, when George was called to preach at the Congerville church, he and Clara decided not to leave the farm. Since George was not always in good health, she did much of the farm work. She could "plow, disk, harrow, plow corn, drive four horses on the binder, cut corn, shock oats, and husk corn." She was grateful to the Congerville church people for the help they gave with the farm work. Those were the "good old Congerville days."

They took their family trips in the old Ford. On a visit to relatives in Arkansas, they camped along the way, cooking wieners and boiling eggs in the hot water from the radiator. They slept in farm yards, spreading their comforters on the ground.

In 1924, after twenty-two years of farming and preaching, George accepted a call to preach at the Meadows church. Then, in addition, he was asked to be administrator of the Meadows Mennonite Home "for one year." In 1925, the family moved into an apartment on the second floor. This home for the aged had been in operation for two years with fourteen residents. The men ate at one table, the women at another, and the Gundys and their family at a third. There were usually more women than men.

Some of the residents could help with the work. One baked bread and coffee cake, another had a special interest in raising and preparing the potatoes. Some acted like children, and the Gundys kindly reprimanded them as if they were children. The Home was sponsored by four congregations in the area. Women from these churches came in for spring and fall housecleaning.

In the year after they moved to Meadows, two tragedies occurred at the railroad crossing in Chenoa, just four miles east of Meadows. One involved a neighbor family, of which several persons were killed. The other took the life of the Gundy's son, Ralph. After having lunch with a group of high school friends, he was riding back to school on the running board of a car. He was killed when a freight train backed into the car. That happened three days after his sixteenth birthday. "It seemed so hard to give him up so young."

At the Home, the Gundys kept cows. They produced enough to sell cream, cottage cheese, and milk by the syrup bucketful. Always the sociable neighbor, Clara enjoyed passing on little jokes with those who came to buy. One of the small boys came for milk and stayed to visit, then reluctantly said, "I guess I'd better go home or my milk will turdle." Clara saw to the making of butter and buttermilk for the Home residents.

White linen tablecloths and napkins

While her husband was minister of the Meadows church, as well as farmer, bookkeeper, public relations director, and maintenance man, Clara was minister's wife, cook, laundry maid, housekeeper, mother, gardener, and milkmaid. During the depression years of the 1930s, the board considered the financial condition in good shape if the monthly report showed a balance of only a few dollars.

Cooking was done on a cob-burning cookstove, laundry in two wringer washing machines. When someone asked her, "Why do you do things the hard way?" she answered, "Is there any other way?"[2]

John Gundy remembers his grandmother as a "tireless, hardworking, uncomplaining, loving lady. She had a strength that I cannot duplicate today. . . . As a small boy staying at the Home to go to Bible school, I remember waking very early in the morning to the realization that much wash was already hanging on the outdoor clothes lines. Most of the wash was done before breakfast. We enjoyed spreading cloth napkins, handkerchiefs, and wash cloths on the grass to dry. (The tables were always covered with fresh white linen and cloth napkins!)"

Mary Bertsche, whose family had been close friends of the Gundys, said that Clara was delighted to be able to retire the flat irons when the electric iron came into use.[3]

What her relatives and neighbors remember especially about Clara was her generosity. The custom of serving tramps continued from her grandmother's time. Unless they were dirty, vagrants were served in the dining room. John said:

> She always had a soft spot in her heart for all people. She was a real example for me. Anyone who needed something was always blessed by making the need known to her. She had to send at least a dollar to any organization that requested funds. She always helped anyone she thought had a need. She gave away more produce and canned goods than most people used. Anyone who visited her never left without something. She corresponded with many people around the world. Her list at Christmas was beyond belief—and everyone got a multi-page letter.
>
> We spent virtually every Sunday at Grandma's. She always had dinner for many people. Any visitors at church were always invited. I learned to know many district conference pastors around her table. And such scrumptious meals, always. But she never ate a great quantity herself.

One of the treats at the Gundy home was ice cream, and Clara was generous with the cream.

The piano was so full of pictures of children in the church and of her own family that Clara declared that she would have to get another piano to hold all the pictures. When Clara wrote a note to the parents of new babies, she often enclosed money.

---

2. Hilda Troyer in a talk given June 4, 1975 at the Meadows Home for a program highlighting Clara's ninety years.
3. From an interview in April 1984.

George would have liked to have had a daughter. The church had a project of bringing children from Chicago, "fresh-air kids," to stay in homes of the members for the summer. For a number of years the Gundys kept a girl whom they would have adopted had her mother been willing.

The Gundys went to the farm people to gather up food for the Home. When they came to the Bertsche's home where Mary's mother had been ill for a long time, they spent the day. Clara did Mary's mending while George visited with her mother.

Clara wrote, "Father [George] had always said that after he had preached forty years he was going to retire, and one day he came in and said he had bought a house."

In 1947, Florence and Frank Mitchell took over the Home and George and Clara moved to their house nearby. "We soon moved into the first home we ever could call our own and you will never know how happy we were to live in our own home by ourselves." He preached at Meadows church for four more years.

In August 1951, while they were helping Don move to Woodburn, Indiana, George had a severe heart attack and died five weeks later. "It was an awful thing to go home and be alone," but she was grateful that her Aunt Lina was with her and for the neighbors' help during that time.

Work was a solace. "We had such a good crop of nice potatoes that year, and it was a relief to get out and dig a bushel when the going got too hard. . . . I was thankful too for the days when I could help at the Home when they had extra work to do."

She welcomed the invitation later that fall to do kitchen duty at Camp Friedenswald for a few weeks. She slept in the first cabin constructed there, the one she and George had helped to build.

After George's death, she received a pension of fifty dollars a month from the church. Clara lived alone in Meadows for sixteen years, making her garden and keeping in touch with her many friends. She mowed her own lawn with the push-mower until she left for the Home, although her sons and grandsons sometimes tried to take the job from her.

Back to the Home

One day she lost her balance on the cellar steps while carrying a basket of laundry. She wondered if it was time to think of moving. In 1967, when her sister Barbara moved to the Meadows Home, she decided to move also.

Sorting through a lifetime's accumulation of possessions in preparing for a sale, she made up a large box of things she considered useful. That box went for ten cents. But to her surprise a little toothpick holder to which she attached no value, and which she had used for years, went for seven dollars. She watched her bedding, piano, and African violets sell, and when there was not a thing left, she felt free to go to the Home. By nature, she enjoyed the sale day for its sociability, as a reunion of family and neighbors.

During her years as a resident rather than an administrator of the Home, Clara had opportunities to relax and enjoy the many activities, especially the religious services.

Clara's years at the Home were happy years, but there were times of sadness when first her sister Barbara and then her son Gerdon died. During the last six months of her life, a grandson and the wife of another grandson died of cancer. John wrote, "She often asked why she who was ready to go could not die instead of those two who were so young and had so much to give." She would have gladly given her life for theirs. When her own time to die came, she remained alert throughout much physical suffering, never losing her sense of humor. She died February 26, 1979.

The Home that the Gundys took over in 1925 is now more than eight times larger. "They were here the longest of any administrators to date, and the good will they created in good relationships with people and churches is a good part of the reason for the continuance and growth of the Home," Hilda Troyer said.

At the Queen for the Day celebration of Clara's ninetieth year, Hilda Troyer had this to say before nominating her for sainthood:

> Many people think about Mrs. Gundy as a human being. They realize that she does get provoked, she does get angry, she worries once in a while. But God wouldn't have made human beings if he hadn't expected them to act like human beings. Sometimes the fact that a person acts like a human being emphasizes the fact that a person does not give a life of service without sacrifice and it helps the rest of us to realize this.

And then Saint Clara was presented with one dozen long-stemmed roses.

Mary Smucker: She was the first woman from her farm community to go off to school.

10.
Trusting During Hard Times

Mary Jane Stauffer Ebersole Smucker
1886—1971

A number of women of Mary Smucker's generation kept journals, some charming, some graphic, a few showing a real gift for expression. Few in our Mennonite communities wrote as a way of earning a living. But Mary Smucker did that for a short time.

When her sons left off newswriting for the local papers to go on to other pursuits, Mary took over. A love of words was part of a family tradition, passed on to the next generation.

Mrs. S. K. Mosiman told how Mary's young grandson came to her door with a request: "May I have some anticipatory cookies?" Mrs. Mosiman smiled at his use of such a literary word and rewarded him with the cookie.[1]

Born in a granary

Mary's father, Elias Rutt Ebersole, was born in Lancaster County, Pennsylvania. He moved to Sterling, Illinois, where he married Barbara Stauffer. Land was already hard to come by in Illinois, so, in 1885, the Ebersoles, with their five children, moved to Ayr, Nebraska, where some of Barbara's family had already settled. There Mary was born on December 22, 1886. At that time, the family was living in a granary, waiting for their five-room house to be built. Brother Ben was born three years later.

---

1. In a letter from Sylvia Pannabecker to Benjy Sprunger, April 1978.

When Mary was nine years old, her mother died. For a time, Mary's older sister Kate supervised the household. When Kate married soon after her mother's death, Esther, with Mary's help, took over.

She had two memories of Esther's mothering: she made Mary a tam-o'-shanter and she put up Mary's hair in rag curlers for special occasions. By the time Mary was twelve, she was capable, during Esther's absence, of preparing a full meal for seven corn shellers, neighbors who came in to help for the day.[2]

Mary and Ben were congenial playmates. They hunted for baby mice in empty corn bins; they strung binder twine from tree to tree in the windbreak to make "rooms"; in the empty hayloft, they played church, using cutouts from *Christian Herald* for Bibles. She enjoyed being outdoors with the two brothers near her age and tended to disappear with them at dishwashing time, for which thoughtlessness she received her only spanking.

Lunch in the livery stable

Summers were pleasant with such chores as "fetching the cows" from the pasture where the children would pick daisies. But Nebraska winters were harsh. The walls of the kitchen were exposed to winter winds on three sides. The children undressed in front of the coal stove in the living room before running to their frigid beds upstairs, stowing heated flatirons at the foot to take off the chill. Straw was used under the living room carpet to reduce the drafts. But "there were no complaints," said Mary, "since this was the pattern of living at that time in the nineties and later."

One of the high points of her life was to drive seventeen miles to Hastings, the county seat, to buy those special items that could not be found in the small town of Ayr. Her father did not like to hurry the horses, so they had to leave early to get to town. "Our first stop was at a livery stable where the horses were fed and kept until we finished our shopping. We also ate our lunch in the waiting room. Whew!"

"We gazed in wonder at the counters filled with merchandise." Purchases that impressed her were a brown coat with two circular capes and wine-colored cashmere that Esther made into a dress. "But the most enticing things were the change carriers floating back and forth from the counter to the upstairs office. We tried that at home with button-hooks and cord on the stairway."

---

2. Mary Smucker wrote a two-page manuscript, "My Childhood Days in Nebraska"; it is now in the Mennonite Library and Archives, North Newton, Kansas. Carl and Irene Smucker and Donovan and Barbara Smucker added information.

The family attended the Roseland Mennonite Church. With the twenty-five cents that Mary won for reciting a Bible story, she bought a Bible which she kept all her life. She continued faithful in Bible reading to the end of her days.

The trip to church was by spring wagon. "Top buggies were coming into use and how I wished my father would buy a 'surrey with a fringe on top,' as one of our friends possessed one and drove by our home with two handsome driving horses. Later my father bought a one-seated buggy."

Mary's interest in church may have been expressed in terms of horses and buggies, but from their parents and the community the Ebersole children received a strong religious faith. Her sister Kate married a minister, and Esther and her husband George Lapp became missionaries to India.

Learning from the Lutherans

School was two miles from the Ebersole home. Mary's brothers took her in the two-wheeled cart in cold weather. "Our school was largely made up of *Blatt Deutsch* Lutherans who had many unusual customs," such as taking coffee breaks and making blood soup after butchering. The Lutherans also introduced the Christmas tree to the community.

Mary's father, Elias Ebersole, was the oldest of nine children. His younger brothers were among the first of the Mennonite young people to obtain a higher education. Mary's brothers all went to college and entered professions, and Mary was the first woman from her farm community to go off to school. She attended Goshen Academy, receiving a diploma in education in 1906. The tribute in the college yearbook read, "Her lively looks a sprite!y mind disclose."

At Goshen, she learned to know Boyd Smucker. He was the youngest of ten children, the only boy. Born in 1879, in Wayne County, Ohio, Boyd had, like Mary, caught from his parents a strong religious faith. His father had died in a farm accident when Boyd was a teenager, and he had made his home with his sisters.

He went from the farm to Goshen Academy, graduating in 1905. From there he went to Kings School of Oratory in Pittsburgh, Pennsylvania, where he received a master of oratory degree in Elocution. Returning to Goshen College in 1907, he took courses and taught Elocution.

Donovan, in writing about his father, said, "Goshen College had a full array of literary societies where he became an outstanding performer. His great claim to fame is this: He was the first teacher of dramatics and theater of any American Mennonite college. Goshen permitted the declamations, but Boyd restricted the drama to the living room of homes where he gave monologues in which he took all the characters."

Mary and Boyd had in common the fact that their parents were no longer living and they had no parental home to return to after college. Mary taught for two years at West Liberty, Ohio, and they were married September 19, 1908. Boyd continued teaching at Goshen College. Orden and Carl were born there.

In 1913, Boyd moved the family to Toltec, Arizona, where he was a sales representative for aluminum cooking ware. In 1915, the Smuckers were asked to come to Bluffton College where Boyd worked as field secretary and professor of public speaking. Donovan and Bertran were born in Bluffton, Ohio.

"Surely one of the reasons for leaving Goshen was its taboo on plays," says Donovan. "When the call came to Bluffton, he was told he could produce plays 'as long as they had a strong moral teaching.' My mother loved these plays and delighted in his pioneering work as a director. Soon he was into Shakespeare and morally acceptable Broadway plays."

Living below the poverty level

Money during the Bluffton years was never abundant. The standard salary was $800 a year for a single person, $1,000 for a married man with an additional fifty dollars for each child. But there were times when the college did not have enough cash to pay even this much. During the Depression the college was often in such dire straits that the cash in the till at the end of the month was divided equally among the employees.

"Dad's salary was sometimes forty dollars a month," Carl recalled, "but I never had the idea that we were in poverty."

All the boys were able to graduate from Bluffton. Mary was not the aggressive mother who told her sons that they were to become college professors. "But she was an inspiration in the way she led us along and encouraged us and supported us. She was so positive all the time. Both she and Dad were teachers and happy with teaching."

In later years, when Donovan went to Mississippi as president of a black college, she never asked him not to go to that turbulent area at the center of the civil rights struggle. Her children remember her as a stable, steady person, not given to the ups and downs of depression or emotional highs.

She never complained about Bluffton's low salaries. Although the pocketbook was often empty, life in general was overflowing with activities, and life on a college campus was stimulating. Both Smucker parents were busy in community, school, and church doings. Boyd was mayor of

Bluffton for a time and a member of the Bluffton-Richland Board of Education. Mary was president of parent-teacher association and taught Sunday classes for single women for many years.

Then Boyd's health began to decline. He died in 1936 of kidney failure. Mary was forty-nine at the time, with a son at home to see through high school and college. A life insurance policy paid off the house, but she had no other income. She not only had to deal with the grief of her loss, but she had to find her own way through the country's economic depression of the late '30s.

Mary rented the second floor of her house for seventeen dollars a month to Miss Naomi Brenneman, the English teacher at the college. A nephew helped out with groceries from his store. When there was no money to pay for groceries, she could count on her sons who had jobs to help. Short of money as she was, Mary found ways of sharing with others. At one time, she opened her home to a daughter-in-law's niece who needed board and room.

"Trust was the theme," Carl said. "You just trust in the Lord that it will be all right."

The Smucker Associated Press

All her sons had been correspondents for local newspapers in high school and college as a means of earning money, passing the job down the line as one moved on. (Donovan, in 1934, had written up the Dillinger bank robbery in Bluffton.)

Finally, Mary took over from the boys. She taught herself to type as she wrote her stories. She was a stringer for the Toledo, Lima, and Findlay papers, paid by the inch. She and the boys chased police, fire, and all the news stories they heard about. A grandson took over the job when he was in high school, and then a daughter-in-law. The Smucker Associated Press must have had quite a wide readership in its time.

In 1946, when she was nearly sixty years old, she began a new career. Gordon Bixel, the Bluffton optometrist, asked her to become his secretary. She was ready with her self-taught typing skill to take over the job. After seven years with Dr. Bixel, she was able to retire on Social Security.

In 1954, Mary's youngest son invited her to visit Europe. He was working for CARE, stationed in Germany. Mary spent two months in Europe, staying for a time with Bertran but going on her own to Vienna. She wrote a detailed journal of her experience, giving accounts of history, politics, scenery, geography, architecture, art, and music. Her observations were articulate and perceptive. She had a good backlog of material from which to prepare talks when she returned to Bluffton.

Family gatherings

Years of retirement followed during which she enjoyed her grandchildren, entertaining everyone at family gatherings in her house on Lawn Avenue in Bluffton.

Orden taught in Bluffton high school for ten years before going to Ohio State for a Ph.D. in sociology. He then taught for twenty-two years at Michigan State. Carl worked for eighteen years for the State Welfare Department of Ohio and thirty-four years teaching social work at Bluffton College. Since retirement, he is an educational consultant on aging in the Ohio Department on Aging.

Donovan taught at Mennonite-Bethany Biblical Seminary for ten years while he studied for the Ph.D. at the University of Chicago. He has taught at Lake Forest College, Spelman College, and Conrad Grebel College. Bertran worked for Mennonite Central Committee in Vienna, and then for twenty years directed the overseas operation of CARE, the cooperative relief society started by the three historical peace churches. He traveled in eighty countries for that organization.

Carl, in commenting on his mother as a career woman, said, "My mother was completely happy in her role as wife and mother." In expanding on this comment, Donovan wrote:

> The college women of my mother's era did not seem to have the restless dissatisfaction of the current generation of educated women. For one thing, the wife of a college professor entered fully into the cultural and religious life of a Christian college. She attended lectures, concerts, workshops, and student events very faithfully. My mother was a member of the Century Circle Club which called for one *major* paper every year on a serious semi-scholarly topic. There was rich fellowship among the faculty families where these women like my mother felt part of a peer culture of college people.

In 1966, Mary moved to the Mennonite Memorial Home in Bluffton and rented out her house. She enjoyed her life there and was always pleasant to visit with. In her last years, she depended on two heart pacers. She spent more and more time living in the past, continuing to read her Bible. She would tell visitors, "Well, I'm teaching the Sunday school class."

She died December 21, 1971, still interested in words and the Word.

11.
She Remembered Missions

Susanna Theresa Nickel Schroeder
1888—1966

In many ways, the life of Susanna Schroeder was typical of many Mennonite women among the first generation born in America. She saw dramatic changes during her lifetime, with moon rockets overtaking the horse and buggy. Like many others, she was one of a large family, and the fact that she lived in a small town rather than on a farm made little difference in the dawn-to-dark work expected of a young woman.

After her marriage, as the wife of a prominent church leader, her life took a different turn. While many of her school friends lived all their lives in one place, she lived in twenty different houses in several communities.

Growing up in Mountain Lake

Susanna's father and mother, Theodor Nickel and Susanna Janzen, migrated, before their marriage, with their parents from the village of Rudnerweide in South Russia to Minnesota, in 1878.[1] Theodor was twenty-one and Susanna fifteen when their families settled on neighboring farms near Mountain Lake.

Since farming did not appeal to Theodor, he started clerking in his Uncle Henry Dickman's store and eventually went into business for himself. After he and Susanna were married in 1885, they built a small house in what is now downtown Mountain Lake. Rooms were added until it was a

---

1. Mrs. P. R. Schroeder, *My Memoirs*, 1964. The manuscript was compiled by Celeste Schroeder Dehnert and is in the Mennonite Library and Archives, North Newton, Kansas.

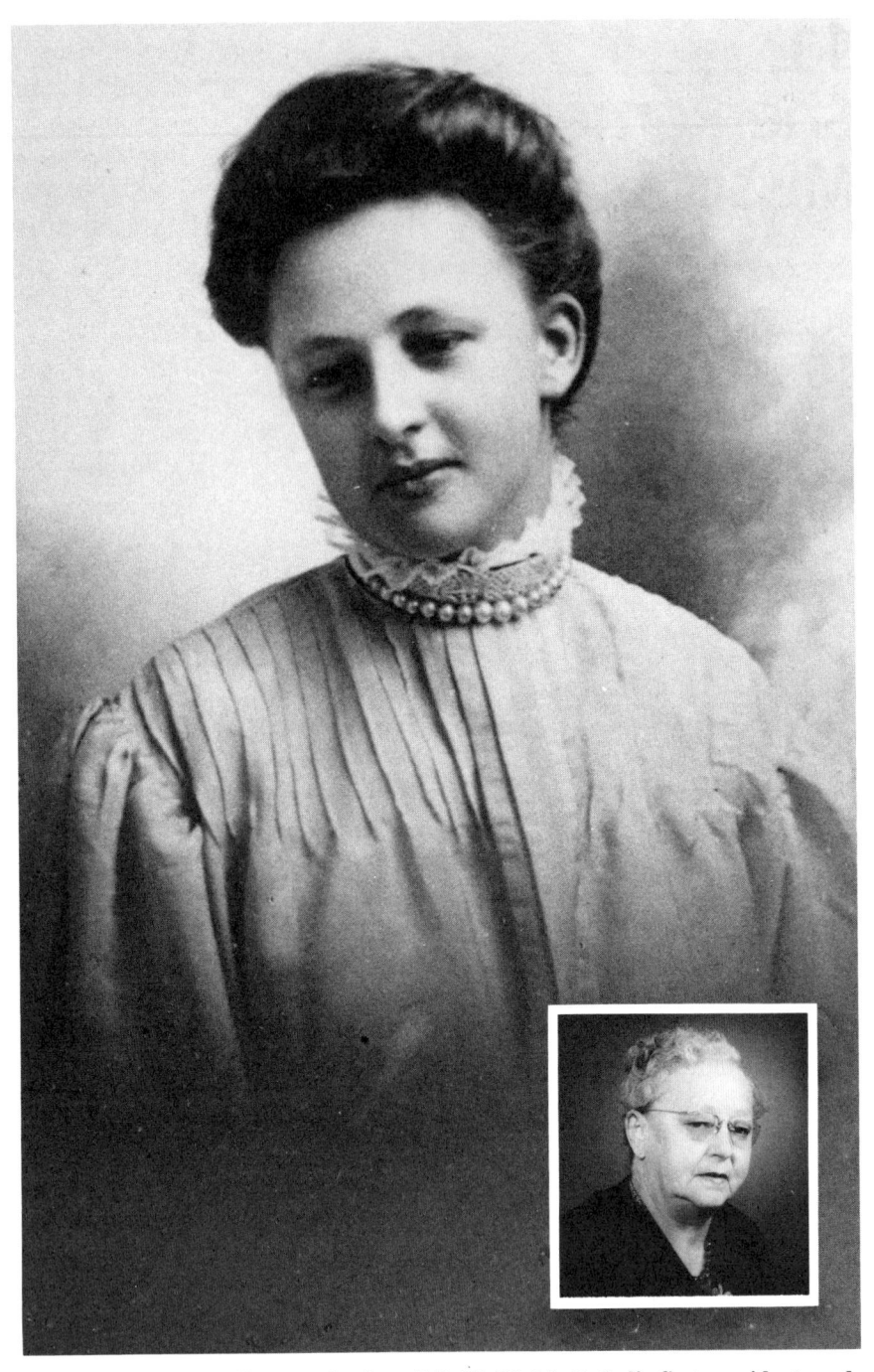

Susanna Schroeder: "I sat at the feet of C. H. Wedel, Bethel's first president, and took in the wisdom and beauty of his teaching."

substantial and comfortable house with four bedrooms. The family enjoyed good clothes, plenty of good food, and a well-heated home.

The Nickels' first born children were twins, Theodor and Jacob, but both died soon after birth. Susanna, to be known as Susie, was next on April 17, 1888, and then four brothers, Theodore, Jacob, Peter, and John, and finally to Susie's delight a sister, Elizabeth. Then Frank, Helen, and Lyllian. Susie used the newswriter's sign (XXX) to describe the end of the childbearing: "That made it 30! We were a big family."

Susie's mother did all the sewing from underwear to overcoats, but she did take advantage of the knit union suits when they became available in the stores. All panties, underskirts, and nightgowns were edged with crocheting, as were the pillow slips.

They had no bakeries, no canned meats except salmon and sardines, no cake mixes. But from grandfather's farm they got hams, beef, and poultry. A quarter's worth of beefsteak from the local butcher shop was enough for the family dinner, with enough left over to eat cold for supper. All the breads were home baked. Yeast was homemade and kept growing in the basement. Also in the basement were a barrel of apples, the root vegetables, and a stone jar of homemade sauerkraut.

Padding the rug with fresh hay

The family used gas lights until Susie was nearly grown, but they had no indoor plumbing. Every Saturday night, the washtub was set on two kitchen chairs facing each other, and Susie's mother would scrub each child, starting with the youngest, dipping warm rain water from the reservoir at the back of the range.

The furnishings of the home were typical of those of a middle-class, small-town family. Susie was delighted when the drayman delivered a beautiful reed organ with a mirror. Later, in 1903, a set of red upholstered chairs and a love seat arrived for the parlor. A flower-patterned carpet stretched wall to wall, padded with hay. Every spring, the carpet was taken up and hung on the clothesline to be beaten. Fresh hay was put down and the carpet relaid with carpet tacks. It was swept with a broom, and sometimes her mother would use spoiled sauerkraut as a sweeping compound.

Susie wondered how her mother accomplished all she did, but noted that she belonged to no clubs, nor did the children. After school, they came home to chores, homework, and reading. There were no school athletics, only occasional programs. On Sundays, they did not change to their everyday clothes after church, but behaved circumspectly and did no work.

Stories told on grandfather's farm

Her grandparents played an important part in her life. The Janzens lived on a farm about five miles from Mountain Lake that provided ideal entertainment for grandchildren: a creek, a hen house, animals, an orchard, barns, swings, "and a hundred other interesting things—*that mattered*! Grandma often 'relieved' Mother of us." The house and barn were attached in the Russian style. Her grandfather, a blacksmith by trade, told stories of Russia with skill and humor.

Susie's youngest uncle was just four years older than she. He was her special pal. At milking time, Pete would see how accurately he could squirt milk into her open mouth.

All of the family gathered at her grandparents' home on the day after the religious holidays: Christmas, Easter, and Pentecost. As many as thirty-three first cousins filled the house for Christmas. Each child received a sack of treats and a gift from the grandparents.

Mission fests with a Christmas flair

The school was three blocks away. Susie loved it. A German class was taught from first grade on, along with the regular subjects. By the time she graduated from eighth grade, she could read and write German as well as English. Adept at drawing, she sketched her teachers as they swept around the room in their bustles and long skirts with stiff gored flounces all around.

Susie described herself as being a willful, determined child, curious, and an avid reader, good at memorizing and ready to speak pieces at school and church programs. By the time Frank, Helen, and Lyllian came along, she was old enough to help raise them.

After grade eight, she wanted to go on to the German School, but Helen was born that September. She resented having to stay home to help, but three years later she was able to take the two-year course. Her pastor, J. J. Balzer, taught grammar, reading literature, Bible geography, ethics, Bible and world history, apologetics, logic, psychology, and Bible doctrine. Under his teaching, "I really came to life and simply drank in all the wonderful Bible and church instruction he gave us."

Regular attendance at the Bethel Mennonite Church was taken for granted. Susie remembered the Missions Fest/Kinderfest as being of equal importance to Christmas. The festival was an all-day affair, with the church decorated "with branches even unto the horns of the altar" (Ps. 118:27).

Visiting missionaries or mission board members spoke. At noon, the congregation adjourned to the lumberyard, which had also been decorated with branches, for a traditional meal of rye bread, *zwieback*, cold cuts, and coffee, the adults being served first. The afternoon was devoted to the children's program, followed by another meal of coffee and *zwieback* at which the children ate first.

Susie understood the importance of this occasion for the church: "Our leaders were alert and it didn't only *happen*" that the first foreign missionaries of the General Conference, P. A. and Elizabeth Penner and H. J. Brown, came from this church.

Giving heart and life to Jesus

W. S. Gottschall came to hold a series of evangelistic meetings and asked her to sing duets with him every evening. The songs were in English and one was "Is He Yours? the Shepherd, the Pilot, the Savior?"

"It was then I realized that I needed all of these and I gave my heart and life to Jesus." After catechetical instruction, she was baptized, weeping much over her past sins.

Ever since P. A. and Elizabeth Dickman Penner had gone to India from Mountain Lake in 1901, Susie had felt, even at the age of nine, that she was being called to full-time Christian service. She knew she needed more education, but didn't know how her parents would react. She wrote a ten-page letter expressing her feelings and put it under the top of her mother's sewing machine. (Later when her mother died in 1930, she found this letter among her "treasures.")

To her surprise, her parents approved of her plans; a friend loaned money for her to go to Bethel College in 1908. But she had another incentive for going to Bethel. She was engaged to a young man from the neighborhood, Peter Reuben Schroeder, and he had attended Bethel College the year before.

She spent the next two years at Bethel, loving the professors, the study, the place. "I sat at the feet of C. H. Wedel, Bethel's first president, and took in the wisdom and beauty of his teaching. He was a member of the General Conference mission board, and since Peter and I were accepted missionary candidates for India, we became better acquainted with him than did many of the other students."

Honeymoon in a Dakota sod house

They were married in September 1910. Her aunt made her wedding dress "of a pearl pink soft material, very delicate colored, like egg shell. . . . I wore no veil but I did wear a wreath of live blooming myrtle." The whole church was invited and afterward came to the wedding lunch at her home.

The cakes had been made by her friends at a cake-baking frolic. After a few days, they left by train for Driscoll, North Dakota, where P. R. was to take a home mission church and teach school for one year before they finished their work at Bethel.

Driscoll was a village about fifty miles east of Bismark. A small group of Mennonites had migrated from South Dakota to homestead fifteen miles north of Driscoll on cheap, rock-infested acres. After repeated crop failures, they had little to show for their back-breaking efforts. "We were to see much of privation, sacrifice, ingenuity, and stubborn determination."

The newlyweds moved into a parsonage unlike any they had dreamed of, two rooms built of sod with a sod roof and a small wooden shed attached around the one doorway. The walls of the house were about two feet thick with small barnlike windows. The walls were plastered and papered but there was no ceiling, just bare rafters. P. R. bought building paper and nailed it in place. They were never cold. From her home, they had brought a sewing machine, a three-burner kerosene stove, and a Round Oak heater. To this they added a desk, table and chairs, a dresser and a kitchen cabinet.

The mail carrier sometimes stopped there to warm up. The first time, he looked around and said, "I never dreamed you could fix up a sod house like this." She had her oil paintings on the wall, white curtains at the windows, their new furniture, and, most elegant of all, a tall gas lamp with a bright green shade. Their main problem was bedbugs, ever present in the sod walls.

Since they had no buggy or car, they walked to the school, three-fourths of a mile away. Peter preached in two different schoolhouses. The neighbors gave them transportation when the weather was too bad for walking. These friends also shopped for them when they went to town, but Sears Roebuck and Montgomery Ward supplied many of their needs, even groceries. Susie substituted in the school on the few occasions when Peter had to be gone.

In May, school closed and they packed up, selling much of their household goods. On the day before they left, Peter put up a wash line on which she hung all the bedding and clothing to be sunned. They left without taking a single bedbug. But the Schroeders departed with many regrets, for they had come to love their first congregation. From the eighty-five dollars a month salary, they had saved a sizeable sum toward their next year's schooling.

A song for the future

The General Conference Home Mission Board asked them to go to Langham, Saskatchewan, for the summer months to conduct a German Bible School. In August, they attended General Conference in Bluffton, Ohio. At one service, they sang, "The Days Are Going By."

"The refrain still rings in my ears:

'They are going, going, going,
Never more will they return,
And the time for work is shortening as they fly.
Let us then be up and doing
Helping men of Christ to learn,
While the days are going by.'

"I believe our future was sealed with the singing of that song!"

S. F. Sprunger asked them to stop to see the new church at Berne, Indiana, but they had to hurry back to Newton for their last year at Bethel College.

While P. R. completed his senior year, Susie enrolled in the college Bible course. They were the first married couple to attend Bethel College. P. R. preached in neighboring churches. He graduated in 1912.

The Schroeders were asked to spend the summer at the Berne church where P. R. was to fill the pulpit vacated by J. W. Kliewer, who was to replace C. H. Wedel as president of Bethel. Since they were planning to attend Oberlin Seminary in Ohio, this seemed to be a good move. P. R. preached in the Berne church the day after they arrived in Berne, just two months after the new church with seating for 2,000 had been dedicated.

"It humbled us, but it also challenged us. We felt we were in an entirely new world." They brought their High German to this community with its Swiss dialect. The young people spoke English, but the church services were in German.

The Schroeders were impressed by Berne's spiritual life. They were introduced to tithing and saw what that can do for a church. The Temperance Society, the way the people brought the *whole family* to Sunday school and church, the outstanding ministers and Bible teachers for special meetings, stress on evangelism and revival, these "did something to our lives that will never be destroyed. There was a deep loyalty to Christ and the Scriptures."

Giving up India for Indiana

The time for a hard decision came when the church extended the call to them to stay at Berne indefinitely.

The Schroeders had thought they were called to go to Oberlin to prepare for the India mission field. "Are we not acceptable?" they asked. Were not the missionaries there waiting for them to come? The decision to stay was more difficult for Susie to make than for P. R., and it bothered her for years.

She had to remember her wedding vows that "where thou goest I will go," and follow her husband in his call. After so much planning, she was never to see Oberlin or a foreign country, but she said that she always felt like a missionary at heart.[2]

They moved into another home, this time buying sturdy, solid furniture that would last the rest of her life. Celeste Evangeline was welcomed in April 1913, named as a heavenly messenger. "What fun that was!"—planning for the new baby, making all the clothes.

They moved to still another home. Susie's sister Helen came to live with them to attend high school in Berne and then to attend college. When her father died, her mother and Lyllian came. The family had to move again, and yet again, and, then, decided to buy their own home, an old house that needed much remodeling.

They began by having the house turned around so that the kitchen faced the backyard rather than the street. The walls had been insulated with hand-hewed sticks and mud mortar and the architect said it was the *heaviest* house he had ever moved. They installed a number of innovations, such as a dumbwaiter and an attached garage. Amid the different moves, Vernelle was born in 1915 and Louise on moving day in 1917.

Shadows around a burning cross

With World War I, they experienced the war's upheaval. Peter was gone a great deal visiting draftees. When the Ku Klux Klan burned crosses on the church lawn, the family watched from the living room window as the white sheeted Klansmen moved about in the shadows. German was forbidden and services were changed to English.

Prices went up to the point where they could no longer make payments on the house, so they sold it and moved back to a rented place. At that point, the church decided to build a parsonage next to the church, and Esther Ruth was born there in 1920. This was to be their last home in Berne, their seventh move.

The next eight years were busy ones, with four girls of different

---

2. Bessie B. Koontz, *Refreshing Rays from Western Slopes* (Newton, Kansas: Allen Publishing Co, 1965), no page numbers.

personalities growing up, lively and energetic. The family developed a strong wanderlust. They went on outings to the state penitentiary, the insane asylum, the county poor farm, city missions, Skid Row in Chicago, the Chicago World's Fair, factories, state parks, and Lake Michigan's sand dunes.

Family devotions were an evening event, and the Bible was read through aloud twice in the children's time at home. Celeste wrote, "We felt that our parents could cope with any situation and we were confident we could too."

Susie wrote, "Daddy had many calls to conduct special meetings throughout the conference and was often gone from one to three weeks. I had to do a lot of the bringing up of our girls by myself and the failures and neglects will have to be placed against my account."

Plea for missionary prayers

Susie made an early contribution to the church by suggesting that a nursery be started. She also recommended that the Sunday school hour be changed from the afternoon to the forenoon. (The suggestion was opposed by S. F. Sprunger because it would give the youth too much free time on Sunday. What would they do with it?)[3]

Susie was elected secretary of the Women's Missionary Association of the General Conference. In 1926, as secretary, she became the editor of the new *Missionary News and Notes*. She wrote in the first issue:

> It is a long recognized fact that we must first know a thing before we will pray for it and when we have begun to pray for it, we shall also be willing to sacrifice for it. And that shall be the sole purpose of these News and Notes, to further missionary interest by imparting information and pleading for the prayers and gifts of our missionary friends.

This involvement was to be shared by the whole family for the next three years. *Missionary News and Notes* often took up the dining room table, and the girls had to work around it. Although most of the copies were printed in English, Peter ran off the German edition on his mimeograph, charging one dollar a month for his half day's time and for the stencil and ink. The family helped fold and mail the 300 copies.[4]

---

3. Naomi Lehman, *Pilgrimage of a Congregation* (Berne, Indiana: First Mennonite Church, 1982), p. 71.
4. Gladys V. Goering, *Women in Search of Mission* (Newton, Kansas: Faith and Life Press, 1980), pp. 43-45.

Buyer and seller of buttons

Susie also helped to finance the project. Metal buttons, to be used in making garments for India, were sold at ten cents a dozen for the small ones and fifteen cents for the large. Susie took charge of button sales. She bought lots of them. Her daughters wore these buttons on their underclothes for years.

Besides the correspondence concerning *Missionary News and Notes*, Susie wrote and received letters on other WMA business: filling offices, getting speakers for conferences, making reports. The executive committee wrote extensively about choosing speakers for conference meetings, presenting reasons why someone should or should not be asked.[5]

In 1928, P. R. was asked to become president of Freeman Junior College in South Dakota. "It was a hard decision to make. Berne was so much a part of us, but there was also considerable tension." To understand this, one needs to know something about the currents within the General Conference Mennonite Church at that time.

Finding modernism in the camp

As early as 1914, Susie had watched her husband's struggle with "a vicious bug called liberalism." He had been attending the University of Chicago, then considered the hotbed of critical theology. When one of the professors urged him to be either fundamental or modern, but not a fence straddler, surprisingly, the challenge led him to choose the conservative cause.

"From then on, his preaching took on a new tone of deep conviction, fearless proclamation, a joyful and victorious attitude and a deep concern for those of his colleagues who did not share this faith. He always had been very determined, and now he often was too impatient and intolerant with his friends. This was very hard on me although I shared his convictions entirely."

In 1922, a questionnaire was sent to colleges to determine whether they had modernist leanings. Bluffton College sent back a long reply with much explanation that did not remove the doubts of some of the church deacons at Berne that Bluffton was indeed in the "modernist camp."[6]

President Mosiman implied that the Berne council had no authority to say whom the colleges should hire. This caused quite an uproar, and in 1928, P. R. compiled his pamphlet, *Evidences of Modernism*. Later he

---

5. Unpublished WMA correspondence, Box 1, Folders 10 and 11, Mennonite Library and Archives.
6. *Evidences of Modernism*, a pamphlet in the MLA.

wrote an apology to the churches of the General Conference saying that he had dealt with Bluffton and Dr. Mosiman in an unloving way. He was apologizing for the way he had handled the situation, but not for his fight against modernism.[7] After P. R. had taught and preached in South Dakota for a number of years, his views changed.

But in Berne in 1928, many church members felt that their pastor and some of their deacons were using heresy hunting tactics against Bluffton College, listening only to those who opposed the college. Susie, of course, was in the middle of this controversy, and at one time pleaded, "Pete, the church leaders are against you."[8]

Finally, the term of the pastor was to come to a vote, but before the final outcome could be decided, P. R. had a call from Freeman Junior College as well as calls from Bethel College and Bethel Deaconess Hospital.

Theirs was, in spite of the controversy, a much-loved family. They left with the good wishes of thousands of people from the church and the community. At the farewell, they sang the hymn that had brought them to Berne. P. R. quipped, perhaps to relieve the melancholy, that their road from Berne to Freeman could be marked by the trail of chicken bones from the packed lunches presented to them.[9]

To a new work in South Dakota's dryness

They left in the fall of 1928. South Dakota in August was "hot and, oh, so different from Indiana. Everything was dry and there were only small stands of dry, leafless trees. We drove to the college and there in the car dedicated ourselves to the new work that we had come to take over."

Freeman with four teenage daughters was a different experience from Berne with four little girls. And Freeman was a different kind of town. After two years, P. R. was asked to preach full time at the Salem (South) church, and so once again they moved, this time to the country.

P. R. left the presidency but continued to teach Bible courses at the college. The girls attended the academy and junior college and then went on to other schools, Celeste and Vernelle to Wheaton and Louise and Esther Ruth to Bethel. Because of the Depression, money was scarce, but they survived by living simply.

During a snowstorm in the winter of 1936, Susie had the harrowing

---

7. Bob Waltner, "Rev. P. R. Schroeder," a research paper in the MLA, pp. 6-9. The letter of apology was found in P. R. Schroeder's personal effects.
8. Lehman, p. 73.
9. Celeste Schroeder Dehnert, "Peter R. Schroeder—Pastor and Conference Worker," *Mennonite Life*, July 1949, p. 40.

experience of locking herself out of the house while wearing only a house dress and sweater. "The blizzard was raging and no one could hear me call. How I prayed!" She happened to think that perhaps the basement door on the other side of the house might be unlocked. She waded through waist-deep snow and found that it was open. She stumbled to safety. "I knelt down and thanked God for my deliverance. I had looked death in the face."

Dust storms were almost as bad as snowstorms. The dust blew into the house, even obscuring the pattern of the rug.

In 1936, P. R., as president of the General Conference, attended the World Mennonite Conference in Amsterdam. It was a valuable experience and he shared his excitement with the family when he returned.

All four girls taught country school for a year or two. They changed off teaching and going to college so that they could help each other through school. Celeste married George Dehnert, an agriculture teacher. Eventually, he was to teach at the University of Wisconsin.

Vernelle and Orlando Waltner were married in June 1939. They were ordained as missionary candidates for India the Sunday following their wedding. Susie felt that it was a satisfying answer to prayer when her sister Helen could serve in India for twenty-five years and Vernelle and Orlando for seventeen years. "I can truly say it was harder to give up going to India than it ever was to be willing to go. In God's own way, he healed my disappointment by allowing three of my loved ones to serve there instead of only me."[10]

Stunned by grief and loneliness

In August 1939, P. R. became ill. The surgeon found that he had cancer of the colon, and performed a colostomy. He made a rapid recovery, and the Waltners left for India as planned. But the next June, the cancer returned. After further surgery, he revived. When they moved to Mountain Lake, after a call from the Bethel church, P. R. took up the work with enthusiasm. But his illness recurred and he died in April 1941.

The family was stunned. When Susie and her three daughters returned from the hospital that morning, they found that the verse for the day in their devotional book was Psalm 116:15: "Precious in the sight of the Lord is the death of his saints," and they were comforted.

Susie was fifty-three. Her life was completely changed. Not only was there the void left by the loss of the husband she dearly loved and depended on, but she found herself without her vocation as pastor's wife. She had no

10. Koontz, unpaged.

home and no income. "But I still had my God and many kind friends and my children."

She went to live with Celeste in Lodi, Wisconsin, for the winter. After the sad news that Vernelle and Orlando had had a stillborn son came the blessing of the birth of Peter Schroeder Dehnert, Celeste and George's first child. He was a comfort in her loneliness.

Then the Bethel church in Mountain Lake called her to be their church worker. "It was the kindest thing they could have done for me, and it gave me the feeling that there was still a purpose for my life." That summer (1942), Louise and Elbert Koontz were married and left for Bonebrake Seminary in Dayton, Ohio, to prepare for missionary work in Sierra Leone.

In February 1943, Louise died of a kidney infection and heart failure. "Oh, those were hard days and weeks. It all seemed like a terrible dream, but it was only too true." Elbert came to stay with her the next summer.

Writing a tract for young mothers

Susie moved to her eighteenth home, an apartment in Mountain Lake. While the Waltners were home on furlough, Orlando attended seminary and Vernelle and her two boys lived with her. Vernelle and Orlando's Carol Louise, her only granddaughter, was born in Mountain Lake. Another happy occasion was the wedding of Elbert and Esther Ruth in August 1944.

Susie's duties at the Bethel Mennonite Church were not clearly defined, but she made a position for herself by visiting the sick and the young mothers. A little tract that she wrote entitled "Whose Image and Superscription Is This?" based on Luke 20:24, was given to the mothers. This tract was also used by some Mennonite pastors.

She also wrote conference reports for the pastors; taught adult Bible, teacher training, and Sunday school classes and one year of released-time Bible class in the grade school; and brought up to date the church records. Retaining her interest in missions, she assisted the relief committee in sending huge shipments of food and clothing to people in poor countries.

Matchmaking for Mennonites in Reedley

Susie made one more move before retirement. The year 1953—1954 she spent as housemother of the staff home of the Kingsview Mental Hospital at Reedley, California. Young people were serving there in lieu of military service, and learning to know them was a rich experience. She enjoyed observing the matchmaking and thought it was an "excellent way of blending the different shades of Mennonites together."

She moved back to Mountain Lake to her twentieth home, this time above the North Star Telephone Company. She wanted to die before she became senile and dependent. "But," she said, "God will take care of me. He has all my life." She had suffered a heart attack after their move to Freeman and she had had a radical mastectomy for cancer while serving the Bethel church.

Girls, remember missions

After she had suffered a series of light strokes, she went to convalesce with Esther Ruth in Hillsboro, Kansas, with arrangements to enter the retirement home. Susie insisted on attending a special service in the church Elbert was serving, and they took her against their better judgment. She returned home tired.

Esther Ruth asked, "Well, how was it, Mother?"

"I knew I'd get along just fine."

"Well, I wasn't too sure of that."

"Going to church has never hurt me!"

The next day they took her to the hospital. Celeste came to spend three weeks with her, reading from the Bible and singing from the *Gesangbuch*. She died of heart failure on February 23, 1966. The funeral was held in the Bethel church in Mountain Lake, the church of her youth and her last years.

Her will included a short page of instructions and the words, "And, girls, remember missions."

Bessie Koontz, the mother of Elbert Koontz and a minister in the United Brethren Church, wrote a tribute to her friend with whom she had shared sorrows and joys. "In the darkest hour of our experience I heard her sing songs of faith that gave courage and strength to both of us. There are no uncertain notes in her song of life."[11]

---

11. Koontz, unpaged.

12.
Always Curious About the World

M'Della Moon
1890—1963

M'Della Moon began teaching at Bluffton College in 1921 at a time when few women taught in the field of science. English, music, and elementary education were acceptable areas for women professors, but here was a woman who could coach men's basketball and teach biology.

Furthermore, she kept abreast of changes in her profession as they developed. Just a few years prior to her retirement, she was taking courses and teaching in the field of environmental education.

From the Trenton tradition

Born September 9, 1890, near the village of Seven Mile in Butler County, Ohio, M'Della Moon was one of a number of well-known educators and church leaders to come to the Bluffton community from the Trenton Mennonite Church. The first child of James and Wilhelmina Augspurger Moon, she was born eight years after their marriage.

She wrote in her autobiography:

> I came from a rather mixed parentage, since my mother was German and my father was English. Both parents were born and reared on the farm and had little formal education. Another outstanding difference was that in my father's family the men were all volunteer soldiers in the Civil War except my father who was too young to go. My mother's people were pacifists (Mennonite). Hence there was con-

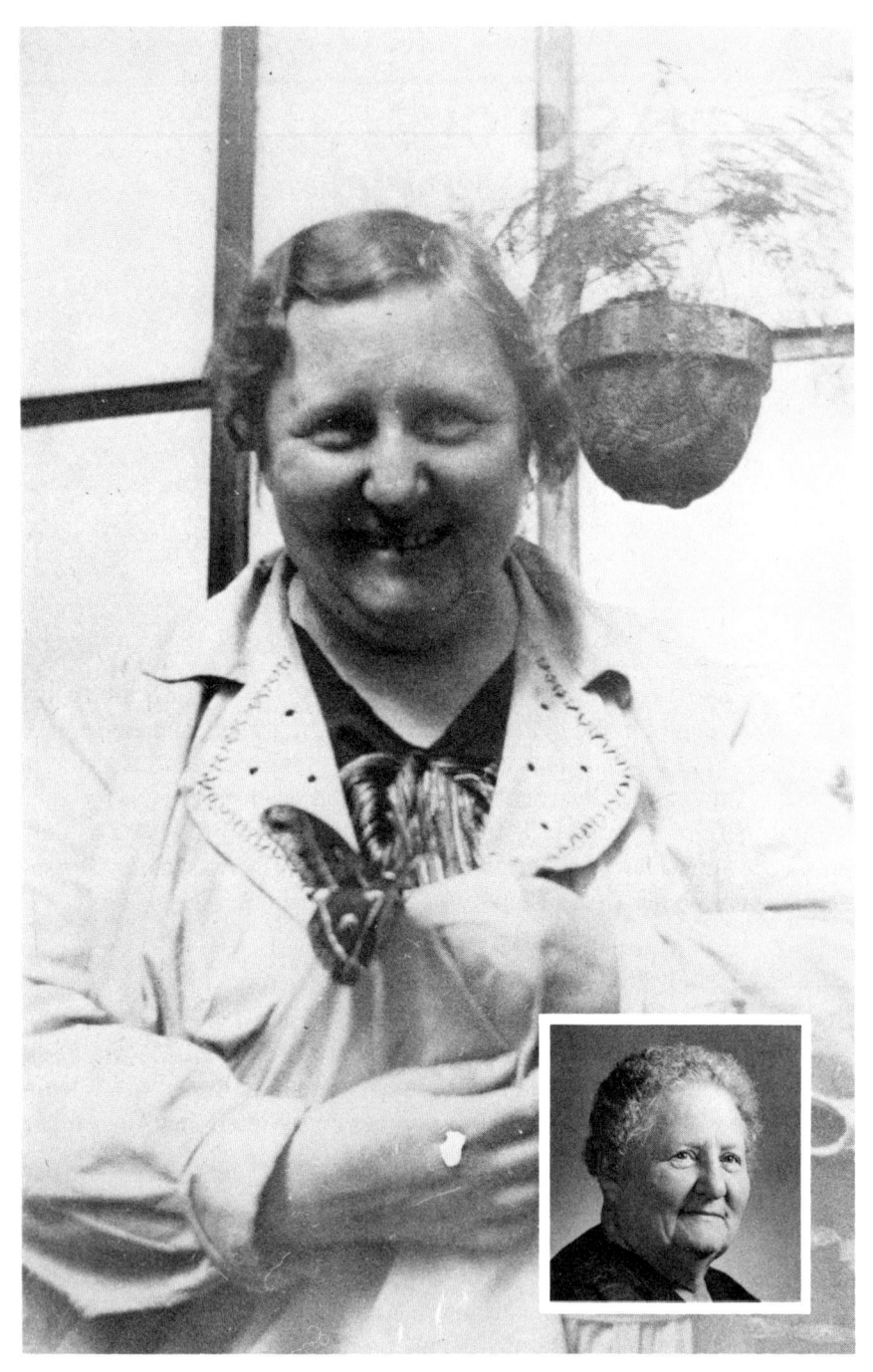

M'Della Moon: Her students were expected to use the greenhouse where she nurtured exotic plants. But the ordinary interested her as well as the extraordinary.

siderable objection to my mother's marriage, not by her parents, but by her grandparents and their families. They objected to my father on three points—he was not a Mennonite, he was not German, and he had very little money.[1]

M'Della was the first grandchild, oldest daughter of the oldest daughter for five generations. Although she considered herself spoiled by her aunts and uncles, she felt that she had received very strict training from her parents and learned obedience without argument, a training she felt was invaluable.

In an era when parents could spend little time with individual children because of their large families, M'Della was read to by her mother and was told stories by her father. They sang together; and M'Della sang solos in church at the age of four. Because she had few playmates, she was very fond of pets: dogs, lambs, chickens, even frogs.

The joy of learning

She found school to be the joy that she had anticipated, although she did not do well the first two years. She preferred playing and listening to the other students recite to doing her own assignments. But in the third grade she learned from a teacher whose methods were ahead of her time, "a really wonderful teacher," who became M'Della's inspiration. This teacher and the Moons started a Sunday school in the schoolhouse. Most of the people in the community attended.

Then her parents bought a farm near Middletown, where M'Della was welcomed by another good teacher. She took piano lessons, but "never became very proficient at it, simply because I was too lazy to practice as I should!" However, she continued singing.

When M'Della was ten, her sister Helen was born, the only other child in the family. Her birth was an important event, but the girls were too far apart in age to be close until they became adults. Helen grew up to have a lovely voice, so they sang duets together while they lived in the same community.

M'Della finished grade school by passing the Boxwell examination, a test that lasted for eight hours and covered a dozen subjects. Her parents continued to encourage her to read. Her father took pains to teach her to read aloud, correcting her pronunciation and expression. He would also discuss with her the ideas presented by the material, helping her to pick

---

1. *Autobiography of a Retired Teacher*, 1962, p. 1, published in manuscript by the Alpha Tau Chapter of Delta Kappa Gamma Society; this copy was contributed by LaVera Hill, Miss Moon's student and close friend.

out the important points and express them in her own words. This exercise prepared her well for high school.

M'Della drove a farm horse the three miles to Middletown High School. Evenings were spent with chores, then studying and piano practice, then singing, checkers, or Flinch. Her parents were opposed to playing cards.

The English-Scientific course was not a college preparatory course. M'Della liked English, disliked mathematics, but she took extra courses that were not required: German, Latin, chemistry, physics, botany, and zoology. Seeing that she was a voracious reader, her English teacher started lending her books and talking college. M'Della's parents, and particularly her grandfather, "thought that a woman's place belonged to *Kirche*, *Kinder*, and *Kochen* (church, children, and cooking). In other words, I should marry and settle down."

Poet and speech maker

Several factors persuaded M'Della's family that she should go to college. One was the influence of the teacher whom the family respected. Another was that the poem she entered in a contest was chosen to go into the cornerstone of the new high school.

Lastly, M'Della was selected by the faculty to write and present an oration at the commencement exercises. The oration, "The Upward Trail," was, she felt at the time, "a wonderful piece of literature!" But when she read it over years later, "how I did laugh over what I had written. The remarks of an unsuspicious and innocent child on attaining an abundant life!"

Nevertheless, her grandfather was proud of her and gave one hundred dollars to Central Mennonite College which secured a scholarship for her. In the fall of 1910, her mother took her to Bluffton. The institution was a junior college, destined to become Bluffton College in a few years. M'Della had dreams of being a medical doctor.

> But that was terrible—a Mennonite woman to become a doctor which was distinctly a man's field. Impossible! Actually there were not too many Mennonite women who went to college at all, to say nothing of completing such a course.

She was counseled to study for a more ladylike profession, such as teaching English. She also wanted to take vocal lessons. Her parents had had a hard enough time scraping money together for her education and said that music lessons were too expensive. Without telling them, she got a job washing dishes and paid for her own lessons.

Choosing science instead of gold and Greek

After two years at Bluffton, M'Della returned home, not knowing what she would be doing. Her former grade school teacher asked her to teach music in some of the schools that had never had a music teacher. From 1912 to 1918, she drove, usually by horse and buggy, to seventeen schools in the country, almost twenty miles each day. Most of the children knew nothing about music, had never seen an instrument, and could not carry a tune. At the end of six years, they were giving little musical programs and singing.

During this time, M'Della was going once a week to Cincinnati to take voice lessons and to attend symphony concerts. One summer, she attended Bluffton College for a class in harmony and counterpoint. She seemed headed for a life's work in music.

Then she took off a summer for a trip that included a stopover in Kentucky where she was talked into signing on for a year as a substitute teacher. Besides a full load of academic courses, "and don't laugh any more than you can help," she was in charge of athletics, even boys' basketball. Her basketball team won the twelve-county championship and so did her chorus. She returned to Ohio after that strenuous year to teach physics and other sciences at Brookville.

M'Della wanted a college degree, and since Miami University was only seventeen miles from home, she went there for summer school. She was not thinking seriously about becoming a science teacher, but since she needed more science for the degree, she took a botany and a bacteriology course. When Dr. Fink, her teacher, asked her to become his assistant for the coming winter, she agreed, provided she could afford it. He found a job for her testing the milk, used in the college dining hall, for butterfat and bacteria.

M'Della always took extra course hours. That year she took Greek. She did so well that she was asked to take a second year and compete for the Elliot Greek prize, fifty dollars in gold. Choosing zoology and geology over the enticement of gold and Greek, she did not compete. During her two years at Miami, she was on the girls' championship baseball team and the hockey team. She enjoyed campus life, again praising her teachers.

An invitation from Bluffton

In thinking about a career, M'Della decided that she wanted to teach. But the head of the education department at Miami University called her in to tell her that, of course, she could not teach: she had not taken the education classes or practice teaching. A few days later Dr. Mosiman, president of Bluffton College, asked her to head the department of biological science at Bluffton. With some hesitation, she accepted the challenge.

When the head of the education department at Miami University called to tell her that she had better reconsider her decision not to take education courses, she had the very human satisfaction of telling him that she already had a position in a college. "I think he almost had apoplexy."

She went to Bluffton College in 1921. She would retire forty years later in 1961. Her training continued during summers. She took a leave of absence in 1923-1924 to work on a master's degree at Ohio State University in plant ecology; she received the degree in 1927. A year's leave in 1929 and again in 1940 were used for further study.

House mother to the men

As her tenure was extended, so were her duties. Her teaching load appears staggering to a present-day teacher, but with her newly-won master's degree, she was also given the responsibility as house mother for the new men's dormitory. As the nation prepared for war, she listened and advised students who were making decisions about how to register for military service.

In 1940, M'Della was named chairman of the Division of Material Science and continued in that position until her retirement. She also took her turn on other college committees: Administration, Curriculum, and Physical Education. She was Dean of Women for many years. As the dormitory head resident, she was counselor to both men and women.[2]

Biology, her first love

But her first love was biology. Students were expected to use the greenhouse where she nurtured exotic plants, but the ordinary interested her as well as the extraordinary. Her former students commented on her approach to her subjects. "She didn't look at animals and plants from a biological point of view. She could get excited about them," Maurice Kaufmann said.

"She could get emotional about trees," was Carl Smucker's comment. "She loved that stuff, and taught that way, and the kids she taught learned to love it too. She had no difficulty with the creation story. She knew that God was Creator. You didn't have to have it spelled out how all these things happened. She had no trouble believing the Bible and science at the same time."

2. *Bluffton College Bulletin*, October 1963, p. 4.

Oliver Diller remembered an exercise that she gave him. He was to draw a circle with a a diameter of three feet and tabulate everything he could find within that circle: vegetation, insects, and soil. It was the beginning for him of a long and outstanding career in forestry.

Her field trips were long remembered. Students first learned to know their own campus, especially the trees. Until her later years she was able to accompany them. She had a genial disposition and could enjoy a joke, even when it was about her size. On a field trip on Indian Lake, she fell out of the rowboat and had to somehow be rescued and dried out. She could laugh about that experience and probably heard the remark that the lake rose by a foot when she fell in. She had excellent rapport with her students, although it was said that she seemed to favor the men more than the women.

Bluffton College made a name for itself for the large number of students who continued their work into graduate school. M'Della and H. W. Berky, the chemistry teacher, guided their students from the time they entered the college so that they would be prepared for further education in the sciences beyond the baccalaureate degree.

LaVera Hill wrote, "She was my professor and close friend. Although I knew her for only seven years, I am thankful that God gave me the opportunity to come in contact with such an inspirational person."

M'Della tried to keep pace with changes in her field. She wrote,

> As I look over the years of my own teaching, I can see that there were different cycles of emphasis. For example, in botany, classification and structure was most important; then we began to think about function, which brought the physiology of plants to the front, and immediately it was evident that more chemistry was needed, so that the physiology could be understood; then the field of genetics opened up and was concerned with morphology (structure) and physiology, as well as plant chemistry, and later biochemistry. Added to this general picture, interest arose in the relationships of plants to each other, and to animals and man. Here were background materials for research with drug producing plants, food plants, what to do with products such as cellulose, which was considered waste material. . . . This is the beginning, but the end is not in sight; someone is always curious.

In 1953, she became interested in conservation. After attending a workshop on environmental studies, she introduced the course into the curriculum.

Great joy in teaching

M'Della's autobiography reveals much of her philosophy about work and a fulfilled life, her attitude toward God and the church, and her state of singleness. Nowhere does she write about herself as a single woman or of having to cope with loneliness. That was not a subject for open discussion in her generation. But what she says about her beliefs gives clues to the way she dealt with life as an unmarried woman in a society of "church, children, and kitchen."

She believed in her profession; she loved teaching. "From the time I taught first graders to sing a simple song to the time when I was getting college students ready to enter graduate school, or to go into some profession, I have gotten great joy out of my work."

She cherished the experience she had had of growing with the college as it achieved North Central Association affiliation, expanded areas of scholastic training, and increased enrollments and facilities. She had enjoyed school, the studying she did in the libraries, the hobnobbing with people in her field.

M'Della believed in reading and study. "I would like to add a word of advice here. Read and read, not only in your own field, but in many fields. Read plays and poetry, biography and novels. Read what is happening in the world today. . . ." Her former students spoke of the magazines she subscribed to and brought into the classroom for them to read.

M'Della thought everyone should have two hobbies, "one to occupy him while he is still active, and another of the sit-around variety." Her active hobby was her interest in plants and conservation. What her sit-around hobby was she didn't say.

She had a close relationship with her parents until her father's death at the age of eighty-four and her mother's death four years later. She and her sister became close friends in their adult years, but Helen died at the age of fifty-one, twelve years before M'Della's death. M'Della spent her vacations with her sister's family and with cousins. "I never feel that I am alone," she wrote.

The faith of a happy person

Possibly she was a disappointment to her family in the early years because of her unconventional desire to study and enter what was at the time considered a man's world. Today we recognize that she had a wholesome combination of feminine and masculine traits: she enjoyed English and music and lacy, feminine things and little fancy rings, and she had the warmth and empathy needed to be a good counselor; but she moved in what was considered a man's world of science.

She was grateful for her good health. She thought of herself as a happy person:

> When things did not go as I wanted or expected, [I was] able to say to myself that I have done the best I could, and to take the days in stride and go on, repairing my mistakes where I was able to do so, and to guard against repeating them. I have never thought that the Lord expects perfection, neither do I think that He overlooks carelessness in doing the things expected of one. . . but He does require from all of us that we meet our problems in the best way possible to each of us . . . and with the certain knowledge that He is there to help and guide us.

M'Della not only professed, but also lived out her belief in God. Lloyd Ramseyer, president of the college, said, "The more she learned about the laws which govern nature, the more love and respect she had for the one who set these laws in motion and continued to be the ruler of His creation. . . . As she taught, she conveyed this faith to her students."[3]

While maintaining her membership in the Trenton Mennonite Church, she taught Sunday school classes at the First Mennonite Church in Bluffton and sang in the *Messiah* and in the Vesper Choir until her voice failed.

M'Della's community interests included the Mennonite Memorial Home for the Aged in Bluffton where she was on the board. She held memberships in the Business and Professional Women's Club and many other community organizations. In 1955, she was listed in *Who's Who Among American Men of Science*. A list of other professional academic organizations to which she belonged is impressive. She was honored as Bluffton's Woman of the Year in 1962.

Officially, her retirement began in June 1961, with its attendant tributes and gifts from faculty and students. Forty years of college teaching is a milestone to be celebrated. Her colleague, Naomi Brenneman, retired at the same time. Later they were both honored when the new women's dormitory, Brendell, was named for them.

With a money gift from former students, she bought a Boston rocker (for her retirement), a new radio (for keeping up), and *Birds of the World* (for her professional growth). One should be able to picture her rocking away in her Boston rocker (along with President Kennedy), but she was asked back to the college to teach Local Flora in summer school, Human

---

3. *Bluffton College Bulletin.*

Anatomy the first semester, and Bacteriology the second. She taught again the next year. Two "men of science" were hired to replace her, according to Maurice Kaufmann who began teaching that fall.

Death came unexpectedly and kindly on September 16, 1963. She was receiving treatment for cancer, which was not considered immediately serious, but she died of a blood clot in the lungs. Her friend LaVera Hill was with her at the hospital at the time.

"Even up to the last minutes of her life she was of a jovial disposition, facing her last illness with faith and courage. She invariably spread good will rather than gloom."[4]

Perhaps her greatest contribution to Bluffton College, outside of her professionalism, was her presence among the small group of long-term, devoted men and women who provided loyalty and stability to the college during the years of its growth and difficult times. She, along with other faculty members, hung on through the debt crisis, struggled to bring standards up to affiliation requirements, and remained steadfast during assaults on its theological integrity.

President Ramseyer acknowledged this in his memorial tribute: "Christian institutions are usually built through the sacrifice and influence of great Christian personalities. Miss Moon was one of these individuals who helped to make Bluffton College a powerful Christian influence on young lives."[5]

4. *Bluffton College Bulletin.*
5. *Bluffton College Bulletin.*

13.
Intrepid Traveler and Teacher

Emma Mary Ruth
1891—1965

In the history of the First Mennonite Church, Reedley, California, is found this comment: "Women's names appear only occasionally in the minutes of the annual meetings of the congregation and of the Church Council meetings, with one exception. Emma Ruth was the one woman whose varied gifts and talents were recognized and used to the fullest."

For many years, she was pianist and organist; she was often a delegate to the Pacific District Conference; and she was involved in migrant work. "In 1940, she was the first woman ever to work on the heretofore exclusively male Finance Committee.[1] Later Emma was appointed to the Church Stewardship Committee.

Along with a commitment to her congregation, she had an enthusiasm for going places and doing something worthwhile when she got there.

Bavarian ancestry

The ancestors of John A. Ruth, Emma's father, were Swiss Mennonites who fled into Alsace-Lorraine, then to Upper Bavaria. John was born in Eichstock and came with his parents to West Point, Iowa, in 1852 when he was seven. In Iowa, John met Clara Eymann, born in Ashland, Ohio, also of German background. They moved to Summerfield, Illinois, in the year

---

1. Ted Loewen, ed., *Reedley First Mennonite Church: The First Seventy-five Years, 1906-1981* (Reedley, California: First Mennonite Church, 1981), pp. 26f.

126 | ENCIRCLED

Emma Ruth: She had an enthusiasm for going places and doing something worthwhile when she got there.

of their marriage, 1870. After fifteen years, they moved to Halstead, Kansas, where Emma Mary was born on September 26, 1891. She was the youngest of their nine children.[2]

When John and Clara moved to a farm near Hesston, the family joined the Garden Township Mennonite Church. This congregation was made up of families who had come from Mennonite churches in Halstead and Moundridge.

Parlor organ lessons

As a child, Emma took lessons on the parlor organ. This beginning, simple as it might have been, sparked her interest in music, and she continued with lessons and singing whenever possible. Music was an important part of the Garden Township church life, with many singing groups such as family quartets.

Emma attended the country school, District 49 in Harvey County, and upon graduation from eighth grade attended Bethel Academy for the school year of 1908-1909. After passing the teacher's examination, she received a certificate so that she could teach in District 49.

A year later, she returned to Bethel to finish high school and then to attend college. After a year of college, she graduated from the Teachers Certificate Course in the music department. Emma gave piano lessons in the community until the family moved to California.

Her Bethel years were most satisfying. Social life with the "Garden Bunch" and the "Bayerish [Bavarian] Bunch" was enjoyable, as were performances with the ladies' glee club, octet, and quartet. And she played tennis.

Exacting as a music teacher

In 1915, at the age of twenty-four, Emma came to Reedley, California. She found here a stimulating community, one that appreciated her music. In the summer of 1916, she started working toward her degree at the University of California at Berkeley. She finished her studies there in 1925. Even after receiving her degree, she continued her music education, attending workshops and summer school courses.

Emma soon attracted a class of serious private piano students, and teaching piano became her career. She was a careful and exacting teacher. Along with fingering skills, she taught appreciation of good music, how to listen to concerts, and what was going on in the world of music. "Anyone

---

2. Unless otherwise noted, this information comes from Clare Ann Ruth Heffelbower, Reedley, California. It includes letters written by Emma and a biography by Clare Ann. This material is now in the Mennonite Library and Archives, North Newton, Kansas.

taught by Emma Ruth would not be slipshod," according to her niece, Ruth Dettweiler Kope.

The high school students to whom she taught piano received academic credit. Her expectations were high. "While in some ways she was intimidating because of her high standards, she had a remarkable power to inspire her students to want to do well," says her niece, Clare Ann Ruth Heffelbower.

Her knowledge and interest in music was well used by the First Mennonite Church of Reedley where she was a member. As director of music, she was at various times church organist and director of a women's choir, a youth choir, and a junior choir. She accompanied the famous men's chorus of that church for thirty years.

As far as anyone could remember, an organ had always been used at First Mennonite. When the church purchased an Estey pump organ that could be pumped either by the organist or another person, Emma chose to pump it herself. When the Estey organ was replaced by a Wicks organ, the John A. Ruth family donated most of the money for it. Emma Ruth was the principal organist until she left for India in 1947. Since then, a number of Emma's students, including at least two nieces, have served as organists.[3]

Emma naturally exposed young people to the music she cared so much about. Ethel Harder commented on her work as youth choir director: "Oh the excitement when one year she introduced us to some beautiful new Christmas music—'Lo, How a Rose e'er Blooming.' " Ethel remembers her as "a sweet lady, always proper, the beautiful Emma Ruth with the deep brown eyes."

Elsie Lichti, one of the young people, wrote, "She was always a friend to everyone. No one ever spoke against her—this is unusual. *Everyone* liked her."

Clare Ann said, "She didn't hesitate to speak out if she disapproved or questioned things she saw. People experienced her as an authentic person. She didn't give praise too often—and when she did it was real. She was straightforward and to the point—she could say things and be heard that many people could not get by with saying."

With Christian Endeavor in Berlin

In her church, Emma also established herself as a friend to young people, a relationship that continued all her life in any place she lived and worked. She was involved in Christian Endeavor programs at the local, county, and state levels. She counted one of the highlights of her life a trip to the

---

3. *Reedley First Mennonite Church*, pp. 58f.

World's Christian Endeavor Convention in Berlin in 1930, attended by 15,000 young people from all over the world. Her first ocean voyage was "endured but not enjoyed." She took the opportunity to visit the ancestral homes of her parents in South Germany. Visiting Rome, she was especially interested in it as the city of the Apostle Paul.

From 1928 to 1942, Emma served as field secretary of young people's work for the Pacific District Conference, which involved considerable travel throughout California, Oregon, Washington, and Idaho. She was, in fact, a woman who traveled more than most of the women of her time. She made a trip to Alaska in 1936, up to the Arctic Circle, and a pack trip to the top of Mount Whitney. Because of her love of mountains, she spent much of her free summer time in the Ruth cabin near Cedarbrook.

Why she never married

Her friends and relatives speculated about why Emma Ruth never married. She was good looking, personable. Clare Ann said, "It would be consistent with Emma's personality and approach to life to simply feel too independent and surrounded by friends to 'need' a husband. She did her own thing. It seems quite possible that she simply didn't have time to get married. Also, few men would have been able to keep up with her."

Emma's father died in 1919, soon after his retirement to Reedley. Her mother lived until 1937. When the opportunity came in 1947 to go to India to teach, Emma was free to respond. Her interest in missions had always been a part of her life. She had encouraged her dear friend Christena Harder Duerksen in the early 1920s by providing the money she needed for an operation and for study at Bethel College to prepare for the mission field.

The parents of two of her piano students planted the idea of teaching abroad. J. N. C. and Anna Hiebert, missionary parents on furlough in Reedley, were so impressed with Emma's piano teaching that they suggested she apply to Kodaikanal School in South India. They knew that the school was looking for a teacher and they wanted to have their own children study with her for another few years.

When Anna Hiebert presented the idea, Emma said no. She had a large class of students and could not possibly leave. Emma didn't say that she was fifty-six years old and past the age for going to a strange country and taking on physical hardships. Probably that thought never occurred to her. But, on thinking it over, Emma decided to apply and was accepted. The idea of traveling in India and teaching in a school for missionary children appealed to her.

After the decision was made in the fall of 1947, she found another piano teacher to take her students and live in her house. She made plans to travel with the Hieberts, along with Christena and J. R. Duerksen and Aron and Kathryn Jantzen who were returning to the General Conference field. There was the usual anxiety about the visa for India, but it came through in true cliff-hanging style. Emma felt the guidance of God in this endeavor and the intercessory prayers of a host of friends who wished her well in her new adventure.

To India with eighteen pieces of luggage

With her eighteen pieces of luggage, she boarded *The Swallow*. The ship was hardly beyond the Golden Gate before it was rolling with the swells of the sea. Except when she was trying to eat crackers and dill pickles, because they stayed down better than any other food, she spent most of her time in her bunk. This ordeal lasted for two weeks, but after Yokohama, food began to taste good again. Experienced travelers said it was the worst voyage ever.

In Singapore, she invested in a *topee*, the pith helmet that was the badge of the India missionary. Emma was one of over one hundred missionaries traveling on this ship. She wrote lively accounts of her bunk mates in the dormitory-like sleeping quarters. Some of these women were strong-minded, and their little spats broke the monotony of the trip.

The trauma of going through customs at Madras proved less painful than anticipated. But other ordeals were in store. Consider the following incident as an example of the many adventures that were to occur during her sojourn in India.

Mr. Hiebert was to accompany her to Kodai, but his customs clearance took longer than Emma's. She was advised to go ahead to the railway station with her eighteen pieces of luggage. She had to deal with the coolies, the beggars, and the helpful people whose English is a foreign language. At the railway station a kind Indian man helped her to find her coach. The heavier pieces of her luggage were being sent over on a truck pulled by coolies. Would it arrive in time for the six o'clock train? Would Mr. Hiebert arrive in time for the six o'clock train? The baggage arrived and was loaded, but then the message came that Mr. Hiebert could not make it and had changed the reservations to the eight o'clock train. The baggage was unloaded and she and the coolies all went back across the overpass to the station.

At that point her helpful friend told her that "he was station Masta No. 3. He was having lots of trouble with me and would expect a nice present." The train came in; the station master and the coolies went up and down the platform looking for her name on the list outside each carriage. There was no reservation for Emma Ruth; the ticket agent had assumed that she would be Mrs. Hiebert, and they found the reservation listed in that name. The kind station master found her reserved seat, and her baggage was stowed in her compartment. The station master insisted that she count the pieces of luggage, not only those in her compartment but the heavier pieces back in the express car.

Finally, Emma wrote, the station master said, "Now all is finished. We have much trouble," and she agreed. The whole troop of coolies, seven of them, stood breathless in front of her waiting to be paid. Now what was she to do?

"You pay the head one—they divide," the station masta informed her.

The head coolie stepped up. "How much?" she asked.

"Fifteen rupees, madam." To herself, she said five dollars seems like a lot of money (three rupees to a dollar), when the station masta whispered, "It is too much—ten rupees is enough."

So she handed it out and off they went. Now it was time for the *present*. So she settled with him for the five rupees the others had asked for, since she didn't know how she would have gotten along without his help. He seemed pleased and thanked her very much. But on a second thought, he remembered that a friend of his had also been helpful to her in the station, would she want to make him a present too. She used the advice he had given her before and told him to divide. So he thanked her again and bid her good-bye.

Now the question was: If Mr. Hiebert didn't arrive on time, should she go on alone or have the coolies unload her luggage again? She decided to go alone, but then Mr. Hiebert arrived with five minutes to spare. He found his compartment in the men's section at the end of the coach and got his luggage on the train. From there on, the journey proceeded according to plan, and her reception at Kodai was "all anyone could wish." The vicissitudes of the journey became a good story and a preparation for further travel in India.

Poor pianos, advanced students

Soon Emma was immersed in teaching piano in a boarding school of 250 students. She gave thirty-five lessons a week. "I have a grand piano class, but poor pianos," she wrote as soon as she arrived. She found the students musically advanced, ready to tackle difficult material, more boys than girls. They were European and American with a few Anglo-Indians. She had limited contact with Indian people.

It was during the long winter vacations that Emma learned to know

India. Her Christmas letters were full of the lessons she was learning in Poverty Education, Studies in Contrasts, and Economics of Maharajas. She was often joined in her travels by a colleague from Kodai, but sometimes she traveled by herself. She visited fellow missionaries at the Mennonite mission stations; in the winter holiday of 1950-1951, she helped to celebrate the Golden Jubilee of the General Conference missions in India.

Moved by her tour of the mission field, she wrote, "These experiences will never be forgotten, nor the loving hospitality shown us by our dear missionary friends. I shall ever count it a special grace of God that I was privileged to witness what God has done through them in India in the past fifty years."

Emma attended workcamps with Kodai students in North and South India. She and her friend Elizabeth Baehr stood at the southernmost tip of Cape Comorin and dipped their fingers where the waters of three seas are mingled. She went several times to Darjeeling for views of Mount Everest, and once, as reported in the *Reedley Exponent* of January 23, 1953, she went with a party on a fifty-five mile trek back into the high mountains, riding a horse appropriately named Red Indian.

She was sixty-two years old that year. Wearing the same blue jeans she had worn to climb Mount Whitney in 1937, Emma and the jeans were untiring. The thrill of that climb, however, came when they met Mr. Tenzing Norgay who had accompanied Sir Edmund Hillary as the first to set foot on the summit of Everest. Emma was impressed almost as much by Mrs. Tenzing.

> By now he does not look like a hillbilly, but quite a polished gentleman that appears on TV and hobnobs with kings and queens and all the great of the land. His wife, a typical Sherpa woman, round of face with rosy cheeks, broad shoulders, full skirt with Tibetan apron, many colors, walking along with him. She hadn't changed her ways or costume. She doesn't want to be spoiled by this new life into which they have been catapulted by his success.

She met and was impressed by other noteworthy people, among them Dr. Ida Scudder, founder of the hospital, medical college, and school of nursing at Vellore. On another adventure, Emma flew to Ceylon, sitting beside the pilot, taking pictures from the cockpit. But traveling in India was usually by rail, "With ten in a party, traveling third class becomes sport, and the cost with concessions, negligible. Five thousand miles for about $20."

She took a furlough to Reedley in 1953, and then returned to Kodai by Dutch freighter accompanied by her upright piano.

Retirement came in 1958. The trip home by boat was one of those "if anything can go wrong, it will" travel disaster stories. Lost reservations, riots in Ceylon, a missed boat from Ceylon because it left a day early, a misplaced health certificate, a lost passport, but finally in July 1958 she arrived in Reedley for welcome home dinners and the demand for personal appearances and talks.

Return to India

After a few months at home, she wondered, "What of the future? Should one retire only because of having passed a certain landmark in age?"

Of course not. Woodstock School in North India beckoned and the way opened for her to return to India, in the Himalayan Mountains this time, a colder, more rugged place. "Kodai reminded me that in the ordinary course of events it was time to retire. But God's time does not always coincide with human calculations." Less than a year after returning to Reedley, in May 1959, she embarked on the freighter *Flying Enterprise*. Even the name of the ship was exciting.

Woodstock was a school of 500 students, kindergarten through high school. Teaching was her paramount duty, but "I take my turn at bell ringing, study hall, meal and playground supervision, and innumerable other things that are connected with a boarding school."

This time she studied Hindi. "It has given me fresh understanding of the learning process and more patience with my students and an appreciation of the first terrific hurdle that confronts every missionary to a foreign country. But there has also been the thrill of becoming literate. It has been a wonderful experience!"

The only indication that she was slowing down came during a trip to Delhi when she accompanied five students on a sightseeing tour: while they climbed the 379 steps of the Qtab Minar, "I watched the handbags!"

Emma met the Dalai Lama of Tibet when he visited the school on behalf of his refugees. She was at the airport with 20,000 Americans and Indians when President Eisenhower flew in, and she was impressed by his speech on world peace. She was sorry to catch only a fleeting glimpse of Mr. Khrushchev as he passed by to the airport after his inspection of the Bhilai Steel Mills, a Russian project. But she heard Queen Elizabeth speak at the Republic Day celebration in 1961.

Fifteen wonderful years

Her short furlough in the winter of 1961-1962 was made by plane, her first trans-ocean flight. By 1963, Emma was having health problems. Surgery for a cataract was successful, but the doctor thought it best that she return to the United States for further attention. Also she was prohibited from climbing, and that was a necessity at Woodstock School. So after five years at Woodstock she returned home in June 1963, counting the time in India as "fifteen wonderful years."

Much as she missed her work and friends in India, she found compensations in the daily life of Reedley: renewing friendships and family ties, FM radio, trips to the Sierras, "heat at the turn of a key and twenty-four-hour hot water service at the tap."

"Instead of calling for coolies, my slogan has become, 'Let the Rambler do it.' " The next year she had further eye surgery.

Back to Reedley meant back to church and community activities. She was again on the Church Building and Stewardship committees, involved in women's circle and mission work. She gave her souvenirs from India to the women's circles to sell for the mission budget. Her niece had thought that Emma knew how to do everything, and was amazed to discover that she didn't know how to sew. Emma bought a machine and Clare Ann taught her to use it. Clare Ann was one of the piano students challenged by her excellent teaching. "She was probably the most organized person I have known."

Her retirement was brief. On April 19, 1965, she died of heart failure following surgery from an abdominal obstruction. J. R. Duerksen, husband of her friend Christena of Reedley and India, was one of the ministers at the memorial service, in which music played a prominent part.

The letters written to the family speak of "Aunt Emma" or "Miss Ruth" as the "best piano teacher"; of her "eternally young spirit"; and of her generosity. A frequent comment was, "She was the most important person in my life."

Clare Ann said, "I saw in her the kind of person I wanted to be. I think in many ways she was a pioneer, refusing to fit into the mold of the traditional woman of her day." In a tribute to her aunt, Clare Ann quoted Anne Ortlung:

> Don't be known to the people as just an organist; be known as a godly person. Music isn't where it's at: God is where it's at. Music is a great vehicle, but it's only a vehicle, a carrier.[4]

Clare Ann said, "Emma was not just an organist or musician—she was a godly person who through her music pointed other people to God."

---

4. *Up with Worship* (Ventura, California: Regal Books, 1982), p. 166.

14.
Her Father's Daughter

Elva Agnes Krehbiel Leisy
1891—1982

On an October day in 1900, H. P. Krehbiel decided that his pretty eight-year-old daughter Elva should ask President McKinley for his autograph. The president had his temporary office in his home in Canton, Ohio, at the time. The Krehbiels were about to move back to Kansas, and this seemed to be the ideal time to get McKinley's signature.

Elva's father placed an autograph book in her one hand and a huge bouquet of dahlias in the other. Taking her to the front walk of the spacious white house, he gave her instructions to go in alone.

"At eight, I was quite an unsophisticated little girl. Probably I thought the president himself would open the door. Instead it was a black butler!"

He took her book and bouquet and returned to lead her to the president's study. McKinley introduced her to the several men around the table and she gave her little speech: "I am Elva Krehbiel and we are moving to Kansas and I would like your autograph before I go, please."

He signed her book, and then he sent her with the flowers to see his wife. Mrs. McKinley treated her graciously and gave her a carnation which had come that morning from the White House.

When the butler let her out the front door, "I ran happily down the sidewalk to show my treasure to Papa and I am sure told my adventures with bubbling excitement."[1]

---

1. Elva Krehbiel Leisy, *Remembering*, a 2-volume manuscript, p. 35, in Mennonite Library and Archives, North Newton, Kansas. Most of the material comes from this source.

Elva Leisy: Ernest said, "Thank you for your picture. I would like to keep the original for life."

Henry P. Krehbiel was not timid, nor was Elva, his only child. She apparently did not hesitate to do what he asked and enjoyed this unique experience. She had respect for and trust in his authority and joined him in his wide interests.

In the doctorless town of Halstead

H. P. was the son of Christian and Susanna Ruth Krehbiel who had come from Germany to Halstead by way of Iowa and Summerfield, Illinois. In Halstead, Christian Krehbiel was a pastor, farmer, and conference leader. H. P. was one of twelve living children.[2]

Elva's maternal grandfather was Adolf Kruse from Hamburg, Germany. Walking across Germany en route to a job, he stopped at a Mennonite community in Galicia where he met and married Margaretha Rupp. After eight years in the Crimea Urich wheatland country, they decided to try their fortune in New York. In 1872, David Goerz and Bernard Warkentin persuaded them to move with their family of four children to Kansas to build homes for Mennonite immigrants from Germany. Margaretha became a busy midwife in the doctorless town of Halstead.

In 1878, when H. P. and his brother John stepped out of the cattle car they had ridden from Illinois, the first person they saw was Matilda Emilia Kruse, a black-haired, black-eyed little girl who was picking up coal along the track. In November 1887, H. P. and Matilda were married.[3]

Elva was born on December 1, 1891, in the five-room Krehbiel cottage in Halstead. The family disapproved of the "foreign" name chosen by her mother, but her father was placated with the middle name of Agnes, although he would have preferred Minnie.

H. P. Krehbiel had thought first of being a doctor, but his father, suspecting that all doctors were atheists, denied his request for money. H. P. borrowed funds to start a hardware store. As a Sunday school superintendent, H. P. soon realized that he wanted to study for the ministry, so, in 1892, he moved with his family to Oberlin, Ohio, to attend seminary.

Here Elva spent a happy childhood with an early start in kindergarten, for Oberlin had the second kindergarten training school in the United States. She began her religious training in a Baptist Sunday school. At this time she also began what was to be a lifetime of edifying travel. Her parents took her, at the age of two, to the Chicago World's Fair of 1893.

---

2. See Christian Krehbiel, *Prairie Pioneer*, for his autobiography, and Mary Lou Cummings, *Full Circle*, for a biography of Susanna Ruth Krehbiel.
3. Elva Krehbiel Leisy, *Henry Peter Krehbiel*, manuscript in MLA, p. 4.

Mind-stretching in Ohio

Her mother found the life at Oberlin a stretching experience and considered those years the happiest of her life. "She had come as a very unsophisticated young woman of thirty, into the intellectual and socially proper small college town." H. P. and his brother-in-law, Henry Otto Kruse, were stimulating conversationalists when they got together. "So Mama was not new to wide outlook and strenuous debates. But how to act in high society? She was timid at receptions."

After his graduation, H. P. was called to a Mennonite church in Canton, Ohio. He chose this church rather than a Congregational church because he wanted to stay with the denomination of his ancestors.

When Elva was three, her father taught her to read from McGuffey's primer. She maintained a fondness for McGuffey for its interesting stories, as well as for Aesop's *Fables* that set high moral standards. Elva had spoken only German until she met Oberlin playmates, and then learned to read in English. She entered school at the age of five and was enrolled in the second grade. During the three years in Canton, as an only child, Elva accompanied her parents to all the events that they attended, be it church, lectures, or the public library.

Looking back, she was grateful to her parents for introducing her to the world of thinking people who were known for their accomplishment, such as Carrie Chapman Catt, then *the* feminist of her day. "I remember nothing of that speech, probably sat restlessly inattentive. But I have never forgotten that I saw her and possibly imbibed some of my feeling of independence from her." In her home, "table talk was always illuminating and mind-stretching. Perhaps that is why I find conversation about food and fashions boring!"

The first year of the new century brought heartaches for her parents. Their baby boy died after four days, a "blue baby." H. P.'s cousin, H. J. Krehbiel, then minister at Trenton, Ohio, came to conduct the service, and Elva and her father "sat sorrowfully alone in the front pew." Her mother almost died of uremic acid poisoning. Mrs. Krehbiel blamed the baby's death on herself. "My heart was broken and I think that is why the baby didn't live. My inner unhappiness while I carried him made him frail."

Later Elva could only surmise that the cause of the unhappiness had been the dissension in the church. "My father was always a controversial figure. To me, he was always kind and loving. But when he took a stand on something, he couldn't be budged. . . . I think my father was right. Tactless, perhaps, and determined." An invitation from Christian Krehbiel, his father, to return to Kansas and rescue his brother's bookstore from bankruptcy came at this time, so H. P. felt he could resign gracefully.

No come-hither look for Kansas

Back in Kansas in the fall of 1900, they found a house in Newton; and for the next eighteen years, Elva became involved in the town, school, and college communities. Her father, along with his management of the bookstore, became involved as publisher with his brother C. E.'s German Mennonite paper, *Das Volksblatt*, forerunner of the *Mennonite Weekly Review*. The two brothers were to be associated for some thirty years. H. P. also preached in neighboring churches.

Elva enjoyed being surrounded by her Kansas relatives. She learned respect for her carpenter grandpapa Kruse and later saw his artistic flair handed down to her children. On the other side of the family, she spent many happy times at Krehbieltown, her grandfather's sprawling farm, school, and orphanage. Three of the Kruses had married Krehbiels, and Elva was to have four double cousins. A fourth Kruse had married a Krehbiel cousin. One of the uncles taught at Bethel College, so Elva became well acquainted there.

H. P. Krehbiel had stirred controversy in the church at Canton, Ohio. When they arrived in Newton, he taught Sunday school and preached occasionally at First Mennonite Church. But he was forbidden to teach or preach there after he gave "an entire sermon without mentioning the name of Jesus." Thus Elva became aware of the dispute about fundamental and liberal theology.

About this time, her father helped to organize the Burrton church where he preached for forty years. He was later criticized for entering politics to become the state representative from Harvey County. He served for only one term, having gained the experience he wanted.[4]

Elva seems to have admired all her teachers. Her parents took an intense interest in her education. "I was not brilliant, but I enjoyed learning, and applied myself." In high school, her teacher gave out a list of thirty books to be read. Elva had already read all but one.

With her earnings from working summers in her father's store, she started a savings account. She did not spend her money on clothes. When her mother suggested that she put on a fresh dress to go to town, she said indignantly, "No, you're just trying to make me very clothes conscious." But she was aware of what was socially proper. When her cousin came by

---

4. Edmund G. Kaufman, *General Conference Mennonite Pioneers* (North Newton, Kansas: Bethel College, 1973), p. 274.

one hot afternoon to take her for a quick ride in his car, she refused because she was not dressed properly to appear in public.

In 1908, after receiving her diploma from Newton High School, she enrolled at Bethel. "All through high school and now at Bethel, boys did not show a particular interest in me. I was not bad to look at, dressed nicely, had parents with local prestige. Perhaps that was it. Boys were afraid of my father. But there was more. I was not flirtatious, had no come-hither look and tended to be serious. Because of my father's constant interest in important matters, I thought young men would expect me to converse on serious subjects. They didn't."

After three years at Bethel, she went to Oberlin to finish her B. A. degree. She was excited about traveling alone by train. When she found her mother sobbing in the kitchen, she became aware of how much this separation would change her parents' lives.

Mr. Leisy prized her picture

After Oberlin, she accepted a teaching position at Moundridge High School in Kansas for sixty dollars a month. At twenty, she was ready to take on a new experience with assurance. "What thoughts did I have? . . . I had vague dreams of greatness but never set an ambitious goal to attain in the next five or ten years. I think I have always accepted what was offered and have applied myself to doing daily the demands of the day to the best of my ability, trying to be cheerful. Perhaps this stems from having my life planned for me for the first twenty years."

She found Moundridge quiet after scholarly Oberlin and bustling Newton. The next year, she was quite overwhelmed by the offer to teach English at the Bethel Academy. As a faculty member among her teachers of two years before, she felt accepted by all but one of them. "He did not feel that I was capable. In many ways he was right . . . . I had facts, I was moralistic, but I lacked analytical ability."

She was also young. "I was not articulate in faculty meetings, bowing to the wisdom of my elders." That spring, President Kliewer said, "I hear you are planning to go to summer school at Kansas University this summer." The thought had never occurred to her, but she made plans to go.

It was after the summer school session of 1914 that her father's bookstore, The Beehive, burned to the ground along with most of that block of stores. It was at the same time that the events occurred that ignited World War I.

She was back teaching at Bethel the next year. Ernest Leisy, who had come to Bethel from studying at Harvard, was head of the English department. Mr. Leisy dated her occasionally, but not seriously. In the fall of the third year, unexpectedly one of the senior college boys asked for a date, but only one. Later she learned that it was a put-up job.

Walter Niles told her years later, "Some of us decided that Mr. Leisy needed to be speeded up. At first, Ed Kaufman was chosen to ask you for a date but he was becoming interested in Hazel Dester and didn't want to jeopardize his chances. The others were either already engaged or involved so the lot fell on me."

The plot worked. On Christmas night, while they were enjoying the lighted Christmas tree, Ernest thanked her for the box of fudge she had given him. He added, "Thank you for your picture. I would like to keep the original for life." He had waited to ask her until he had paid his debts.

Illinois after three days in the army

Elva and Ernest planned their wedding for August 1917. He continued his work at the University of Chicago and came back with his master's degree to teach summer school at Bethel. The night before the wedding, she lay listening to the pounding rain and her mother's sobs from the next room.

Her father presided at the wedding in their home. She would have liked to have been married in the college chapel with President Kliewer officiating, but she didn't mention her preference to her father.

"I was not a woman's libber, then unknown. But I had asked that the *obey* be deleted. Women were just beginning to be conscious of what that meant, feeling that the relationship should rather be one of mutual relationship and harmony. . . . There was no ring ceremony. I think I felt I would be embarrassed by such a public act."

They began married life on the Bethel campus with Ernest teaching. She taught the little ones in the campus Sunday school and audited a course in German literature.

Ernest was a conscientious objector, and the next summer he was called to Fort Leavenworth. As an objector, he was assigned to latrine duty. "But the combination of broken arches and c. o. status was too much for the authorities and on the third day he was sent home."

Bethel College had already hired someone to take his place. He applied to fifty colleges, and the University of Illinois answered, "Come at once." When she followed him in October, she was greeted by a jubilant crowd at the station who were celebrating the false armistice of World War I.

Starting the Leisy family

They spent five years in Urbana where Ernest worked on his doctoral degree along with his teaching. After the war, the enrollment of the university increased dramatically, and Elva was asked to teach two classes in freshman English. In October 1922, she went back to Newton for the birth of their son Melvern. Her mother thought Elva should stay home; she was much embarrassed to be seen in downtown Newton with her pregnant daughter.

The next move was in 1923, to Illinois Wesleyan University, Bloomington, Illinois, where Ernest was head of the English department. The next spring they left Melvern with his grandparents and went to the British Isles and to Europe to study Mennonite history and to visit the origins of their ancestors.

They spent four ecumenical years in Bloomington. She joined the Woman's Home Missionary Society of Trinity Methodist Church and taught at the Baptist Sunday school because she thought they were doing the best in teaching children from the Bible. Ernest liked to hear the Presbyterian minister, so they went to Sunday services there.

Margaret was born in February 1926, and James came thirteen months later.

Settling down at SMU

The last move came in 1927 with an offer from Southern Methodist University in Dallas. There they found a stimulating community. While Ernest developed a national reputation for his textbooks in college English, she became active in parent-teacher, church, and literary organizations.

Her involvement in PTA was more than the usual mother's monthly attendance. She was instrumental in starting a cafeteria lunch program that even offered choices of food. This group also organized a library in a vacant room of the new elementary school. Margaret remembers working with her mother night after night preparing the books for circulation.

One of their mother's traits that impressed the children during this time was her treatment of other people. Margaret told of her mother's efforts on behalf of a grocery store clerk who was persistently sharp-tongued with the customers. Elva committed herself to help this woman to change, and she persistently spoke pleasantly to her. Each week Elva reported her progress to the family, until finally she could inform them of a change in the woman's attitude. Her children were influenced by her kindness to the cleaning woman whom she supported long after her services were no longer needed.[5]

There were good years when Ernest taught summer school in differ-

---

5. Telephone interview with Margaret Steinegar, May 14, 1984.

ent parts of the United States and the entire family traveled together. Over the years they traveled in forty-seven of the contiguous states, missing only Wisconsin.

Elva's mother died in 1931. In 1935, her father married Katie Friesen, who was just five years older than Elva. In November 1939, her father died and was interred in the mausoleum at Halstead.

She wrote, "Ours had been an unusually close family. . . . Papa talked a great deal at the table about business, or church affairs, or the world. His counsel never was dictatorial, but reasonable." But she was aware that everyone did not share her opinion of her father, and she could understand why. He was "too modern in his thinking" but "twenty years later another group accused him of being far too dogmatic, a fundamentalist. It is true he stood aggressively for his beliefs or plans and could ride roughshod over those who didn't agree. He lacked the winning ways of his brother C. E., which made them successful partners for forty years."

Melvern went to Harvard. When he was drafted, he was sent to a camp for conscientious objectors. He applied for hospital duty and was sent to the mental ward in the hospital at Duke University. Because of this experience, he decided to become a physician. Margaret graduated from Southern Methodist, then went on to Kansas University for a degree in social service. James registered for the draft as a conscientious objector, but Texas did not look favorably on this position. He was assigned to the marines. When he pointed out his objector status, he was assigned to the navy where he helped returning servicemen. Later he finished his degree in business at SMU.

Then came the season of weddings, Melvern to Pegi Hauck, James to Emily McQueen, and Margaret to Jack Steinegar. The Steinegars were stationed overseas in Germany and Iraq with the State Department for a number of years. Then came a time of welcoming grandchildren.

A time to practice patience

Ernest taught abroad for a term at the University of Vienna, and they traveled extensively from there. In 1955, Ernest began his last year of teaching, thirty years at SMU, fifty years altogether. But he was beginning to change. He was "funny" in his lectures, using a humor strange to the students. "He had always been gentle and courteous; now he at times was almost vulgar."

In the spring of 1958, the Leisys spent Easter with James in Palo Alto. While they were visiting relatives, she spent most of her time explaining his peculiar behavior. Tests revealed that he had had slight strokes over a period of three of four years. Nothing could be done except to practice patience and understanding. "That became my motto after getting home."

In 1962, after suffering a broken hip, Ernest was taken to a nursing home within driving distance for Elva. She visited almost every day until he died.

Her own time was spent actively in church and other groups in Dallas or visiting their children. Melvern was a physician in Los Angeles, James a publisher in Palo Alto. Margaret and Jack had settled in Kansas City. Elva realized that the nine grandchildren did not know each other, so she invited them by age groups to stay with her. The two older boys were teenagers, and she enjoyed their inquiring, thinking minds.

In 1965, Melvern and his two boys were killed in a small plane accident. All the family gathered in Los Angeles for the memorial service. "I remember too little of the service. . . . My mind, I fear, was on the untimely and unnecessary death of a son who was so helpful to so many and of the two boys who showed so much promise."

She and Ernest celebrated their golden wedding very simply in Ernest's room at the nursing home. "Did he understand it? Who knows? Did he think of the happy understanding years we had shared, the three fine children we had who had made our home a happy home? Of course there were differences, but usually I was to blame." Ernest died in March, 1968. A memorial service was held at SMU, and then interment in the Halstead mausoleum.

At work in many churches

The significant theme of Elva's life that emerges, along with the homekeeping, is an ongoing interest in the church. She had always been part of a congregation, beginning with those churches where her father preached, and at the Bethel College Church where she maintained her membership for her lifetime, even as she was active in churches of other denominations in the university towns where they lived.

In 1905, after taking the catechism class from J. H. Langenwalter, she was baptized by her grandfather Krehbiel in the Halstead Mennonite Church. "I think I felt a deep, solemn response as grandfather Krehbiel sprinkled water on my head. . . . I wanted to be a worthy follower, obeying always the teachings of Jesus Christ in my thoughts and deeds."

Her first Sunday school teaching began at the Baptist church while she was in high school, and then she took on a class at the First Mennonite Church, Newton, fifteen or twenty well-behaved, "Prussian-trained" boys and girls. They used the same lessons that the adult classes used, which were sometimes difficult to explain to five-year-olds.

After marriage, she continued teaching Sunday school and summer

Bible school. She taught at different levels, especially enjoying the junior high age as she watched children become teenagers. She was superintendent of that department for twenty years.

When much later she was asked to teach a group of older women, she was challenged. These were grandmothers and great grandmothers who could influence grandchildren. "It was with regret that I closed my Sunday school teaching life when the class was discontinued in 1974. . . . I had profited so much from those years of study of the teachings of Jesus Christ."

Elva had been active in the women's missionary groups in the churches she attended and regularly gave mission study talks. She belonged to other literary and service groups, including college clubs for faculty women and mothers of students. She was instrumental in setting up the SMU Scholarship Fund.

Commenting on her many involvements, she wondered if she would be accused of parental negligence. "Margaret told me recently that she remembers many afternoons coming home to find a plate of cookies on the table and a note with a name and a telephone number. Often their father was in his study."

I am a teetotaler

Her aversion to alcohol began when her parents moved from Oberlin, a dry town, to Canton, which was not. There she saw drunken men and their poorly clad children. "That is a sight etched in my memory forever."

Her grandfather Krehbiel once offered her a cup a cider freshly pressed. "Remembering those drunken potters and their frost-bitten children, I drew myself up to my full eight-year-old height of indignation with a positive, 'I am a teetotaler,' and nothing would budge me." This aversion carried over to her adult years.

Writer and activist for peace

Elva Leisy combined her skills in English and German to produce a significant body of writing, although she made little mention of being a writer in her memoirs. Probably the most astonishing for her family was the writing that won a Plymouth as first prize, telling why she liked a new grocery store in Dallas.

More noteworthy to her relatives and of consequence for Mennonite history was her translation of her grandfather Krehbiel's memoirs, *Prairie Pioneer*, from German to English. She and her twenty-six Krehbiel cousins had the book published by Faith and Life Press in Newton in 1961.

She earned her own credits as a writer with a chapter on the history of the women's peace movement in her father's book, *War, Peace, Amity* which he wrote and published in 1937. Remarkable in her statement is a stirring denunciation of mothers who romanticize war, who send their men off with smiles and roses because they would have been ashamed of sons who would not want to be war heroes. Already at this time, before World War II was even a foreboding in American minds, she was denouncing war toys and asking that parents supervise their children's play as they did their reading. She was concerned that children be taught Christ's commandments concerning peacemaking.[6]

In her biography of her father in *General Conference Mennonite Pioneers*, she tells that she was much influenced by her father's stand on peace and nonviolence. During World War I, he refused to install signs in the Beehive Bookstore, saying, "No German spoken here." He felt that too many of his customers would have difficulty speaking English. Because of his resistance to public pressure, his storefront was painted yellow from roof to sidewalk.[7]

Through investments made by her father, Elva was in a position to make substantial gifts to causes she believed in. The building that had housed her father's bookstore was given to the General Conference. She endowed the Ernest E. Leisy Distinguished Chair in English at Bethel College, and both she and her husband took an active interest in the Mennonite Library and Archives at Bethel, contributing financially and materially with archival deposits.

Aging reluctantly

In December of 1971, when she was eighty, she observed that "this was the year I was shocked into realizing that I was old." She was in and out of hospitals and nursing homes during her last years, with eye surgery on one occasion. After a hospital stay, she would check into a recovery center. She enjoyed making new acquaintances as well as the vacation from household chores. When her Sunday school class disbanded, she felt bereft. "So, at eighty-two, ended my useful life."

At eighty-four, "To my distress, I find a growing resentment within me against growing old—an awareness of people's change in attitude. . . . I fight this sensitivity—it is the way to a crabby old age."

Elva was eighty-eight when she stopped writing her memoirs, which became 524 typed pages—quite an achievement.

---

6. H. P. Krehbiel, *War, Peace, Amity* (Newton, Kansas: published by the author, 1937) pp. 302-315.

7. Edmund G. Kaufman, *Prairie Pioneers* (North Newton, Kansas: Bethel College, 1973), p. 274.

She had hoped to celebrate her one-hundredth birthday, but at the age of ninety-one she was glad to be released from the burden of her body. Margaret wrote that she "looked forward to rejoining those who had gone before." She died in a Dallas nursing home on December 25, 1982. The service was in the Bethel College Church where she had her membership.[8] The obituary was headed, "Kansas Pioneer's Oldest Descendant, 91, Dies in Dallas."

She deserved a better headline. The granddaughter of Christian Krehbiel was a person in her own right, with accomplishments in addition to that of longevity. She was an articulate spokesperson of her time, ahead of it in some respects, adapting to it with reluctant grace in others. Living her last years with pain and tragedy, she was nevertheless thankful to God and to all who had enriched her life. She is one of the host of witnesses who passed on the Word.

---

8. *Mennonite Weekly Review*, December 30, 1982, p. 3.

Martha Habegger: She knew she was a philosopher, but she majored in German to make sure she'd pass.

15.
Her Faith Could Smile

Martha Lena Baumgartner Habegger
1892-1983

Can a woman find a place in Mennonite history as a humorist? Phyllis Diller may be Bluffton College's famous funny alumna, but the thoughtful humor of Martha Lena Baumgartner Habegger is more enduring. For her, the serious business of living, loving, and practicing her Christian beliefs was compatible with fun and humor.

Discipleship had meaning

Martha's father, Christian W. Baumgartner, was a fourth generation descendant of Deacon David Baumgartner. Christian's father Peter had immigrated to America in 1837, settling in Adams County, Indiana. Christian was born in 1851 and in 1879 was married to Caroline Riesen of the Linn Grove Mennonites. They were married by Samuel F. Sprunger, the beloved long-term pastor who did so much to influence the Berne church.[1]

Christian and Caroline pioneered on a wooded farm east of Berne. While the family was growing, money was always in short supply. Butter and eggs were for selling and not for eating. Caroline was responsible for most of the children's discipline, but as she was busy with the chickens, truck patch, laundry, and cleaning, some of Martha's upbringing came from her older sisters.

---

1. Most of this material was written by Christine Habegger Purves. Baumgartner family data is from S. H. Baumgartner's *Brief Historical Sketches of Seven Generations of Deacon David Baumgartner* (Indianapolis, 1908), Mennonite Library and Archives, North Newton, Kansas.

Martha was born April 16, 1892, the fifth of six surviving children. Bertha, the attractive oldest sister, married early. Young Martha, seeing some of the frustrations of a newlywed's home, hoped she'd learn before she married "not to fuss over little things."

Her sister Cora had a sense of humor, and Martha learned to respect her tongue; when Martha was found reading under a tree when she should have been peeling potatoes, Cora reminded her of her middle name and dubbed her Lazy Lena. Sarah was sickly, but lived the longest of all the brothers and sisters. Elmer would rather wrestle or tell stories than take the wagon to town to sell vegetables. On the other hand, Martin, the youngest, was a born salesman.

Both parents were devoted to the church. Martha was impressed by how seriously her father took discipleship. He refused to be angry with a brother even if that brother wronged him. Once, on the way to church, the family buggy passed that of a man who had cheated him, and Christian greeted him warmly.

"But Father," his son said, "that man did you terrible wrong!"

Christian nodded. "That's his problem, not mine. Giddap."

Mother Caroline hated saloons and drinking, as two of her brothers had problems with alcoholism. She couldn't tolerate violin music because it reminded her of saloons. Although she had heard that President Lincoln was killed because God was displeased with him for going to the theater, her sense of fairness made her doubt that God would put more weight on this one event than on Lincoln's act of freeing the slaves.

Easy to talk and joke with men

Martha remembered all her life that her mother, usually so strong, was once found crying behind the kitchen door because of the bickering of the three youngest children, Elmer, Martha, and Martin. The teenagers had a conference and decided it was time to grow up.

Martha could not remember how she learned it, but by age five she was reading. She was sent off to first grade along with six-year-old brother Elmer to the Canopa one-room, eight-grade, primary school. Schoolwork came easily for Lazy Lena, who loved recess and friends. B's seemed as good to her as A's.

Despite her outgoing nature, Martha's feelings were easily hurt. She, who walked fast and purposefully, never forgot one teacher who characterized her as "Marthy, walkin' with her dress tail a-swishin'." And in front of her classmates, too!

Her early sense of humor might not have been appreciated by one schoolboy who insisted on walking her home. When they started up her muddy lane, he tried to steal a kiss. She gently put her arm about his shoulders, then suddenly used her young strength to scoop up some mud and plaster it in his face.

Every school day, Martha walked to the Berne High School where she made friends easily. But thoughts about a permanent relationship with a special friend turned toward Carl Habegger. She was attracted by his sense of humor, love of music, kindness to all, no matter what status. She did not consider herself at all beautiful and was straitlaced enough to avoid any hanky-panky. But having been brought up between two brothers, she always found it easy to talk and joke with men.

A thinker wiser than a chicken

After high school, she went to Earlham College for a summer course to enable her to teach primary school. All her life, she quoted what she learned in that short course about school discipline: "Be consistent. Do not allow exceptions to your rules." She credited that practice with the fact that in her second year of teaching in her own crowded Canopa one-room school, she did not have to punish a single student.

Following those two years, she was able to attend Bluffton College with aid from Carl Habegger's father. Again she was a good student but never seemed to care about being at the top. She showed a great aptitude for languages. Later, when she took her first trip to Europe at the age of eighty-three, she was a spokesperson in French, German, and Swiss for the tour group.

Mrs. Mosiman, the wife of the college president, was a great influence on all the college women of that day, especially in the teaching of social manners. Martha was also influenced by Dean Noah E. Byers when he said, "If you ever looked at a chicken and wondered, 'Chicken, do you know you are a chicken?' you are a philosopher." Martha knew then that she was a philosopher, but she majored in German "to be sure she would pass."

She found opportunities to have fun in college. On a sleigh ride, she felt a hand on either side of her reach under the blanket to hold her hand. Surreptitiously, she allowed the hands of the two boys to meet, and they squeezed each other's hands tenderly throughout the journey.

Her contralto voice won her a place in the Choral Society, the Vesper Choir, and the Gospel Teams. The flourishing musical program of the Berne church had trained her naturally good voice. For that matter, her brother Elmer and cousin Chris Riesen were famous for their low E's, evident in songs like "Silent Night" arranged for male voices. Brother

Martin, as well, gloried for years at family gatherings in roaring "Why Do the Nations So Furiously Rage" from the *Messiah*.

In 1915, she completed the four-year college course in three years. Her father and mother came for her graduation. At the pregraduation functions, Martha noticed that Father was wearing his everyday clothing, since it was not Sunday.

> Knowing that the main graduation exercises were also not on a Sunday, I felt sure it would not come to his mind to wear his best clothes. I did not have the courage to tell him myself (he was such a gentle man, one hated to correct him), so I asked mother to remind him. He complied, wore his new broad-brimmed hat and looked the deacon that he was—his first desecration of his Sunday clothes.

After graduation, Martha returned to Berne to teach high school. She discovered that she was more of a perfectionist as a teacher than she had been as a student and consequently more nervous about school. She loved teaching music. But when she married Carl Habegger in June 1916, she was content to forsake the classroom for the home, as tradition demanded.

Father was a trouble shooter

Both Martha and Carl were born into a church which had gone through a great deal of religious confusion. Settlers in the Berne area had come from various church backgrounds. Dissensions had arisen and the compromises that were made left scars. Fortunately, the leadership of J. W. Kliewer and S. F. Sprunger had brought the church together in better harmony.

Martha's father was a deacon for many years. Her impression of a deacon was that he was a trouble shooter rather than a policy maker. Neighbors came to him for counseling when they could not settle disputes.

The Berne church was large, over 1,400 members. Women and daughters sat on one side, both on the main floor and in the huge balcony. Men and sons sat on the other side. The curved balcony made it possible for the young people to see easily those on the other side. As he ogled, many a young man decided which girl he would ask to take home after evening church.

However, good behavior was expected. Once when a group of young people were talking in the the balcony, S. F. Sprunger stopped his sermon to point a long finger at them and cry, "Shame on you up there!" Punctuality at church was emphasized. A member walking in late to Sunday school might expect a public lecture from the Sunday school superintendent.

All children and babies came to adult church, for there were no nurseries. If babies cried too long in church—and mothers differed in their opinions of how long was too long—the babies were carried out to the *stubli*, a little room set aside as a retreat. Some mothers were embarrassed to have to take babies out; some would give small spanks to show they knew how to discipline; others were proud and arranged the baby's pretty, long dress to hang just so over their arms as they walked out.

Martha's talents surfaced early. Every Monday, the family dog was required to watch small Martha imitate the noses, mouths, manner of breathing, and tilt of head of various members of the congregation whom she had observed at the long Sunday services.

Church sermons and Sunday school were in German until World War I. Then, until World War II, every fourth Sunday included a German sermon. Most people spoke English with a heavy Swiss accent. Sunday school classes met in the main auditorium with perhaps one bench between classes. The teachers would shout the lessons, and while the regular members were used to the noise, a visitor was heard to wail that it "sounded like a chicken coop."

Faith and humility for a wounded church

Martha accepted the faith her parents taught about a just God and his Son, Jesus Christ, the Savior. She absorbed the atmosphere of sincerity of her parents and other church members. As the church went through difficult times from the 1920s to the 1940s with some controversial leadership, Martha began to feel that too much of the teaching was negative.

From her childhood, she remembered that once a minister had refused to marry a couple because the bride wore a bit of red braid at the end of her apron strings. And there was the memory of having other children shout to her that she would "go to hell" because her mother had sewed a few flowers on her hat. There was much about what *not* to do if you wanted to get to heaven and less about what *to* do. She decided that she would "keep an open mind, neither accepting tradition as the whole truth, the ultimate, nor rejecting new ideas as no good."

Although as a married woman she was in demand to direct the ladies' choir or help with the Women's Missionary Society, she was not permitted to teach Sunday school because she would not promise never to go to the movies. Later, she observed that when television came in, many who were against movies were the first to purchase TV sets.

Some of the church leaders doubted that a person with a college education could really pray. Yet neither Martha nor Carl rejected this church of their childhood, and in their home, family worship before breakfast each morning was memorable for the three children. Eventually, a new pastor, Olin Krehbiel, helped to heal the wounds the church had suffered in those earlier years.

In her collection of favorite sayings was one that expressed her faith: "The glorious traditions of the past should stand beside the rich possibilities of the future in the spiritual world as well as the secular."

But she tempered her judgment with humility. Among her collection of thoughtful sayings was this one: "I have great sympathy with the low. They're as good as I am any day. It irritates me quite a lot to find they, too, feel that way!"

Mother learns as children grow

After graduation from Oberlin College, Carl came back to Berne to edit the *Berne Witness*, but for most of their married life he headed the family business, The Winner House, manufacturers of clothing. Martha and Carl lived with his father, a widower, for seven years before they moved into their own new home.

Martha did all the things young wives did: cooked, sewed, canned, gardened, cleaned. She did some things all young wives did not do: she exercised to phonograph records and took voice lessons from a Fort Wayne teacher. Martha, for all her college education, knew little about a good sexual relationship, holding the prevailing belief that a virtuous woman should keep a husband at arm's length as much as possible. Carl, basically kind and understanding, bought her a book on the subject and she came to fully enjoy that part of marriage.

Much as they wanted children, Martha did not become pregnant for over a year; and then after a difficult pregnancy, Christine was born in September 1919. About a year later, they heard of the plight of a poor young immigrant father who had been left a widower with four boys. Martha and Carl offered a home for five-year-old Jules. When Christine was five, they took Ruth, also five, from an orphanage. Both children were free to stay in touch with their own families, so little strain was ever felt on that point.

Martha was a firm believer in the power of the environment to conquer any hereditary problems. Her success in dealing with children as a teacher had led her to believe "she knew how." Many years and many tears later she was not so sure that environment could solve all problems. There were times when Martha felt that she was a failure as a mother, but she tried.

When Christine and her high school friends' social life became too boisterous, Martha lectured on the values of quiet conversation. When, on the other hand, Christine and her date became too quiet on the downstairs davenport, Martha did not hesitate. From upstairs thundered the contralto voice: "Christine, I want to see you up here a moment!"

Jules was a popular and good-looking basketball player with charming Martha-taught manners, much sought after by the girls. By Martha's high standards, his teenage escapades were not the behavior she expected. One day, Jules, probably chafing against the strict rules of the house, complained that he did not have enough clothing to keep up with his friends. Martha's answer was to sweep into his closet and dump seventeen pairs of pants onto the floor. An orderly young man, he was left to pick up the clothing he said he didn't have. At times, Martha wished he were five years old again, when her main problem had been his swearing in Swiss with words like *donner und blitzen*.

Eventually, Jules married Betty, moved to California, did well as a salesman, and raised a family with many of the same values he had seemed to ignore as a teenager. During Martha's final illness he telephoned often to inquire about her.

Ruth's problems were not so normal. From the beginning it was obvious that she was no ordinary child. In a store, she could add a bill upside down and tell a clerk if she had made a mistake. In school, she could not pass a mathematics test. Not much was known about special education or learning disabilities at that time.

Her excitability, refusal to share, violent language, flashes of brilliance but utter helplessness in school studies were at first accounted for by environment at the orphanage; but as the years went on, the new environment was not solving the problem. Relatives soon lost patience and suggested that they "send her back to the orphanage," but Martha and Carl could not do that.

Eventually, because of attempts at suicide, Ruth was committed to an institution. Martha stayed in touch with visits and once-a-week letters. Ruth remained loving and grateful for the attempts to help her, but she was unable to live outside the institution.

Christine's interest in music took her to her father's college, Oberlin. There she met and married Jack Purves, a musician. They lived in New York during World War II while Jack was in the Coast Guard.

Taking naturally to grandmothering

After the war, housing was in short supply. Martha and Carl took in Christine and Jack, Jules and Betty and their three daughters. There were some tense moments, especially at dinner time, as the three families tried to blend into one household.

Martha thought Jules' wife spoiled him by offering him whole jars of her home-canned peaches. She thought Jack was careless when he helped with the painting and carpentering. On the other hand, the young couples thought Martha was too much the perfectionist. However, politeness was the rule of the house and there were few hard words spoken. On the whole, group living formed a closer bond.

When both Christine and Betty became pregnant, it was time to find other housing. By the time they moved from Berne, Christine and Jack had three daughters, and Martha had taken naturally to grandmothering. She sewed and visited, and when she visited she cooked and cleaned.

Along with her interests in the Garden Club and Bird Club, Martha continued her interest in the church. She belonged to the women's organization and was director of the Mennonite Ladies Choir from 1932 to 1945.

About this time Martha began to be in demand for her authentic Swiss Day readings. She wrote all of them herself, drawing upon her background of growing up in a Swiss-settled town in the United States. She could mimic the angular up-and-down Swiss accent that carried into the English language. Children in her Swiss skits had names like "Chaqueline Francile," or "Cheromy Elmer." They came down sick with "bronical ammonia," while their parents felt an "automatic" pain in the joints or suffered from "very close veins."

The Winner House had been a thriving business, but in the 1940s, Carl began to see the large business conglomerates gobbling up smaller firms. He tried to fight the trend. He was called to Washington, D. C., several times to testify in congressional committees for small business. The Washington newspapers called him "the grey-haired Hoosier philosopher."

Eventually, his refusal to deal with the huge garment-making industrialists led him to close down his small factory. Martha was never heard to complain or express fear for their financial future. She trusted Carl on these matters and she trusted her frugal upbringing to help her manage, knowing that they could live on less money than before.

The move to Bluffton

Meanwhile, Carl began to have a series of strokes. Eventually, they decided to sell the big colonial-style house and move to an apartment in Bluffton where the Purveses were on the Bluffton College staff.

The story of Carl's death and Martha's moving in with Christine and then the move to the Mennonite Memorial Home is best told in her published poem, parts of which are included here.

On Not Being a Pessimist After 80

I wasn't ready to come to the home.
Oh, I was aging, but not aged.
I didn't want to live
        in our big house any more either.
You can't reenact the past even
If you still have the home.
The past isn't there.
It's in my memory.
And I can take that with me
        wherever I go. . . .
But the big house was too much to clean.
Reading was much more fulfilling.
Yet I felt guilty.
Cobwebs must be hanging
        in those unused rooms.
Windows were dirty in others.
To read? To clean?
A disturbing question. . . .

Carl had always been well
And could work.
One day he had a little stroke—
Wires in his brain got crossed.
He had to quit work.
That did it. We sold the house
And moved to a college town
Where our daughter and family lived—
        into a neat apartment.
Carl liked it.
He would say,
"Aren't we lucky!"
He was always an optimist.
I wasn't a pessimist,
So I said, "Yes."

In 1970, he "crossed the bar."
I was alone.
I did what I always said I wouldn't—
        moved in with my daughter's family. . . .
They gave me charge of the kitchen.

I did the shopping—
I liked that very much.
But the time came when my daughter said,
"You spoil me, Mother.
I must get into that kitchen again."
"No room for two cooks in any kitchen,"
        we both said.
I applied at the Riley apartments.
There was no opening.
I said, "I'll wait."
I wasn't aged.
I felt tops.
Oh, maybe a little clumsy,
But I did almost anything I ever did—
        only slower. . . .
No opening came.
But another birthday did!

One day, I looked in the mirror and said,
"Who do you think you are?
You look just like
        all the other biddies at the home.
Better go join them."
So I did. . . .
Surprised my folks.
Pleasantly, I think.
They never told me to go
        or even hinted. . . .
But, yes, they were glad—
I would have been too.
Children should honor their parents,
But parents should respect their children's time too.
        And not be selfish.
They haven't the easiest life
In this day of pressure.
If I would go to the home
They could answer a need in Africa.
That's where they are now—
And I am here.
At first, I thought they had a lot of nerve
Leaving poor old tottering me.

Only I wasn't tottering,
Everybody says,
"You walk too fast;
You will ruin your heart
Or get a stroke."
I say, "So what?
Let me walk fast or any other way"
       (I'm getting a bit pigeon-toed). . . .

So now I'm here.
You know what?
We're all funny.
We forget,
We forget names and sometimes other things—
Like what day it is. . . .
Like what they already told you
Many times before.
       (Notice I say *they*.)
Such as why they can't sing anymore
But once could reach high A.
How they broke their leg
Or had an operation—
The most interesting ever.
To them—not to me.
Mine was more so. . . .
But it's nice here.
People remember us.
They show us dogs and babies.
They give us a strawberry feast—
Big, big luscious ones!
So big they can be peeled for those
Who can't eat seeds.
And don't need Serutan. . . .
We get good food.
They even bring us seconds—
Sometimes too late, like when
We already had dessert. . . .
Some gobble their food.
Others dally—not too daintily
       (rather clumsily).
The kitchen help and waitresses are patient.

It's hard to please us.
Some want cottage cheese
Instead of salad.
(The same ones that don't need Serutan.)
Some want pudding
    instead of peaches.
An egg on Tuesday
    instead of Wednesday
And pat it to see
Whether it is soft
    instead of hard.
If it's hard they shake their head
And call the waitress. . . .
They sing "Happy Birthday" to us
Whether we want it or not.
They're nice.
We have a sing-a-long.
Anybody can go there
Whether we want to or not.
    (Sometimes the "nots" go for a little while.)
We have Wednesday evening church service.
Anybody can go there
Whether they want to or not.
Most want to—
Because we all need that.
We learn from each other here.
How we want to be like some
But others not at all!
But still we must not judge.
We thank God for a place like this.[2]

Ruth Naylor described the circumstances under which the poem came to be written. Ruth had been asked to conduct a poetry workshop at the retirement home, and she had hoped that Martha would attend, but she did not show up. Ruth said to her, "I was hoping you were going to come write some poetry for me."

Martha, who if the truth were told, didn't like being organized into group sessions, was a bit flustered and explained, "Well, I deliver the mail here at that time and I didn't feel I should ask anyone to take my place."

---

2. *Christian Living*, March-April 1983, pp. 48-51.

Later she approached Ruth and with a slightly apologetic tone told her that she *had* written a poem; she knew it probably wasn't any good; would Ruth just look at it and tell her what she thought about it.

Then, when the Home was planning for its twenty-fifth anniversary, Ruth asked Martha to read her poem, which, with a little coaxing, she did. Ruth reported, "She was the hit of the program. Absolutely delightful. Afterward, an official from the state association of retirement homes asked for her name. He wanted to use that lovely, lively octogenarian at other state meetings. . . . She possessed a deep abiding faith that helped her to see life's possibilities rather than its threats, to focus upon life's blessings rather than its disappointments."

Martha is adopted by the Shetlers

In the First Mennonite Church in Bluffton, she found a great freedom to express herself. After Christine and Jack left for Africa when Martha was eighty-five, the Bluffton church made a public statement that it would be family in a true sense to anyone left in the congregation with family elsewhere. One church couple, Luther and Geneva Shetler, "adopted" Martha. She grew to love them dearly.

Her granddaughters, too, kept in close touch. Greta Holt came from Cincinnati with flowers and teased "Grandma Hobby" about being "decrepit" and "not touching your capital," referring to Martha's thrifty habits. Mary Liechty brought her children from Indianapolis, and Jean Lehman telephoned from Denver regularly and later wrote, "I couldn't accept Grandma's thanks for the calls. I called because I wanted to. I needed those periodic perspective-giving conversations and her gift of laughing at herself."

In her last letter before Christine and Jack came home, and a month before she died, she wrote, "So you are sixty-four, Christine. No wonder I'm ninety-one. We await your coming. Our arms are open! Hurry, but take your time. Love, Mother."

In October 1983, on leave from Africa, Christine and Jack took Martha to visit Mary and her family in West Virginia. Martha was not quite as energetic as she wished, but she played quiet games with the children and dug into a pile of mending. Mary wrote, "Grandma, my mother, and I giggled over the advice of a home makeup saleswoman who insisted she could take ten years off of Grandma's age with the proper facial applications."

In recalling what her grandmother's life had meant to her, Mary wrote, "The way Grandma relayed events of the past was entertaining and informative. And it was always spiced with humor. Thinking of Grandma makes me smile—and that feels good. . . . She reinforced for me that a living faith is one that challenges us to question and discuss our beliefs so that we might become more convicted in them."

Back in Bluffton, Martha entered the hospital for tests, but she developed pneumonia and did not respond to treatment.

Christine wrote, "About the third day while I was sitting at her bedside I noticed she was rather pensively looking at me. 'What tender thought is she thinking about her only daughter, here all the way from Botswana?' I wondered. Then she opened her dry lips and said quite clearly, 'Well, you got a brown spot on your face in exactly the same place I got my first brown spot.' Mom hadn't changed much."

After a long drawn-out three weeks of discomfort, during which she responded with pluck and wry humor to the doctor's and the family's efforts, Martha died. Christine got the call just as she was preparing to go to the hospital. " 'I'll be right over,' I said. I thought, 'Good for you, Mom! You did it!' "

For her eightieth birthday, Jack Purves, her son-in-law, wrote a fitting eulogy that sums up Martha's many years:

> Someone has said that the *liberally educated* person is one who can entertain herself, can entertain another person, and can entertain a new idea. . . . [Martha] daily entertains herself and others, and she daily tests new ideas. She daily acts upon the results of her testing with an appreciation of the pure, the lovely, the gracious, and the praiseworthy.

16.
Bonding White and Hopi People

Polingaysi Qoyawayma (Elizabeth Q. White) 1892—

I accept the reasoning of my white friends. They say that I am a good example of what takes place when a person is uprooted and forced to adjust to a new way of life, because I was an ordinary Hopi child at the time education was brought to us through the white man's schools, and because I had only limited experience with white people.

Polingaysi Qoyawayma dated her birth by the arrival of H. R. Voth at her village of Oraibi, Arizona, in 1893, when she was one year old and took the birthday of her friend Elizabeth Schmidt as her official birthday. She tried to meet the expectations of two sets of parents, Fred and Sevenka Qoyawayma, and J. B. and Aganetha Frey. She knew she was a Christian, but how could she discard all that was good in the Hopi culture?[1]

Hopi life in Old Oraibi

Born in Old Oraibi village on Third Mesa, her home was a one-room, stone hut with a leaky brush and mud roof. It was her grandmother who cared for her while her mother worked in the field and at the grinding stone. Her toys were sheep-bone dolls and bits of broken pottery for dishes. Her games were "begging for food" and a version of cops and

---

1. Polingaysi Qoyawayma, as told to Vada F. Carlson, *No Turning Back* (Albuquerque: The University of New Mexico Press, 1964), in the foreword.

Elizabeth Qoyawayma White: Even the broken pieces of her pottery were sought after.

robbers with Hopi against Navajo. Her chores were to carry water from the spring below the mesa and to care for the younger children.

During good harvests, they ate well of sweet corn, melons, and blue *piki*, the bread used for celebrations. When the harvest failed, they heard their mother say, "I will take a drink of water to weigh me down."

Fred Qoyawayma, her father, belonged to the clan of the Kachina, those supernatural beings who came up from the valley for the ritual dances and returned to the San Francisco Peaks at the end of the day. Once she went to the end of the mesa, hoping to follow them from a distance as they filed west in the valley below. But they never appeared. "She had no idea that the dancers had removed their masks and costumes, discharmed themselves, and entered the village from another direction. She took it for granted that they had made themselves invisible to human eyes."[2]

Her father was not afraid of the white people. He worked for the H. R. Voth family who lived in the valley below her house. Voth had recognized Fred's keenness of mind and had taught him to deliver babies, pull teeth, and do simple carpentering. The villagers had given him the nickname of "Little White Man's Rooster."

Polingaysi attended religious services led by the Voths, learning the missionaries' songs. She sang "Jesus Loves Me" in English, not knowing what she was singing: "*Deso lasmi, desi no.*" The children thought they were singing, "The San Juan people are bringing burros," and giggled at the silliness of the white people.

She combined her parents' way of worship with white ways, not understanding either. She had been taught to be thankful for food. "Getting up at dawn and going to the mesa's edge to voice one's thankfulness for life and all good was part of the established Hopi pattern." She would have been shocked to know "that the missionaries considered [the Hopis] wicked and unsaved."[3]

No turning back

The missionaries cooperated with the government to set up a school. The village was divided into conservative and progressive elements. Mother Sevenka hid Polingaysi when the white men (whom they called *Bahana*) came to catch the children and take them to school. The white men, not able to speak Hopi, brought Navajo policemen who terrified the children.

No one knew what school meant, but Polingaysi, an intelligent child, was curious about it. The children came back from the school laughing

2. Qoyawayma, p. 12.
3. Qoyawayma, p. 16.

and singing. She was attracted by the striped ticking dresses and the promise of a noon meal. One day she allowed herself to be captured. After that, there was no turning back.

The children were given English names, and Polingaysi, whose Hopi name means "Butterfly Sitting Among the Flowers in the Breeze," was given the less poetic but more pronounceable name of Bessie. (Later she was called Elizabeth, and she will be referred to as Elizabeth from here on.) The children were forbidden to speak the Hopi language or use Hopi names. They began to learn also the sinfulness of their ancient beliefs. Her mother told the children:

> We must not allow the bad behavior of the Bahana to cause us to act in the same manner. We must try not to think bad thoughts, because bad thoughts are like jabbing at the thought-of one with a knife. . . . We must be peaceful and unresisting. Otherwise how can we be pure-hearted enough to offer our prayer to Cloud People and the Rain Gods? And if we do not offer prayers and Rain Gods forget us, then surely we shall starve.[4]

But the Hopis did not always live up to their tenets. A battle was fought between the progressives who wanted the school and the conservatives who did not want anything to do with the white men from Washington who did not live up to their promises. This was a push war, because an agreement had been made that no blood was to be shed. When the conservatives were ordered out of the village a hand-to-hand battle ensued, and the progressives were pushed out. They retreated to establish the village of Hotevilla, seven miles away. Another faction, torn between the two, established the village of Bakavi. Elizabeth's parents, uneasy on the mesa, moved down to New Oraibi where the government had built the school.

Songs to sing in California

Elizabeth was one of the children sent to Sherman Institute in California; she was eager to go to "the land of oranges." Her mother refused to let her go, but her father consented and gave her three silver dollars, his wages for six days. She had never seen so much money before.

Her introduction to dormitory life was shocking. For one thing, she had to remove her clothes to take a shower. She was afraid that the stream of water might contain the spirit of the Water Serpent, who by breathing upon a woman could cause pregnancy. The matron did not understand her

---

4. Qoyawayma, p. 30.

fears. Elizabeth was the only Hopi girl in the dormitory. Although she had declared that at fourteen she was too old to cry, she dived beneath the pillow and wept—for weeks.

"Song was her salvation." Polingaysi had a sweet soprano voice and good lungs. She could memorize easily. At first terrified to appear in public, she came to enjoy performing.

One of the teachers asked her to live with her family and help with the housework. Elizabeth could have become one of the family, but she found it difficult to emerge from her shell. But she learned the homemaking skills of the white woman, cooking and sewing, and her English improved so that she became more confident.

Cottonwood growing on gift site

After four years at Sherman, she went home with some dread. She knew she could not settle into village life. Her mother urged her to marry and have a family, but Elizabeth, who loved children, was not ready to bear them. And for no man would she grind corn on her knees. She envied the girls who were satisfied to do that, but she could not.

She scolded her parents because they had no table, no bedsteads, and her mother sighed, "What shall I do with my daughter who is now my mother?" When Elizabeth made an apple pie and threw away the peelings, a neighbor asked what she was doing. "She is being a white man. It is their way to waste food, you know," her mother said.

Unable to convert her mother to Christianity and feeling unappreciated, Elizabeth accepted Missionary Frey's invitation to live with them at Moencopi, near Tuba City, about forty miles away. After her father had placed her belongings on the wagon in readiness for the trip to Moencopi, he asked her to look at a plot of ground near their home. He offered it to her as a site for the home she hoped to build some day. A young cottonwood tree that her father had planted grew there, and the site was pleasantly situated with its backdrop of mesa. She promised her father that she would build a house there among the other members of her family.

Not ready to be a missionary

Elizabeth felt at home with the Freys and their three children. J. B. and Aganetha treated her like a daughter. The Hopis had mistrusted the Freys at first. "They still smarted under the methods of H. R. Voth, who had delved into their most esoteric rituals and made his findings public."[5]

---

5. Qoyawayma, p. 80.

But the Hopis were impressed with Frey's practical advice, his skill in farming, and his habit of sharing, an important symbol to the Hopi people. Elizabeth was so impressed with the religious faith of the Freys that she became overly zealous in trying to change the cultural pattern of her Hopi elders.

A plan was formed for her to attend Bethel Academy in Kansas. The summer before her first year at the school, she worked for the John Frey family and discovered how hard the women worked; she didn't know who was more to be pitied, the Hopi or the German. She compared the solemn, long depressing sermon at their church to the "flash and color and rhythm of Kachina dancing."

At Bethel, she earned her way by working in the kitchen and dining room. The work was tiring, but she did it cheerfully. She liked to laugh with the other students. Her classes in voice and piano enriched a talent that was recognized and enjoyed by others. A friendship developed with Elizabeth Schmidt that was to last a lifetime. Since Elizabeth Qoyawayma had no birthday, Elizabeth Schmidt shared hers with her friend.

The next summer, she returned to Arizona eager to see her family, but she was shocked to see how unkempt they were. She knew that she must lead them to Christianity and was frustrated when they did not respond. She gladly returned to Bethel. Another summer was spent in visiting churches with Frey.

After a third year at Bethel, she did not know what her future was to be. She knew she was expected to be a missionary to her own people, but her work was not satisfying and by then she did not feel that she was competent to be a missionary. An opportunity came to teach Navajo students at Tuba City, and she saw teaching as a way to earn money for building her house.

The Freys were saddened to have her give up the missionary vocation, and asked her to try one more time. They sent her for a course at the Bible Institute of Los Angeles where she sang often in the churches in the area and enjoyed working with the older people. But she did not like city life.

Building her dream house

When Elizabeth returned to Moencopi, she was in her late twenties. The Freys had good news for her. She could buy an old mission building and use the material to build her own house. While working at the mission, she could supervise the building of her house. Her brothers agreed to build the house, and for a time it was her main interest.

Still she was not completely happy. She felt useful and her relationship to the missionaries was good, but she found "often she was arguing with them rather than agreeing spontaneously that all things Hopi were wrong." She sat down for the first time to think through what she really believed about herself and her people. She realized that she could not go back. She had changed but the Hopis had not.

> Actually, she had but one consuming desire: to achieve a good life, independent of both white people and her own Hopi people, but esteemed by both. The struggle was not "to be a white man" but to keep from rejecting everything good she had learned at such cost of time and energy from the white man's world. . . . "A true Hopi is a part of the universe and must keep himself in balance," she had been told. "All things, animate and inanimate, have life and being. A true Hopi tries to be aware of the deep spiritual essence that is at the heart of all things. All things have inner meaning and form and power. The Hopi must reach into nature and help it to move forward, harmoniously and beautifully."[6]

In 1924, an offer from the government school in Hotevilla interested her. Her mind said, "Take it, take, it," and she did. The Freys were stunned and disappointed, but they treated her as their daughter and did all they could to help her; there was harsh criticism from others.

Breaking new ground

She was soon teaching the beginners and despairing over the material. What could the story of a train mean to a Hopi child who had never seen one? What meaning did the story of Little Red Riding Hood have? She began substituting the songs, stories, and legends they had grown up with. The parents objected, but she continued.

She entered a time of self-confidence and fulfillment, spending weekends working on her house in Oraibi. She bought a piano. People laughed at her house with its place for a bathroom and kitchen sink when water could not be brought into the village until years later.

When it was finished, she was not happy with the look of it because it was not in harmony with the other houses in the village and did not blend into the landscape. After a year or so she tore off the hip roof and added more rooms. The house began to look like a pueblo dwelling. She was chagrined that even in building a house she had resisted the Hopi culture before she realized that she could use it.

Caroline Burkhalter, a missionary friend, had helped her to prepare for an examination for Indian Service teachers, and she was able to pass

6. Qoyawayma, pp. 127, 128.

the test to become a bona fide employee of the government. An educator with the Indian Service came to observe her teaching and was impressed by her methods of leading the children from Hopi to English. She was transferred to other schools, finally to one in New Mexico.

A home and a husband

In the late 1920s, when she was approaching forty, she realized that she wanted a home, a husband, and children. She knew she should marry a Hopi, but she was not attracted to anyone, and the ones she knew disapproved of her, a Hopi woman teacher.

Lloyd White was part Cherokee, and when he proposed marriage, "her heart spoke more loudly than her good sense." They were married in 1931. She was happy with him, and he did not object to her teaching. When school closed, they went to her home in Oraibi.

She built a house for her parents with running water, linoleum, and good beds and then she enlarged her own house so that she could take in paying guests during summer vacations. Mrs. Harold Ickes visited and told her that she should be teaching among her own people. Shortly after her visit, Elizabeth was transferred to Polacca and then to Oraibi.

But with the transfer, her marriage suffered. "She could not adjust to marriage with a man whose interests were so foreign to her own. She had been independent far too long to be able to take second place in her own home. So she and Lloyd parted.

Indian commissioner John Collier eventually gave her the greatest support in her teaching methods. He changed the teaching procedures for all teachers. From thinking of their students as "benighted children of nature," the teachers were to think of them "as worthy parts of the whole 'web of life.' "

When she was transferred to Oraibi, she was not well received. Another teacher had been removed to make a place for her, and her failed marriage was held against her. But the principal of the school, Guy Dickerson, and his wife received her warmly. She went through a time of despondency until she resolved not to run away from it.

She remembered the Hopi tenet of nonresistance: "Don't fight. Don't think spiteful things about others. Don't try to get even when they hurt you. To seek revenge is to hurt yourself more than you hurt them."

She realized that this was also the essence of the teaching of the missionaries. But they had been unable to see any good in the Hopi culture whose teachings were so similar.

The next summer she was chosen from all the Indian Service teachers of the nation to demonstrate her teaching methods to teachers and supervisors in Chemawa, Oregon.

When her father developed diabetes, Elizabeth took him into her home to give him good nursing care. He delighted in talking about the old days. He was the only one of the family who by that time had not accepted the teachings of the missionaries. Finally, he too became a Christian.

"Always I have been standing at the door," he remarked, "but now I can come inside with my family." He died before she felt she had gotten to know his inner ideals and beliefs, and she regretted that she could not ask him some things she should have asked long before. Her mother, too, died soon after.

Conflict in the church

As early as the late 1920s, a controversy had developed among the missionaries, the mission board, and the Hopi Mennonite Church. It centered on Frey's theology. He was accused of universalism. This controversy over a doctrinal point eventually split the Hopi Mennonite Church as well as the white churches in Oklahoma. Of course, Elizabeth was sympathetic to the Freys.

In 1949, the mission board had met with Frey and they had forgiven each other and shaken hands. But in 1953, Elizabeth's sister died and was refused burial from the Hopi Mennonite Church. The funeral was held in the family home, and when Frey rose to speak, the other missionary walked out.

Elizabeth wrote to the Board of Missions:

My people are being required to make tremendous speed in transition almost from stone age in one generation into white man's pattern of life. Which causes much mental disturbance. Now the spiritual confusion among the missionaries, the Hopi people question. "What is the fight about? Where and what is the love of Christ?"[7]

Elizabeth began to think of retiring, but she needed the salary check which made it possible to aid her nieces and nephews who wished to go on to college. But in 1954, she gave notice. At her retirement, she was presented with a bronze medal from the United States Department of the Interior.

Then she had time for a second career. She had wanted to work with clay, to write, to do something in music, but she didn't know where to begin.

7. Lois Barrett, *The Vision and the Reality* (Newton, Kansas: Faith and Life Press, 1983), p. 49.

The scholarship fund

She found that her work in education was not over, for people came to her for advice and help. The Hopi people who had earlier opposed education were asking for help in getting their children into college. In 1959, Elizabeth told her needs to Dr. and Mrs. Carroll Fenton. They made a generous donation to establish a scholarship fund to be administered by Northern Arizona University. By 1982, over $100,000 had been contributed and over 300 Hopi students had benefited from it.[8]

Elizabeth wrote, "It has been our long Indian history to this day, to rely upon the Bureau of Indian Affairs, to follow its set patterns, regulations, and dictation, while our minds lay dormant in passiveness. The time is here that we must encourage our young people to rely upon themselves."

Her niece, Ida Murdock, was the first to use the fund. Ida then taught music and lower grades in several states and has now retired to her family home near Elizabeth's house. Elizabeth had always stayed in close touch with her family. She had taken the three children of her nephew into her home for a number of years when their mother died. Brothers and their wives kept in touch while they were living.[9]

Recognition as a potter

Her second career as a potter was begun after retirement from teaching. Her pottery became "desperately sought after," even the broken pieces. Most valuable are the pinkish corn maiden wind bells and the pots with the raised ear of corn. Even her early experimental pieces are collectors' items. She took courses in ceramics at Northern Arizona University and became known for her new techniques and her use of unusual clays.

Her first book for children, *The Sun Girl*, was chosen as one of the fifty best books of the year for children. First published in 1941, it was reissued in 1978. The story of her life, *No Turning Back*, was written with Vada Carlson and published in 1962, and another book, *Broken Patterns* is to be off the press soon.

Elizabeth kept adding on to her house until it was described as a mazelike, bed-and-board pension. She seemed to have had open house continually for her friends, many of them artists who came to paint or sculpt. Others came to her yard to study native American culture under the cottonwood tree. She had a particular interest in the anthropology students

---

8. "Polingaysi," letters compiled by Jo Linder to honor Elizabeth White on her ninetieth birthday in 1982, p. 25. A copy is in the possession of Evangeline Hiebert, North Newton, Kansas.
9. Jo Linder in "Polingaysi," p. 5.

who came from Arizona and the surrounding states. Sometimes she housed groups of twenty-five or thirty.

A story told by one of her friends is revealing. She had come to the Sears store, where he was working, to buy paint for her house. She came back in a couple of days to report that the paint was peeling off her wall. "What started out to be a quiet talk changed to raising her voice and stamping her feet. We got the manager, who gave her more paint with a different oil base."

On a later visit she noticed that the paint salesman was absent and learned that he was at home sick. She got his address and took him a good meal of chicken. He became one of her students of Hopi culture and her "official" photographer. Later she helped him chose his wife. He reported that Ernest Hemingway thought she was the best storyteller he had known, that Margaret Mead had visited her house, as well as eighteen anthropologists from Europe.

Included in her book of letters written for her ninetieth birthday are ones from Karl Menninger of the Menninger Foundation and from Senator Barry Goldwater. But there are letters from many not-so-well-known people who might have been important only to Elizabeth. Some of these letters refer to her deep faith in the Creator and in the Lord Jesus. They write of how the summer under the cottonwood tree changed their lives.

A chance to live again

In January 1971, when she was nearing eighty, she was the victim of an accident that nearly took her life. While she was walking on the sidewalk in Winslow, a pickup truck driven at eighty miles an hour went out of control and hit her. She was later told that the doctor pronounced her a "bottle of blood."

She heard the Navajo nurse rush from the room crying, "Death, death," in her native language. "Then there was a wonderful floating weightless feeling completely devoid of care or pain, just 'out of the body.' She was eagerly anticipating meeting her Heavenly Father. But then the voice of her little great niece called to her and she felt she must return."[10]

Elizabeth wrote, "To have been given another chance to live again is more than a privilege. In humbleness I thank God for it and each moment should count to fulfill this purpose."[11]

She recovered and did return to her home in Oraibi to care for her nephew's children. In 1975, while she was in Phoenix to give testimony in

10. "Polingaysi," p. 9.
11. Letter to Evangeline Hiebert, March 19, 1973.

the litigation against the driver of the pickup, her house burned down. She lost both her house and the court case.

She wrote, "I don't need that home to remind me of the wonderful things that happened there. . . . Ask never to regard my personal misfortunes as they regard the trials and tribulations of Job. I'm so much richer than he was. And it's beautiful that I can't be bowed down now by material things."[12]

The next year a group of young people from a church in California designed and built a new house for her. She cooked a dinner for the thirty-six workers, including a non-Hopi dessert of lemon meringue pie. They presented her with the keys to her new front door which was decorated with the stained glass Hopi Sun symbol.[13]

There was still another award. In 1975, she received the Outstanding Alumni Award from Bethel College. Evangeline Hiebert, who wrote the citation, reported later, "There was a moment of glory when everyone stood in recognition of her achievements—it had never happened before."[14]

Now in her nineties, having suffered a stroke in January 1985, Elizabeth still lives in her house under the cottonwood tree. She remembers the glimpse of the world that she had after her accident and says she is ready to return to that world.

As Polingaysi, she can remember her Hopi girlhood and the refrains from the grinding song:

> Oh, for a heart as pure as pollen on corn blossoms,
> And for a life as sweet as honey gathered from the flowers,
> And beautiful as butterflies in sunshine.
> May I do good, as Corn has done good for my people
> Through all the days that were.
> Until my task is done and evening falls,
> Oh, Mighty Spirit, hear my grinding song.[15]

As Elizabeth White, she also remembers and appreciates what she had learned from the missionaries, particularly the Freys. At one point in her life, Elizabeth said, "I'm sorry they cannot see [the truths of the Hopi faith], but I'm grateful to [the missionaries]. Because of them, I do not await the coming of Our Brother as my unconverted people do. For me,

---

12. Letter to Maggie Wilson, "Polingaysi," p. 145.
13. Letter from Bob and Jeanne Mowers, "Polingaysi," p. 112.
14. "Polingaysi," p. 65.
15. Qoyawayma, p. 5.

and many others, He has come. I have given Him my heart and soul; what have I to fear, except my own lack of understanding?"[16]

Her grandmother had predicted that Polingaysi would be the bond between the Bahana and the Hopi people. Elizabeth said, "I am Indian enough at heart to believe that her prophecy has been fulfilled."[17]

16. Qoyawayma, p. 155.
17. Qoyawayma, Foreword.

Sylvia Pannabecker: She read a pamphlet that "probably influenced my life more than any piece of writing outside the Bible."

17.
Prayer—Her Most Important Work

Sylvia Tschantz Pannabecker
1893—1979

Sylvia Pannabecker, when she was speaking about her experience as a missionary in China, said, "I asked God for patience in China and he sent me a cook who couldn't cook, so that was the way I learned patience."[1]

Besides her Chinese cook, Sylvia had a variety of teachers. From her father, she learned to enjoy doing practical things: picking cherries, making hay, driving a team of horses, milking the cows. From her mother, she learned appreciation for the beauties of the farm: sunsets, bird songs, flowers of the garden and field. The outdoors were always more enjoyable than washing dishes or making beds. Her first lesson in faith came from praying during thunderstorms.[2]

Her treasure house of books

She counted her blessings in the shape of an attic full of old books and magazines and a Sunday school library, "a treasure house for youngsters." When she helped with haying, she tucked a book away in a corner so that she could read while she waited for the next load to come to the large bank barn.

---

1. An interview with Edna Ramseyer Kaufman, 1984.
2. Much of this information appeared in talks she gave to women's groups; copies are in the Mennonite Library and Archives, North Newton, Kansas. Richard and Wanda Pannabecker, and Rachel and John Pannabecker also contributed information.

Sylvia Tschantz was born on an Ohio farm near Dalton on January 23, 1893. Her family was a part of the Sonnenberg community, a group of Swiss immigrants who had come to Wayne County from 1820 to 1850. She was fifth in a family of six.

In her childhood, Sunday was seen as a change from the routine of farm work and a time to meet her friends. Little thought was given to the spiritual value of the Sunday service, but "unknown to the recipients, lives were being molded through the influence of all that the house of God offers." She found the missionary books interesting and occasionally heard missionaries speak at the Salem church, without any stress being given to go to foreign fields. At the age of eight, Sylvia "wished with all my heart to go out there to relieve [famine in India] providing Father and Mother would go along."

Each day, her father led the family in devotions immediately after breakfast. "Sometimes I chafed under them, but as I grew older I realized what an important part they had in molding our characters."

The Swiss dialect was used in the home, but the language of church and Sunday school was High German. When she was twelve, her class of girls persuaded the church fathers that they should be allowed to use English, the language they used in school. The sermons continued in German, and the young people got little from them. Christian Endeavor was conducted in English. "For that reason Christian Endeavor has always had a very warm place in my heart."

When she asked her parents if she should join the church following catechism instruction, they counseled her, " 'Join church only after you know Christ has come into your heart.'

"That evening when the pastor explained how to become a Christian, God spoke to my heart. Christ seemed to be standing outside of the door of my heart (I had seen pictures of that) so I invited Him to come in. . . . He came in and swept down all the cobwebs, so it seemed at that time. I shall never forget how happy I was. I was born again."

Leaving her parents

School had been a trial during the first two years, but after that she wept if she had to stay home to help with the work. Three years in Dalton High School were followed by a year at the Academy at Bluffton. Because of her closeness to her parents, leaving home was a painful experience for her. If she had thought about it, she would have considered it physically impossible to leave home for service on the mission field.

After her Academy course, she stayed another year for college work.

During those two years, I was under the influence of Mrs. Mosiman's fine personality. In a Bible course on the Four Gospels, much mention was made of the importance of carrying out God's plan for one's life. Our duty is to discover his plan and then be willing to carry it out.

Mrs. Mosiman had shared her own life story with her students and indicated that she had had a long hard struggle before committing herself to the Lord. "That helped me greatly, for I, too, had a long struggle because I didn't want to go overseas as a single woman."[3]

After her two years at Bluffton, Sylvia taught school for two years, four miles from home. As she drove her horse and buggy to school, she read her Bible. One morning as she was reading Genesis 12, she heard a distinct call.

"Now the Lord said to Abram, Go from your country and your kindred and your father's house to the land that I will show you."

"What, leave my home and my dear parents and family and go to a foreign country? I can't do that. I'd rather be a Salvation Army lassie and stay in this country."

She argued for a year. She couldn't bear the thought of leaving her parents. Missionary terms then were for nine years. And if she married? But the voice continued until finally she said, "Yes, Lord, I'll go where you want me to go."

"Inexpressible peace and joy came. I told my mother immediately and to my surprise she wept tears of joy. 'Why, my daughter, that's what I have prayed for all your life.' "

Sylvia felt that her mother's prayers and Mrs. Mosiman's influence had been the means of leading her to the mission field.

Sylvia returned to Bluffton College for three more years. During that time, she learned to know Floyd Pannabecker, a student from Petoskey, Michigan. When they found that both were interested in foreign missions, they felt this mutual interest was "an indication that God was showing us his plan for our lives." At Bluffton College, she was active in Student Volunteers and YWCA, both with weekly meetings, all pointing them in the direction of mission work. She graduated in 1912.

As Christian Endeavor field secretary

She and Floyd did not marry immediately. Floyd believed that he should not marry until he had all his debts paid. "And it took him seven years to

---

3. In a letter to Sue Sprunger, May 1978.

do it," Sylvia would tell people later. Floyd graduated from Bluffton in 1917 and from Witmarsum Seminary in 1918. He was called to teach at Bluffton in 1918.

In the meantime, Sylvia went back to her home, having promised her parents that she would spend a year with them on the farm. But early that fall she was asked to be Junior Field Secretary for the Ohio Christian Endeavor Union with an office in Columbus.

Her parents were willing for her to go. She felt incapable, but God "reminded me that all my experience in the past—being in charge of two different Junior Christian Endeavor societies in the Bluffton and Salem churches—as well as courses at Bluffton College looked in that direction." She accepted the call. For three years she traveled to all parts of Ohio to rallies and workshops.

When her mother became ill, Sylvia resigned to spend a year caring for her parents. "That was exceedingly rewarding, for I learned much which helped me be a better wife and mother later on, as well as giving me great joy in being with my parents."

Sylvia and Floyd were married August 3, 1921. "We truly felt that our marriage was made in heaven."

For two years, they lived in Bluffton while he taught physics and was librarian at the college. Their first child, Richard, was born in Bluffton, and Sylvia began entertaining students, earning her lasting reputation as a hostess.

With hostessing and attending to the baby, she began to feel harassed. Then she read a pamphlet that "probably influenced my life more than any piece of writing outside of the Bible." It had to do with making a quiet time for oneself.

Finding her own quiet time

In 1923, they were ready for China. Upon their arrival, the first order was a year of language study in Peking and Peitaiho. This was a stressful year. There was the shock of a different culture and the concern about sixteen-month-old Richard being handed over to the *amah* from nine to four every day.

Work on the language was intense. Although she and Floyd had devotions together every day, she had no quiet time of her own. She felt irritable toward her family and discouraged with her study. When they went into the interior to Taming for further study, she made time for personal devotions and found that this time made a difference in her life.

In preparing to go to China, she had realized that she would be facing problems of dirt and disease, but she had felt assured that "My God shall supply all your needs according to his riches in glory by Christ Jesus."

Still, as they waited on the station platform at two o'clock one morning, she felt "terribly bothered" when a group of boys surrounded them, wanting to touch the baby and feed him watermelon. "I feared the germs people talked about back home."

The next day she asked Jennie Boehr, "Why didn't you tell us how dirty these non-Christians are?"

How Jennie laughed! "You didn't expect to be warned about everything new and different, did you?"

Slowly they learned to appreciate one of the finest and oldest civilizations in the world. "Where could one find articles made of copper, brass, cloisonné, wood, ceramics, porcelain to equal those made in China? The language, probably the most difficult in the world; the people, the most courteous; the food—it took me months to learn to really enjoy it, but later I agreed it was as tasty as our American food."

Marie Regier helped her to learn to manage the servants.

> To live a Christian life before them was the most important thing for us to do. My hot temper, which gave me even more trouble when I must deal with servants who got on my nerves, must be submitted to Christ. How can I tell them with love and a Christian spirit to keep the kitchen clean, how to wash dishes properly, to be sure to fasten a piece of cheesecloth over the milk pail while milking so that no goat hair would fall into the milk and make it taste abominably. Keeping house and handling servants was probably the biggest hurdle to leap over. The servants were our modern conveniences and we had to have them.

The cook later became her close friend. When Sylvia was trying to help her bake a cake amid many interruptions, the cook said, "You serve the Lord in the front room, and I'll serve Him in the kitchen. . . . [I serve the Lord] just as much as the Chinese evangelists who go out to preach."

After two years of language school at Taming, the Pannabeckers moved to Kai-chow where they spent the remainder of their time in China except for short furloughs forced on them by the wars. They felt great joy in their work, feeling that they were "in the center of God's will." Their specific work was at the Hua Mei School for high school boys, where Floyd was superintendent and she taught a course in English.

Much of her ministry was with women and students who dropped in just to talk, some with problems, some out of curiosity to see how these white people lived. Some of the young people were led to Christ and to Christian service in this way. "Several people accepted Christ in our home. What a delight."

Two other children were born in Kai-chow, Robert in 1925 and Alice Ruth in 1929. The latter was brought into the world by Floyd's twin brother Lloyd who was a missionary doctor in China during the same period.

Living amid the sounds of war

In 1927, missionary families were separated because of the war, the women and children going to safe retreats while the men tried to carry on the work in spite of disruptions by the war lords.

The family returned to the United States on furlough in 1931, eight years after going out. Floyd completed a divinity degree at Garrett Biblical Institute and then spent another year at Bluffton College in 1933-34 as acting dean.

They returned to China in 1935. The following year the China field celebrated its twenty-fifth anniversary, work having been started by H. J. and Maria Brown in 1911.

Over a thousand church members from the field filled the tent erected for the celebration. "Our Christians were so impressed that there were so many like-minded people in our field. Most of them were accustomed to small groups meeting in homes or small buildings." At that time there were two thousand members of the General Conference Mennonite Church in China.

Again, in 1937, the family was separated. The Japanese entered China to begin a war that lasted until 1945. Then when the school which the children were attending moved to Hong Kong, Sylvia and the missionary mothers from all denominations went along. Two rail passenger cars were reserved for the two-day trip. The Japanese bombed the tracks ahead of the train, and at one point the travelers had to wait for eight hours while the track was repaired.

The school was set up in a hospital, with classrooms and living quarters for the staff and students. The three Mennonite mothers and younger children rented a house about a mile from school. After four months, the school closed for the summer and the families went back to China, spending some time in North China before returning to their stations. The city was under attack, but there was never a direct hit on their mission compound.

In the spring of 1941, the missionaries took the advice of the American counsel, and the mothers and children returned to the United States in the spring. The men with families returned in the fall shortly before the bombing of Pearl Harbor. The Browns, Marie Regier, Wilhelmina Kuyf, and Elizabeth Goertz stayed and were interned by the Japanese.

Choosing between China and Chicago

Back in the United States, Floyd taught at Bluffton College for a year and then went to Yale for his Doctor of Philosophy degree which he received in 1944. That same year he left again for China to do relief work under the Mennonite Central Committee.

During that time, Richard and Robert were in Civilian Public Service and Sylvia and Alice Ruth lived in Bluffton. Sylvia taught religious education in the Bluffton school, grades one through six. She also spoke often in the churches in the area.

For two years, while Floyd was overseas, he and Sylvia, through the erratic mails, had to make decisions about their future. Should they return to China, knowing that it would be for a short time since the Communists were rapidly taking over the country, or should they accept the call of Mennonite Biblical Seminary, affiliated with Bethany Biblical Seminary, in Chicago? Eight missionaries did go back, but they were able to stay for only two years. The China field closed to foreign missionaries.

As seminary hostess

The Pannabeckers decided to go to Chicago, where Floyd was to be dean. When the seminary moved to the Woodlawn area, she and Floyd were host and hostess in the beautiful old house at 4614 Woodlawn Avenue. There were about thirty students, some of whom ate at the common table, and some who lived in apartments nearby.

When Dr. Abram Warkentin died in 1947, Floyd became president as well as dean. In 1958, the seminary made another move, this time to Elkhart, Indiana, to establish the Associated Mennonite Biblical Seminaries with the Mennonite Church. Richard was teaching at Bluffton College, Robert was an insurance executive in Hawaii, and Alice Ruth Ramseyer was a missionary with her husband Robert in Japan.

Floyd retired from the presidency of the seminary and became dean and professor of missions from 1958 to 1964, then registrar from 1964 to 1969, and then archivist and president emeritus. Sylvia was grateful to be able to work more closely with her husband than during the preceding years, and she found the later thirty years more restful and joyous "in spite of our loss of hearing which at times can be exasperating. We are even learning to thank God for that experience."

They were at the seminary in Elkhart until the fall of 1976. While her husband served as registrar, Sylvia acted as hostess and friend to the seminary students and staff and other church members of the Hively Avenue Mennonite Church. When he stepped down from his office, he retired to write the history of the General Conference, the Central District Conference, and the seminary.

But Sylvia found herself unemployed. The loss of the hostess responsibility left a void in her life, but her indomitable will enabled her to find activities to keep going. She taught Sunday school and lengthened her quiet time. She shared her books with the younger seminary students and her grandchildren.

Earlier she had had surgery for breast cancer and she suffered from a heart problem. Walking was prescribed exercise, so she used it purposefully.

Her seminary friend, Frieda Claassen, wrote, "She loved people! She had the gift of praying for them. She walked along seminary drive mornings (something the doctor had prescribed) and prayed for the students and their families living in the apartments."[4] Because she could not hear well, she got little from a sermon. Nevertheless, she attended church regularly and spent the sermon time in prayer for the individual members of the congregation.

The Pannabeckers moved to the Greencroft Retirement Center in Goshen in the fall of 1976. Floyd died in October 1977 and Sylvia on June 2, 1979. The memorial services were held in the Sermon on the Mount Chapel at the seminary.

As she summed up her life toward its close, she wrote: "Always God has laid upon me the responsibility of prayer for the people with whom we have worked—in China, in Chicago, in Elkhart. Probably it has been the most important work I have been able to do. I have not always been faithful to this assignment, but God in His own way brings me back again."

---

4. "In Memory of Sylvia Pannabecker," *The Bulletin*, July 1979, p. 8.

18.
Keeper of the Network

Stella Rosella Shoemaker Kreider
1893—1977

by Robert Kreider

In colonial America, long before conferences or church periodicals, women were the keepers of the Mennonite network. The kitchen door and dining table were open to all visitors: relatives, neighbors, and strangers. It was an oral world with guests and hosts sharing information of family, farm, travel on the road, and life in the church.

In a later day, Stella Shoemaker Kreider was also a keeper of the network. Her kitchen door was open. Guests were often at her table. Daily she wrote chatty letters to brothers and sisters, children and grandchildren, cousins and distant relatives, friends from distant communities.

She was keeper of the memory: names, birthdates, family connections, bits of information from the church papers. She was a keeper of the Mennonite peoplehood, that intangible sense of belonging to a larger Mennonite community. When she died at the age of eighty-four, she had lived in five Mennonite communities, had been associated with three Mennonite colleges and two seminary campuses, and had been a member of three Mennonite conferences. She had become an inter-Mennonite woman.

Visual aids from muslin sheets

Stella Rosella and her younger sister Louella were the "little girls" in a family of nine children. Stella was born November 17, 1893, in a red brick house built before the Civil War. Her parents, Joseph Shoemaker and

Stella Kreider: She was secretary of Girls Activities, a vigorous organization that was shut down by the mission board because these men thought women were beginning to lose a sense of their subordinate place.

Elizabeth Brubaker, had come to Stephenson County in northwestern Illinois just before the Civil War, a generation after Abraham Lincoln had joined a militia which drove out the last of the Indians in the Blackhawk Wars. Stella's mother faintly remembered hearing Lincoln and Douglas debate on the courthouse lawn in the county seat of Freeport.

With the building of the railroad to Chicago, Stella's parents had migrated west from Lancaster County and Germantown, Pennsylvania. Her ancestors—with names like Ziegler, Hunsberger, Kolb, Shellenberger, Op den Graff—had all migrated from Switzerland and the Palatinate of Germany long before the American Revolution.

Stella grew up in a farm world where she learned to make soap, help with the butchering, milk the cows, hitch a horse to a buggy, and prepare dinner for threshers. A half mile west was the one-room Lancaster School, where she and her brothers and sisters attended school and where she later taught. Beyond was the small white meetinghouse where she attended Sunday school and church. Her grandparents were buried in the cemetery to the east of the church. Her father was pastor, also bishop or elder, of this church.

Joseph Shoemaker not only farmed but raised and sold a variety of exotic chickens to customers over a wide area. He and his business-minded brothers had their hands in a water-bottling firm, a condensed milk plant, and a telephone exchange. He was also secretary of the Mennonite Mission Board, one of the editors of the church hymnal, and an evangelist who traveled to many congregations.

Stella listened to the four members of the hymn committee as they used a tuning fork to get the right pitch, singing each hymn before confirming it for inclusion. She helped her father print outlines and Bible verses on muslin sheets which he displayed when giving Bible talks.

Good people do things differently

Her mother gradually became crippled with rheumatism. With their father often gone on long trips, Stella and Louella as young girls helped with the heavy housework. Their mother had gifts in craft arts, particularly in making braided rugs.

Stella respected and loved both her parents but had a particular affection for her mother who was called upon to manage the farm and hold the family together during those extended periods of the father's absences due to church work. Once, as mission board secretary, he made a trip around the world, spent several months in India, and returned to write a book about his missionary adventures. The family subscribed to the *National*

Geographic in which Stella delighted in stories of strange and faraway places.

Stella grew up in a home open to many guests. She remembered a severely plain Mennonite woman from Pennsylvania, a distant relative who smoked a pipe. Stella and Louella stared at her in wide-eyed disbelief only to be taken aside by their mother and quietly told not to stare and to remember that some good people did things differently.

Helping people as a pastor's wife

She enjoyed schoolwork and was the second of her family to go off to Goshen Academy and College to study. There she met Amos E. Kreider from Sterling, Illinois, who was several years ahead of her. They began a cautious, deliberate courtship which extended over seven years.

Preserved is the letter from January 1913 when Amos asked Stella to marry him. A week later came a grateful, restrained letter responding, "Yes, but . . ." Stella explained that she should first pay off her school debt. The courtship lasted four-and-a-half more years.

Meanwhile, Stella taught in one-room schools for thirty-five and forty-five dollars a month. One summer, she and a group of young college students worked at the Mennonite Publishing House in Scottdale, Pennsylvania, in a kind of voluntary service program. Amos finished college, taught in a village school, and completed his seminary studies in Evanston, Illinois.

Stella was twenty-three and Amos twenty-seven when they married September 5, 1917. That fall, they made their home in a small apartment on Eighth Street near the Goshen College campus where Amos taught Bible and related subjects.

Not having finished college, Stella took courses in art and other subjects that interested her. Together, they lived on a salary of $800 for that year. Stella followed the work of the newly emerging Mennonite Women's Missionary Society under the vigorous leadership of Clara Eby Steiner.

In the wartime spring of 1918, Amos received an urgent call from his father to return to Sterling, Illinois, to take over one of the family farms. Having been ordained three years before, Amos returned to be one of the ministers in the Science Ridge Mennonite Church and to manage a 110-acre corn and hog farm.

Those were years of heavy work on the farm and new family responsibilities with the birth of two sons, Robert and Gerald. Robert was born during a great blizzard and the nationwide flu epidemic. Stella and Amos often told with gratitude of how John Conrad had walked across the snowy fields to risk contagion when they both were in bed with flu, to help with the baby, and to do chores.

Stella had the task those years of learning to live in her husband's home community with the demanding expectations of his parents. She also learned the ways of helping people as a pastor's wife. They both developed deep affection for members of their congregation, an affection which continued until the end of their lives.

Mission board shuts off women's movement

However, beyond their congregation, clashes over leadership, practice, and doctrine were rumbling in the (Old) Mennonite Church. Amos finally yielded to urgent requests that he return to Goshen College, which was being severely criticized and was struggling to survive.

In 1921, Stella and Amos sold their farm equipment, packed up their belongings, and drove in their Maxwell from Sterling to Goshen. They purchased their first house, a big square white house on South Eighth Street. At Goshen College, he served as dean of the Bible School, registrar, and business manager as well as pastor of the Goshen College Mennonite Church.

Goshen College was in crisis. A series of presidents had served only one- or two-year terms. In 1923, the college closed. Amos and Stella considered several possibilities: an invitation from Hesston College, a return to the family business at Sterling, graduate study, or an interim teaching assignment at Witmarsum Theological Seminary at Bluffton, Ohio. Their choice of the position at Bluffton had long-term consequences for their lives. As Old Mennonites, they moved into a General Conference Mennonite world.

For three years, Stella and the boys stayed at Goshen and Amos commuted, returning on weekends to Goshen. In 1923, Stella was elected as the first secretary of Girls' Activities in the conferencewide Mennonite Women's Missionary Society. This vigorous organization was shut down by the mission board in 1926 because these men thought women were beginning to lose a sense of their subordinate place.

Those were painful days in the church. People who were getting hurt in church conflicts sought out the counsel of Amos and Stella, who could identify with their concerns.

When the family moved from Goshen to Bluffton, their neighbors were no longer Zooks, Yoders, and Landises, but people with Swiss names: Reichenbach, Badertscher, Hilty. As members of the faculty of this General Conference-related college, there were Low German neighbors like the Schultzes and Klassens; Prussians like the college president's wife, Emelie Hamm Mosiman; former Old Mennonites from Goshen; in the 1920s, refugees came from the Russian Revolution like the Schmidts, Epps, and Warkentines.

Beating army uniforms into pants and jackets

Stella, who had worn a bonnet and covering to worship services, found women wearing hats. The church had an organ, and an orchestra played at the Sunday school opening. German services were held once a month. Stella learned to adjust to the new ways.

In Bluffton, the family lived in four different rented homes. Stella's resourcefulness was challenged in furnishing each new residence attractively and inexpensively. During Amos's serious thyroid problem, which led to two major surgeries in 1930, Stella carried more of the responsibility of parenting their two sons. She read regularly to them.

As a magazine agent, she subscribed at a discount to a wide variety of edifying magazines such as *Hygeia, Parents, Christian Herald, National Geographic, Child Life*, and a dozen more. She carefully selected books for her sons' birthdays: biographies, books of missionary adventure, children's classics, and even Shakespeare. The Kreiders went camping when they were the only family in the neighborhood to take camping trips. Attendance at movies was not permitted unless a good review appeared in *Parents*.

Stella operated a well-disciplined home. The boys had their assigned work. All were drawn into the tasks of drying sweet corn and apples, making sauerkraut, gathering walnuts and hickory nuts, putting up eggs in brine, canning fruits and vegetables, making cottage cheese (*schmierkase*).

Meals were simple. One family standby was cornmeal mush and milk. There was much darning and patching of a few sets of clothes. She did much sewing on her treadle sewing machine. Using army uniforms that someone gave her, she remade them into matching pants and jackets for her sons and spoke of the project as "beating swords into plowshares."

Little was discarded. The family teased her for her systematic ways of saving string, rubber bands, glass jars, and Christmas wrapping paper, a habit she practiced to the end of her days. Stella kept a precise record of every expenditure from the beginning of their marriage. And despite her frugality, she never talked of money or lamented the lack of it.

Even during Amos's prolonged illness, the home was open to many guests, including the tramps who came to her kitchen door, several a week, who learned through their unique communication system that her meals were good and there were no chores.

Letters written to a widening circle

In 1931, Witmarsum Seminary closed. His health now recovered, Amos was invited to become pastor of the First Mennonite Church in Bluffton. Up to this time Stella and Amos had retained their membership in the (Old) Mennonite Church at Sterling. Now, for the first time, they joined the General Conference.

When the family moved into the neglected, rambling old parsonage, Stella wept. This was still the era of the icebox, the kerosene stove, and no running water in the kitchen. The pastor and his wife, living on a corner property with a large publicly exposed garden, soon developed a local reputation as master gardeners. In those Depression years, many members of the congregation had little money to give but were generous with meat and produce for the support of their pastor.

From 1931 to 1935, Stella came into her own right as hostess to a constant flow of guests, some years as many as a thousand recorded on her list. She also recorded menus. She served several basic meals, one being baked meat loaf, mashed potatoes and gravy, canned vegetables, pickled cucumbers and red beets, a salad in season, and canned peaches with a dab of whipped cream. She always declined help from guests in the kitchen, calling instead upon her sons to set the table and mash the potatoes.

A severe blow, the death of her mother, came to Stella in the fall they moved into the parsonage. Since her father, the well-known churchman, had received much attention and adulation, Stella was always quick to speak a word in appreciation of her mother who dwelt in the shadows. Throughout her life, Stella had a particular eye and appreciation for the wives of the much-heralded leaders of the church.

In the Bluffton congregation, Stella taught the Busy Mothers Sunday School class. She accompanied her husband in his calling on church members. Soon she knew every member of the church and the intricate network of family relationships which bound together this Swiss congregation. Both found deep satisfaction in being accepted into the affections of the congregation.

With her sons in high school, Stella had more time to pursue her interests in craft art forms: quilting, braiding and hooking rugs, caning chairs, and refinishing furniture. She was a member of the Book of the Month Club, subscribed to the *Atlantic Monthly* and was an active member of the Alice Freeman Club. In 1933, the Kreiders bought a small farm near Goshen and had much fun planning the renovation of house and farmstead. Meanwhile, she wrote dozens of letters every week to a wide circle of family and friends.

Call for cooperation among women

In 1935, the Kreiders accepted the second invitation from Ed G. Kaufman to come to Kansas to join the Bethel College faculty. Stella quickly made friends with a new set of neighbors. She continued her hosting ways. Among their guests for a week was Poet Edwin Markham, author of "The Man with the Hoe." They hosted the speakers from the Kansas Institute of International Relations: Muriel Lester, Leyton Richards, and Y. T. Wu. Stella taught a class of young married women.

She became a charter member of the local chapter of the Women's International League for Peace and Freedom. Elected to the Literature Committee of the Women's Missionary Association (WMA), she became increasingly absorbed with missionary literature.

Stella continued to keep up an active correspondence with Sterling, Freeport, Goshen, and Bluffton relatives and friends. Her style was to write short newsy letters, "bread and butter letters" she called them, about garden, guests, quilts, sons, campus events, lunch menus. Their campus home became a hostel to the east-west traffic of friends from communities where they had once lived. They urged those who dropped by unannounced, "You must stay overnight. We have a spare bedroom all ready for you."

After eight years at Bethel, both sons having graduated from college and entered alternative Civilian Public Service, the Kreiders accepted a call to Goshen to the Eighth Street Mennonite Church. There Stella renewed friendships from earlier college days and cultivated a new circle of friends. She continued her work on the Literature Committee.

She was particularly appreciative of the inter-Mennonite cooperation of wartime and observed how the walls of separation were breaking down. In 1945, at war's end, she urged in a paper on "Cooperation Among Mennonite Women" presented at a meeting of the WMA, that an inter-Mennonite paper should be launched, suggesting the title, "The Mennonite Woman."

> It need not carry missionary news, since other church publications are doing that for us. It might carry a page for young mothers relating to child health and care; a section for the hospital nurse; news and comments of interest primarily to women; a section on the kitchen, household hints, sectional recipes, balanced meals; a needlework page which specialized in arts and crafts such as quilting, rug making, and knitting of lace; peculiar folklore and stories sought out by the English department in our colleges; a poetry page; some good editorials especially appealing to Mennonite women; a

page of devotional Bible study for spiritual growth . . . an exchange column where a Mennonite woman or girl in one part of the country might find a job in some other locality if she so chooses.

Filling their guestbook with names

In 1944, Amos and Stella bought a farm several miles west of Goshen and moved from the parsonage. Here they had a large garden, chickens, a cow, and a large apple orchard. In 1946-47, while her husband made a trip around the world visiting mission and Mennonite Central Committee programs, Stella found herself doing those things which she had not done for thirty years, such as throwing down hay from the mow and milking Myrtle, their independent-minded cow.

The Kreiders' white house in a grove of sugar maple trees became a stopping-off place for a stream of friends. When a friend or stranger drove on to the farmstead, Stella's first question invariably was: "Can you stay for lunch? Can you stay for supper? No bother. It will be simple." Their farm home eventually became a second home for eleven grandchildren. A highlight of these years was Stella's first trip and Amos's second to Europe, a part of an MCC-sponsored missions study tour.

In their early seventies, they reluctantly moved from their farm home into a brick house across the street from the church in Goshen. For their last years, they moved to the Greencroft Retirement Center, which Amos had helped establish. Again, they had opportunity to become friends in a new community.

They were keepers of the network and the memory. Of particular delight to them were those occasions when they were invited to come to college classes to discuss with students the art and grace of growing old. They continued to host visitors, filling their guestbooks with names. They were diligent in attending funerals, weddings, family reunions, and campus events. Stella remembered birthdays, clipped items which would be of interest to others, and wrote those newsy letters.

Stella was grateful for the biblical interests of her New Testament scholar husband. She read the things he read, and they discussed together what they read. She shared her ideas candidly with him. He respected her judgment. However, she always preferred to look to him to put into words their shared faith in Christ.

Amos died in February 1976 at the age of eighty-six. Stella had always said that she wanted to live six months longer than her husband "so I can get all things in order." She lived eighteen months longer and died July 24, 1977, almost eighty-four years of age.

She lived and moved and had her being in the Mennonite Church.

Although she had experienced deep hurts in the church, her feelings of affection for the church prevailed. She was not only a keeper of the network of awareness and friendships in the Mennonite peoplehood, having moved in so many different communities and conferences, but she emerged as an inter-Mennonite woman. The unfolding of her life may have been a foretaste of an unfolding of an inter-Mennonite sense of peoplehood—"for your people shall be my people, your ways, my ways."

19.
Gifts Given to God

Florence White Fluck
1894—

by Mary Lou Cummings

A child runs laughing along the mountain path worn by her own bare feet and those of her sister. The girls are on the way to Maugie's where they will get a treat of fresh bread and molasses. Maugie (Mrs. Morgan) is the children's only neighbor, and she lives one-and-a-half miles further up the mountain, occupying a "possession house" for the local iron company. It is surrounded by a high fence to keep out wild animals, but never children.

Wonderful childhood in the mountains

This is a mountainous, sparsely-populated mining area in Pennsylvania known locally as the Coal Regions, but the rigors of life here do not impress children. Florence White and her sister are aware only of how extravagantly beautiful their mountain is, with the honeysuckle smells, the wild flowers, and the birds.

They are not impressed by the many snakes (copperheads and black snakes find their way into the house sometimes) or by the fact that their father walks four miles down the mountain to buy supplies and carries them home on his back. The girls are used to walking two miles to the Fountain Elementary School and will walk four miles when it is time to go to Branchdale High School. "I had a wonderful childhood," Florence says.

Now with obvious relish, the ninety-year-old Florence White Fluck tells stories of the carefree girl on the mountain, of the college girl who

Florence Fluck: On the back of each painting she attaches a note to the buyer: "Since I have dedicated my painting ability to the Lord, you, too, now have a share in contributing to His work."

became the 1915 May Queen at Kutztown Normal School, and of the young teacher who began her career in a country school far from home.

A lot of living has happened since then. Not only did she build a good marriage and begin a second career as an oil painter, but she also developed a life of living in Christ's footsteps, always giving, pouring out herself to others.

A gentle person with a quiet manner, Florence is a tall, five-foot eight-inch, frail-boned, and angular *lady*, a term used by various people looking for a better description for her but unable to find one.

As one watches Florence dabbing carefully at her easel with tapered fingers, it is sometimes difficult to see her in the stories she tells of the self-sufficient woman of her younger years who drove the horse and buggy through snow at seven in the morning to her school to kindle coal fires, and who went home to an empty cold farmhouse at four, barely beating the winter dark. Perhaps it is this contradiction between the lady and the pioneer that prompts friend Bonnie Zieseniss to dub her "The Velvet Bulldozer."

Taking on the image of Miss Dove
Florence's father, George Herbert White, had been studying for the ministry at Oxford University in England when his money ran out and his young wife died, leaving him with three children. Later, with his new wife, Frances Fletcher White, he emigrated to Pennsylvania where they tried to eke out a living for his three children and the six that followed. He had hoped to build a better life in the Swatara Mountains where his brother had struck it rich and owned a coal mine.

Education was important to the Whites. To Florence, who was born October 18, 1894, school was a link to the world. She idolized her teacher, Miss Mary Diener, and with the other children, met her each morning as she walked up the railroad track and followed her the rest of the way to school. Florence thought it unlikely that she would become a school teacher herself, as there would be no money for school fees. But she kept working and she dreamed.

When she was a senior in high school, a representative came from Kutztown Normal School (now Kutztown University) to interview potential students. He offered to allow her to pay her tuition and board after she started teaching, an answer to her prayers. Two years later in 1915, she started teaching at Fillman's School, near Quakertown, with a salary of thirty-five dollars a month. It would take her years to pay off her $449 debt.

The man who drove her to school in his buggy that first morning teased her, saying that he hoped she could "handle a stick." As twenty-one-year-old Florence looked over her classroom of fifty pupils that first day, she felt some apprehension, but things went smoothly.

She didn't know then, as she stood on that wooden platform in front of a dark portrait of George Washington, that this country school would set the tone for a teaching career of thirty-nine years which would transform Florence into a Miss Dove image for hundreds of students and co-workers so that whenever they thought of the advantages of a one-room, eight-grade school, they would remember her.

In 1916, Florence White moved back to Schuylkill County, four miles from her home, to become assistant principal at Donaldson High School. Her father was heartbroken when she resigned that job in 1919. "I'm sorry to say I was in love," she shrugs apologetically.

The young man was Victor Fluck (rhymes with look), a sensitive and gentle young man whom she had met back at Fillman's School. They married and lived in Philadelphia for a year where he had a good job in the post office; she worked as bookkeeper for a large oil refinery. City life was a trial, however, to both Florence and Victor. They determined to save enough to buy a farm.

Drawing parents into school life

Florence secured a teaching job for grades five through eight in Tabernacle, New Jersey. She boarded with a woman who stored her crop of sweet potatoes and other staples in barrels in the parlor. Across the street was a tiny country church where Florence felt at home. "I heard 'The Old Rugged Cross' there for the first time and it has been one of my favorite hymns ever since." Victor and Florence saw each other on some weekends, but it was a lonely time.

In 1924, the young couple returned to his home community, Haycock Township, and bought their farm. Their home was an old-fashioned stone farmhouse three miles from Quakertown. Florence lived there and taught at nearby Stover's School, and Victor continued his job in Philadelphia, coming home on weekends. It was not easy. Their dirt road was half an hour from town by buggy. Even mail had to be picked up at Thatcher, over a mile away.

Florence was undaunted, however, and plunged into community life through the school. At Fillman's, she had formed the Literary Society which sponsored a highly competitive adult debating team. At Stover's School, she began a parent-teacher association which was active in improving the school, putting in electric lights, digging a well for drinking water (eliminating the bucket and dipper borrowed from a neighbor), and taking children on trips to historic sites. Parents even volunteered to keep the school grounds mowed in the summertime.

"The key to success was getting to know the parents and getting them involved," says Florence emphatically.

Mother to hundreds of children

During those first years on the farm, Florence watched her pretty younger sister Alice fight tuberculosis (then called consumption). Earlier she had helped pay for Alice to go to business college, after which she had secured a good job in Philadelphia. Then Florence had urged her to come live at the farm to breathe fresh air. After a time at a sanitarium, Alice returned to the farm where Florence nursed her until her death in 1926.

From 1930 to 1944, Florence taught at Tohickon School, where she spent some of her most rewarding years as a teacher. She was busier than ever, working again to make the P.T.A. active. Together they brought the little eight-grade school up to A standard for the county.

By then it was clear that Florence would have no children of her own. Her childlessness was a deep grief to her, but it did not keep her from mothering. In this new school, some thirty to thirty-five of the fifty children lived at the nearby Children's Home and came from broken homes. "I felt I was filling a need in my life and theirs," she says. She became mother, confidante, and encourager to these children. "I had no children of my own, but in all these years I have mothered hundreds of children. When they graduated, I hated to let them go. They were my family."

Irene Lyons lived in the Children's Home for several years. "Our only happiness was in that schoolroom," says Irene. "We couldn't wait for school to start each year."[1]

Helping behind the scenes in quiet ways

Since the children at the Home attended Flatland Mennonite Church, Florence and Victor also began to attend there, becoming members in the 1940s. "I really *am* a Mennonite," she assures her interviewer. "The peace position is natural to me." She particularly enjoyed the intimacy of the tiny stone church and its colonial charm. "We were a family there." The Flucks were faithful and interested church members. She helped with Bible school; he served as deacon.

---

1. Janet Falon, "A Teacher Remembers Her One-Room School," *Bucks County Courier-Times*, November 4, 1979.

The Flucks lived very simply themselves but were generous in giving. "Wherever she and her husband could be helpful, they were. They did everything in a quiet way and never wanted to be noticed for what they had done," says former pastor Wilmer Denlinger.

Congregation member Ruth Frei concurs: "She encouraged me to get certified to teach after my children were grown. She said, 'If you ever need money for school, I'll lend it to you interest-free.' She made the same offer later to my son, and loaned him some money. Another family in the church needed a car, and I'm sure it was she who bought it. That's the kind of person she is. She has a remarkable spirit. She's a very strong person."

At one time, Florence befriended a teacher who had become a paraplegic. A car had crashed into a parade and hit the woman as she tried to protect her girl scout troop. Florence contacted the woman and began paying $100 per month to help her pay for her high medical bills. She continued the payments for ten years until the teacher died. "Kathryn became a beautiful Christian and was an inspiration to many and especially to me. We became good friends. That was the project that gave me the most pleasure and satisfaction."

Because of Florence's natural reserve, much of her love and generosity was offered behind the scenes, known only to the person to whom it was offered. The only evidence is in the wide circle of people who feel that they are part of Florence's family and who keep in close touch.

Hay in the barn for guests

After five years of commuting, Victor finally moved to the farm to begin farming in earnest. He began a 1,000-chicken operation and "did all the hard work." Florence spent her summers peddling strawberries, corn, eggs, and vegetables. She cooked over a wood stove and fed fires in the fireplace and wood furnace downstairs. She was busy, but she thrived on the hard work. Always there was time to stop to see the beauty, the wildlife, the favorite turns of Tohickon Creek; to plant some flowers and listen to the birds nesting in the porch.

The house was always open and full of people. Victor's friends from the post office, Florence's family from the Coal Regions, and other guests came to stay on the farm in the summer, often sleeping on hay in the barn. "I look back now and wonder how I fed them. Did they have enough to eat? I guess so, they always came back!"

Two foster boys also became part of their family. Elmer Anders was the first, staying for seven years until he entered the navy; he is still close to Florence. Robert Neal lived with them for fifteen years until his marriage; he and his family live nearby and are members of a local Mennonite church.

Special pupils close to her heart

From 1944 to 1954, Florence returned to Stover's School to teach. During this period of her career, Florence remembers two special pupils. "One, Richard, was spastic, and had been in several private schools with very little improvement. His father asked if I would be willing to accept him, promising to take him out should he cause any trouble. We took him in, and kept him for eight years. He proved to be one of the most lovable, well-behaved pupils we had, and he wrapped himself around our hearts—mine and the children's.[2]

"Another student was George, who seemed to spend a lot of time thinking up ways to draw attention to himself—tricks that couldn't be passed over lightly [like setting fire to a Santa Claus on her desk]. He was finally sent to a correctional school and I corresponded with him from time to time. After a few escapes and a short prison term, he became a changed young man—so completely changed that several years ago he came to see me and apologized for his behavior at Stover's School and to thank me. So it was a happy ending for two people."[3]

In 1954, until her retirement in 1959, Florence taught only two grades in the fancy new Haycock School which had four classrooms, an office, and a cafeteria. She had taught for thirty-nine and a half years, almost all in one- or two-room country schools. She lived to see almost all the country schools closed, converted to other uses, and disappear. She mourns their passing.

Bringing patience to marriage

How did this fragile, soft-spoken woman handle up to fifty children in eight grades for all those years?

Former students say that Mrs. Fluck demanded respect and got it. Former principal Ellen Werner describes her as an excellent teacher and a good disciplinarian. "I paddled sometimes," Florence admits, "but not often. Being kind and listening worked. The key to it all was teaching the students to help each other, knowing the parents, and involving them in the school.

"I liked new endeavors, adventures, but I also enjoyed my home, being here with Victor," Florence muses about her past. She and Victor

---

2. Florence Fluck, "Walking My Babies Back Home—in 1915," *So Your Children Can Tell Their Children* (Pittsburgh: Geyer Co., 1976).
3. Fluck, "Babies Back Home."

had been married for fifty-three years when he died in 1973. It was a good marriage, according to their friends. "I am strong, but also submissive. It was important to be ready to give in, to talk things over. It was a two-way street we were traveling on.

"The most important thing to learn in marriage is patience, devotion. Give things time to work out, time for each other to see a different point of view. We worked together, we liked wildlife, fishing. We didn't fight. When I realized how easily hurt Victor was, I couldn't scold him."

Gifts for retirement

When Florence retired in 1959, she tried something for the first time that had always appealed to her—oil painting. Bill Atkinson, her patient teacher, encouraged her, taught her, and became a close friend. She paints "places I know," which means the Tohickon Creek, Haycock Mountain, old stone homesteads, her parents' mountain cabin, and Bucks County scenes.

She had never done any artwork before she retired. "We traced everything in those days at school," she laughs. "Bill began by teaching me about the horizon line and perspective." Within a couple of months, people were asking her to paint for them. Since then she has completed over 350 paintings, half of which were sold, and half of which were gifts to friends.

"God gave me painting as a special gift for my retirement," she says, "so I have dedicated my gift to the Lord." Every cent she has earned on her paintings goes back to God. She doesn't even buy supplies from this fund. On the back of each painting, she attaches a little note to the buyer saying in part: "Since I have dedicated my painting ability to the Lord, you, too, now have a share in contributing to His Work. . . . Romans 8:28."

She paints in a fine, clear, brightly-colored style with a faint touch of primitive. "Oh, I'm accurate," she mocks herself, "fussy, detailed. That's me all over. I'm very exact—that's the way I taught school!"

"She's a perfectionist," agrees one of her students, "and she's stubborn. She's not satisfied with anything but your and her own best."

She has taught painting to others at no charge for many years, encouraging people to enjoy themselves as they paint. Her small house smells cheerfully of turpentine (cheerful perhaps only to other painters) and contains small partly-painted canvases propped and drying, awaiting the next lesson.

"My relatives think it's too much for me, but I don't want to give up the painting classes. We have a nice time together."

Florence has had a one-woman show at the Michener Library in Quakertown and has showed her work locally with the Upper Bucks Art League, but most of her commissions come to her privately.

Her telephone rings frequently. In addition to painting, sometimes for six hours a day, she has served as long-time president of the Richland (One-Room School) Historical Society, which maintains a one-room school as a museum and meets for animated fellowship. She is a charter member of the Elementary Teachers Forum of Bucks County and is an honorary member of its executive committee. Art students stop in for classes; committee members stop to pick her up for meetings, and church members check in about Sunday services.

Concerned about imitating Christ

On her eighty-fifth birthday in 1979, eighty-three guests from as far away as Albany, New York, and Silver Spring, Maryland, returned to Quakertown for a huge surprise birthday party. Former students returned to lavish love and kudos on their favorite teacher. Large photo-essays of the event ran in local papers.[4]

Other news features pictured Florence teaching elementary school children as they visited the old one-room school for a day: ringing the bell, teaching from a McGuffey Reader, and showing children what school was like in the old days.[5] The photos remind many local people of the more simple world that now has passed out of all but older memories, a time when the world of church, school, and community were closely knit.

As she looks back, does she feel that she fashioned the life she wanted to live? "Yes," she says. "I think I did. God worked out His plan for me. I wouldn't change one thing in my life if I could."

"I feel sorry for future generations," she says thoughtfully. "There are more opportunities today than we had, but I don't know that people are taking advantage of them. It gets harder to live a devoted life than it was. People are not as concerned about imitating Christ."

Cherishing the model community

Florence has recently experienced the merger of her tiny, country congregation of Flatland with the Bethany Mennonite Church, creating United Mennonite Church of Quakertown. While she has adjusted well, missing the fellowship when she can't get to services, she also has had some

---

4. Dennis O'Brien, "On Her 85th Birthday Retired Teacher Saluted," *Doylestown Daily Intelligencer*, October 23, 1979.
5. Alice Cantwell, "Florence W. Fluck, One-Room School Teacher," *The Quakertown Free Press*, December 5, 1979.

difficulty accepting the conflicts which needed to be ironed out between the two groups. "In past years I just went to church and took for granted everyone was devoted to Christ and would be agreeable, but there are so many disturbances today."

She can no longer attend church as often as she would like, but compensates with devotional books and tapes that people lend her. She enjoys selecting a Bible verse for each day, and keeps her worn Bible and devotional book close by.

She still lives alone in her stone farmhouse. The Haycock Township area, with its granite boulders, streams, and woods, was sparsely populated and undeveloped until recently, when it became a recreation area for Bucks County. Florence loves every tree and pasture of her home and hopes she will not be forced to leave it. Neighbors call in daily to check on her, bring groceries, and fill her numerous bird feeders. Her niece comes for a week at a time to help her maintain her home.

To many, Florence represents the Christian woman who pours out love to others through her profession and her zest for life. She does it with dignity, restraint, and respect for each individual. She is a symbol of a time when the one-room school was a model community where people worked together to meet each other's needs, whether it was to love a spastic child or mow the schoolyard in August.

20.
Making Art Respectable

Lena Waltner
1895—

Lena Waltner developed her artist's eye on the rolling acres of the farm in South Dakota where she grew up. She loved the pasture with its ravine and spring, its trees where the cows could be found when they had strayed from the hills, the gooseberry bushes where she and and her cousins could make a day's outing picking the fruit. Sometimes she could persuade her grandmother to go with her to pick pasque-flowers (anemones) in the pasture just after the snow had disappeared. Lena would fill her apron with blossoms to take home to enjoy for a few days.[1]

Lena's parents had come as teenagers with the Mennonite emigration of 1874 from Dubno, Volhynia, in western Russia. The Johann Waltners had settled near Yankton, South Dakota, and the Johann Muellers had been attracted to a homestead near Freeman. Lena was born September 12, 1895 to Jacob and Freni Mueller Waltner, the last of their eight children, born between 1881 and 1895: John G., Emil J., Anna, Peter (who died at birth), Benjamin J., Edward J. B., Henry Jac., and Lena.[2]

Corn husking holiday from school

Summers were for picking gooseberries, wild plums, cherries, and grapes and then sitting with her grandmother under the box elder tree to prepare

---
1. Lena Waltner, *Recollections*, privately printed, 1983; Mennonite Library and Archives, North Newton, Kansas.
2. Gary J. Waltner, compiler, *The Joseph Waltner Family* (Freeman, South Dakota, 1962), p. 58.

Lena Waltner: She knew as well as anyone that a person choosing a career in art would starve in a garret, but she believed in the importance of art in ordinary life.

them for making preserves. Summers were also for exploring the pasture spring that never ran dry, summer or winter.

Winters were for sledding, feeding the horses their corn and straw, gathering eggs. But it was also for going out at night with her brothers, carrying the lantern while they hunted for sparrows and squabs (small pigeons) for soup. The family made ice during winter to store in an ice house for summer use. In winter when she was just starting to school, her brothers pulled her to the country school house on her sled. Winters were for telling stories of the grasshopper plagues of 1875 and 1876, of the blizzard of 1888 when school children on their way home were frozen to death, of the prairie fire of 1889 that leveled the farm of a neighbor just a mile away.[3]

After her only sister's death when Lena was nine, she was assigned more strenuous farm work, particularly with the chickens and cows, women's responsibilities. When she was old enough to drive the horses, she helped with the haying. "Harvesting grain could not have gone off without my helping with the shocking until the last grain was cut."

For cutting the grain, she rode the lead horse of six. In the fall, school was dismissed so that the children could help with corn husking. Her goal was to fill the wagon box by noon, but she rarely succeeded. "It was not an enjoyable job, especially during cold, frosty days." In the house, she helped her mother at the washboard and with the baking. She was to enjoy baking for the rest of her life.

Searching, praying, sometimes weeping

Her parents ruled with authoritarian discipline. Strict obedience to orders was expected without question. Honesty, responsibility, right use of money were taught. But her father was a generous man, reminding her mother to provide substantial meals for the hired help, and there was hired help most of the time.

"While I was in college and money was needed, sometimes more was given than was asked for, but with the admonition, 'Now use it wisely.' " This early training left its mark: "I do not remember ever having been in debt later in life in spite of hospital experiences, trips, or building my own home."

Her parents were devout. "A portion of Scripture was read daily after breakfast, with prayer on our knees while father prayed. The day was ended the same way." They attended the Salem Mennonite Church five

---

3. Emil J. Waltner, *Banished for Faith* (Freeman, South Dakota: published by the author, 1968), pp. 200f.

miles away. If church attendance was canceled by bad weather, "we had to listen to a sermon read by father from a book of Hofacker's *Predichten*. Needless to say, we were always relieved when it came to a conclusion as the sermon was too theological for our young minds."

The death of her sister had a profound influence on Lena's religious life.

> She was so ready to go and died a triumphant death without fear. Though, basically, I was a good child and not conscious of specific sins, yet there was a fear of death as I felt that I could not die like my sister died. So there began a long period of searching, praying, Bible reading, and sometimes weeping. This lasted several years until I was old enough to be baptized. I could not honestly feel I was ready to answer the questions that would be asked, so baptism was postponed for another year with continuing turmoil in my life. The following year, I joined the catechism class and decided to be baptized, but I was still in a very troubled state of mind.
>
> A few days before the event was to take place, while I was sitting on the sofa of the living room of our home, the most important experience of my entire life occurred and because of which, nothing that happened to me in later life could shake my faith. It was as though Christ in all His loveliness and beauty came through the door with outstretched arms, saying "Come unto me." What relief and joy flooded my soul! Now I really felt ready for baptism and that I belonged to him. He has stood by me through all the many years of my life, leading through some experiences that were far from easy, but there was always the assurance of His presence.

Lena attended country school for her elementary years. Then she stayed out of school to help her mother with the care of her grandmother. After completing her studies at Freeman Academy, she taught at her country school for a year.

An art curriculum for South Dakota

The break with the family came when she and her cousin Edna made the bold step of going to Bethel College together. Lena began on the four-year course and majored in English while her cousin took the shorter music program. In spite of missing one semester because she had to return home during the illness of her mother, she managed to make up the work and graduate with her class. She was, in fact, the first Waltner to graduate from Bethel College.

How did it happen that Lena, the only daughter in the family, was allowed to attend college? Most of her brothers had become farmers with little advanced education. The answer given by family members is that this was one of the most progressive families in the community. They were looked up to in the community as "pillars of the church" and as being "sharp, intelligent people."

When she graduated in 1923, a friend who had graduated a year earlier recommended her for the English position at Redfield College in South Dakota, a Congregational school. Lena taught in the academy and was also housemother at the girls' dormitory.

The next two years were spent at Freeman Academy where she taught English, German, and home economics; she was also assigned to the dormitory as housemother. Although unsettled about what she wanted as a career, she knew she was interested in some type of religious work.

The year 1926-27 was spent in Ohio at Witmarsum Theological Seminary that was associated with Bluffton College. She was one of five women in the class of eighteen. She also took some artwork at the college. Returning to Freeman, she added a course in art to her teaching load. She did not feel qualified to teach the course, but the experience helped her to decide that she would enjoy teaching art as a career.

In the summer of 1927, she joined a group of women she had known from college days for a trip to the Holy Land. They spent a few days in Paris visiting cathedrals and art galleries, including the Louvre. In Cairo, the camel ride, the pyramids, and the art museum were noteworthy. Then the Holy Land. "Two places seemed very real, wading in the Dead Sea and the Jordan River. The open boat ride on the Sea of Galilee left a most memorable impression that evening."

Lena left Freeman after two years to spend the next year, 1929-30, at Iowa University studying art and home economics. After a year of teaching German and art at Yankton College, she decided in 1933 to get a master's degree in art from Colorado State College of Education at Greeley. Her thesis, "A Course of Study for Art in the Grades," was incorporated into the South Dakota curriculum that same year.

"Anyone who has not gone through the experience of working for an advanced degree does not know what it feels like to have the major professor put his signature of approval on your work. The question, 'What if you do not get that approval?' always hangs over you until it is accomplished." She was teaching at Sioux Falls College when Bethel College called her in 1934 to start an art department. She went, hoping that finally this would be a permanent position.

Five flights of stairs for twenty-four years

During her first two years at Bethel, she shared a classroom with another instructor and taught without equipment. Lena protested that art was not a subject to be taught from a textbook. She insisted that she needed a separate room, so a room was fixed up in the east attic of the Administration Building. The equipment consisted of two tables and some chairs which had served their purpose elsewhere, plus a secondhand loom.

"So I began climbing the five flights of stairs, and this continued for the next twenty-four years, asking for additional equipment as the years went on. . . . Trying to build a department was always going uphill, money for more equipment was not easily available. However, I was fully convinced of the importance of art in the life of Mennonite people and others, so I plodded on."

Going uphill was literal as to location and figurative as to financing. Neither constituency nor faculty could understand the need for spending money on an art department. Art was not something that Mennonites in general were willing to pay for. Art for them meant the Old Masters. She knew as well as anyone that a person choosing a career in art would starve in a garret or make illustrations for Walt Disney, but she believed in the importance of art in ordinary life, even that of practical Mennonites.

Lena was to do battle for a real department for the rest of her tenure. She was frustrated by the limitations of place and equipment, and she probably irritated succeeding administrations with her importunate demands. After her retirement in 1962, she was to see the new Fine Arts Center built in 1965. Even though she could not enjoy teaching in the new facilities, she had the satisfaction of seeing a former student, Robert Regier, teach in a building and with equipment she had only dreamed about.

Lena really cared about her students, but she tended to be reserved and unemotional. Her favorite medium was watercolor, and she approved of certain colors and content for paintings. She and Walter Hohmann, the music professor, developed a course in Appreciation of the Fine Arts that was the first of its kind at Bethel.

One of her students, Randy Penner, who went on to make a career of painting, wrote, "As the lone art professor, she had to teach every facet of art; and her students became acquainted with many dimensions of expression. She excelled in the crafts, and her weaving was wonderful. She made no claims to being a great painter; but she did a good job of teaching the basics."

She enjoyed campus life, taking in the recitals, dinners, Christmas banquets, faculty retreats, and lectures. She was also a faithful member of the Bethel College Church that was an easy walk from home. Her nephews and nieces, along with other South Dakota students, were often invited to enjoy the home she had built across the street from Goerz Hall. She later added a large studio for her painting, weaving, and plants. The backyard was an extension of her home as she developed it into a bird sanctuary.

Threads in her tapestry

One of Lena's gifts was her ability to apply her artistic flair to practical ventures. Her house was an example of a pleasing, functional building in a neighborhood with rather unimaginative styles.

She had an exceptional way with flowers and plants that was appreciated by the community. She loved flowers not only for their color and form, but also as an expression of God's creation of beauty in the world. She liked to arrange them and paint them, and she liked to grow them, to make bigger and more perfect blossoms. Working with flowers was for her a religious experience. Besides her painting, she was always busy with craft projects, things that were both attractive and useful.

Her interest in bird watching was shared with Lucile Thomas, the city nurse, and Marguerite Russ, an English teacher from the college. With the Russes, she made two trips to follow the dogwood trail. She and another Newton friend took weekends off to paint in the Ozarks or the Flint Hills. Lena was especially fascinated by old barns and by sunflowers.

As a member of the Western Arts Association and the Kansas State Federation of Art, she attended their annual meetings. She was president of the latter for one year, as well as editor of its official publication. A trip to Mexico with fifteen women was a highlight, and she came back with several paintings done on that excursion. When Gerald and Hope Stucky invited her to Colombia to give a workshop, she also took advantage of the opportunity to study the mission program there.

During her retirement, she took part in a foliage tour through the New England states and an art tour through the Great Smokies. Even though retired, she kept going to art workshops and learning more about weaving. Her weaving showed less restraint than her painting. She used some of the Indian motifs she had seen on her trips to Mexico and South America.

But there came a time when she felt that "a move to where one's roots are would be wise." So in 1968, she moved to Freeman, to live in the "old, familiar community with relatives and friends." She moved to the Salem Home in the summer of 1981, where two of her brothers were also living. She says she is satisfied, although she misses the young people of the college setting. Her failing eyesight is a burden to her artistic temperament, but she is thankful to have had the privilege of being a seeing person for most of her lifetime.

In comparing her life to a tapestry, Lena described the dark threads in the pattern as the deaths of her parents in 1941 and 1942, the death of a close friend, and the hospital stays that she experienced. As a single woman, she also had her times of loneliness. But she felt that the thirty-four years of her life spent in the college environment were her happiest, that she could not have been as happy elsewhere.

> They were years of fulfillment, although at the time it did not always seem that way. To be permitted to live long enough to know that a strong, continuing department has emerged from a small beginning through one's efforts is very gratifying. It has further been rewarding to realize one was able to make a small contribution in developing the talents of those who followed me and have given continuity to the department. . . . Many others of my former students have also developed successful art careers in other areas.

Lena was not the first teacher of art at Bethel; she had been preceded by Mary Wirkler Krehbiel and later by Mary's sister Elizabeth, but in the years before Lena came to teach, there had been no art teacher. She in effect had to build a new department. She was dedicated to promoting art, insisting that the faculty and administration and the constituency be aware of art as a respectable profession, one that should be taken seriously. She helped us to understand that art has a legitimate place in our lives.

21.
To India with Love

Christena Harder Duerksen
1896—1984

A tradition of loving must have taken root among Christena Harder's ancestors. Giving and receiving love provided the theme for her life, with her family, her friends, and the many she touched in her ministry in the United States and India.[1]

Her mother, Justina Quiring, was born near Mountain Lake, Minnesota, and started "working out" at fourteen. She grew up to be a cheerful, optimistic woman, and used her early experiences for stories to tell her own children. Christena confided often in her "dainty little mother" and loved her as a sister.

Abram Harder, Christena's father, came to the United States from Russia when he was four. After their marriage, Justina and Abram started farming a few miles north of Mountain Lake. Christena was born October 6, 1896, the oldest of six children, the last born when Christena was twenty-six. A frail child, Christena suffered from poor health for much of her life. From those early years, Christena remembered her mother's creative ideas for play and her father's interest in music.

Finding serious Christians in Dakota

Theirs was a family on the move. When Christena was seven, they moved

---

1. Most of this material comes from the Jacob R. and Christena Harder Duerksen collection of diaries and letters in the Mennonite Library and Archives, North Newton, Kansas, Boxes 117, 1-9. There were also interviews with her daughter Lois Deckert, school friends, and India missionaries.

Christena Duerksen: Because the mission board had no money, she and J. R. decided that they would sell his inherited land and use the money to finance their first three years in India.

to Langdon, and in two years to Munich, North Dakota, and then looking for better land, the family went to homestead in Scranton. The crops were poor, and her mother had to scrimp with the egg money to order a few books. *Youth's Companion* and Sunday school papers were sewed together so they could be read again and again.

Christena began teaching Sunday school when she was thirteen. She was converted at fourteen, listening to an itinerant Methodist preacher. At sixteen, she was chosen to go as a delegate to a Sunday school convention several railroad stations distant. There she discovered that there were *many* Christians who took their beliefs seriously, and she came home with enthusiasm for her own teaching.

By the fall of her eighteenth birthday, she had taken her teacher's examination, put up her hair, and signed up for a school near home. During that school year, her parents moved to Chinook, Montana. She would have liked to have moved with them, but she felt that a contract was a contract, and she kept it. The next spring she followed them and taught in the Bruderthaler settlement, twenty miles north of Chinook.

Fighting to fit into the Lord's scheme

It was in this school that she felt a call to full-time service in the foreign field, but she did not feel willing to give up teaching. "Many a battle was fought beside school desks when the children had left and I was doing janitor work. I wanted to be willing."

During the summer of 1916 at an Epworth League convention, she rose to publicly answer a call for recruits for foreign service. She felt that having made public her commitment, she would never be able to go back on it. This decision was an important emotional experience. When she told her mother, Justina gave her blessing, telling Christena that she had dedicated her to be a missionary even before her birth.

Christena often discussed the sermons she had heard and her concern about the power of Satan. A friend had sent her a Christmas present. "The book is a romantic love story, the kind that doesn't do a person any good to read!" On the other hand, the theology books she read also troubled her. "Either I have not a great enough faith or I have something which I must surrender that I have not done yet."

After another year of teaching, Christena enrolled at the Bible Institute of Los Angeles to train for Christian service. She took her practical work at the Who-So-Ever-Will Mission and became one of the charter members of the little Mennonite church that was organized there. By that time, her parents had moved to Reedley, California, with William, Joe, and Martha.

At school, she found much to inspire her already well-developed interest in the mission field and her desire to follow the will of God. She felt drawn to China by talk with missionary friends. But when she met a missionary from India, she wrote, "It is getting easier for me to think of leaving for whatever field the Lord has for me but again and again comes that selfish thought, 'A little more time, a little more time.' "

She talked easily about her love of Christ, but she still had great yearnings to be a better Christian. She looked with envy at a girl "who knows her heavenly Father so much better than I do." She was chosen to speak for the women of her graduation class of December 1919.

The two years at the Bible institute were soul stretching, but her health was a problem. "You puny little thing. You'll never live a year in India," a friend told her.

She suffered from headaches and eyestrain. Just before graduation she learned that she was physically unqualified for foreign work. With no money for the extensive operation that she needed, she wondered if the Lord could perform a miracle of healing. Returning discouraged to Reedley, she asked where she fit into the Lord's scheme of things.

The miracle happened in Reedley

Christena found her place in the family, helping her mother with the growing household duties. She became a second mother to Harry, born in 1917, and Bobby, in 1922.

In spite of her interest in housewifely tasks, she didn't let them become too important. She did in fact become bored with her life sometimes. At a birthday party, she deplored the routine: "The men stand around in groups discussing the weather while the women sit around in the house talking about their families and how many chickens they raised."

A year after she returned to Reedley, the miracle happened. Her friend Emma Ruth gave her the tithe of her inheritance for the operation she needed. Then she was able to pass the physical examination for foreign service, but she still needed to gain twenty pounds.

Christena's love story

The family joke was that Christena's father would chase any suitor off the yard who did not speak German. It is time now to tell the love story of Christena Harder and Jacob R. Duerksen. J. R. could speak German.

During the last three months of her stay at the Bible institute, a young Mennonite man had called attention to himself by ignoring the Mennonite women. "That quiet boy from Kansas must have a girl back home," they said.

Nine months after Christena returned to Reedley, she received a formal proposal from J. R., not of marriage, but an invitation to become acquainted. He had sent his application to the mission board, he said, but he did not believe it was the Lord's will that he go by himself. And since he knew that she planned to go as a missionary to some field, perhaps their plans might be the same. Would she let him know what she expected to do with reference to missionary work? The letters that followed were more human.

Later in the year, she moved to Los Angeles to work as a practical nurse and they were able to become better acquainted. Some plans must have been made in June 1920 after his graduation from the Bible institute, but no formal announcement was given since the future was not determined. He returned to Kansas.

Their letters carried a sense of fun along with poetry and prayers, Bible verses, and bits of sermons. Christena was an idealistic person who took the occasions of birthdays and New Year's Eve to write in her diary or in letters to J. R. of her resolve to follow God's leading and to be a better person in every way.

J. R. enrolled at Bethel College to complete work for an A. B. degree. She waited for her health to improve and both waited for the mission board to give them a clear call. In the meantime, she worked. She wrote of cutting peaches, one day cutting 4,260 peaches in half, taking out the pits, and placing them on trays. "But my heart certainly isn't in this work. Still it is a means to an end, even though I earned only $1.20 today."

In January 1922, she was asked to be the pastor's assistant at the First Mennonite Church in Reedley for two-thirds time at sixty dollars a month. Her duties with the church usually involved activities with women and children. Christena visited other churches, went to conventions with young people, made pastoral visits, and taught Sunday school and Bible school classes. She did not preach.

As one of the girls at Bethel

At the suggestion of the mission board, plans were made for Christena to go to Bethel Academy to complete her high school training. Again Emma Ruth came forward to make this move financially possible. J. R. wistfully suggested that they push their plans up a year and be married in 1923. He could get a little house close to the campus.

In her twenty-six-year-old wisdom, she answered: "Some things would be easier to write if we could look into one another's faces and could catch the expression and could hear the tone of voice . . . . I do want to spend the year at Bethel as 'one of the girls' for I simply do not feel ready for the other yet . . . . When I do face [the responsibility], J.R., I'll face it with my whole heart."

"You'd better practice Low German," he warned. "There will be no way out, you'll have to talk it here." Speak Low German she did, with J. R.'s family and in the dormitory. Mariam Penner Schmidt remembers that "whenever the girls in the dormitory wanted a good laugh, they asked me to come down to talk Low German with Christena. Just for the sound of it."

After graduating from the academy, Christena worked at the hospital and then took a six-months' course in nursing. As she watched the death of a young child, she realized that this was preparation for attendance at deathbeds on the mission field.

She returned to Reedley that December to spend the last six months with her family, and correspondence resumed.

Waiting on the Lord and the mission board

The mission board asked Christena and J. R. to go to Montana, but they were reluctant to change plans. Their thinking had been in terms of foreign fields, specifically India, although they were willing to go to Montana if they understood that it was the Lord's will. Furthermore, the missionaries she had been writing to were looking forward to their coming. Christena and J. R. thought of H. J. and Maria Brown as examples of those who heard the call and went independently. They reached the decision that "the mission board is not always infallible."

After their wedding in Reedley in June 1924, J. R. and Christena returned to Kansas where J. R. taught in a two-room school and preached in the Garden Township Church. She continued writing the column for the *Mennonite Weekly Review* that she had begun in January, called "The Children's Sunday School Hour," a substantial piece of writing that was for the most part Bible story telling.

They were discouraged by the delays from the mission board about going to India. There simply was no money. After a pleasant year in Halstead, they made a decision: J. R. would sell his portion of inherited land and use it for their first three years in India. They would save enough for their passage and outfit from their two years of his teaching and preaching, and the sale of the land would cover their first years of language study and get them into the work. Everything would be settled and they could then leave in a year.

They presented this idea to the mission board and to his widowed mother. Both accepted the plan. "We do not see why we should not do this," she wrote to her mother. "If we were going into business, no one would be surprised if we put all we had into it. So why shouldn't we put all we have into the biggest business in the world?"

Dreaming and breathing Hindi

In February 1926, they learned that they were to leave for India in the fall, and so began a round of speaking trips, purchasing and packing, and resigning from school and church. Finally, the time came for farewells, with an emotional leave-taking from the family. As they boarded the train at Newton, the friends who had come to see them off began singing, "God Be with You," and "Blest Be the Tie." They sailed in October and arrived in India a month later.

"We are like children who get their first glimpse of the Fresno County Fair," Christena wrote to her family. Arriving during the Jubilee celebration of twenty-five years of General Conference mission work in India, they had a proper greeting from missionaries and Indians with garlands and songs.

They lived at the Korba mission station with C. H. and Lulu Suckau while they began language study. Although they were apt pupils, they found the language difficult. Her Hindi sentence, "The big oxen have eaten the little trees" came out as "The long hair have eaten the small feet."

By March, Christena wanted to throw her Hindi book into the river. In April, they went to Landour in North India to language school, and by October they were teaching their first Sunday school classes. She wrote out the lesson in English and then translated it into Hindi for the *pandit* (teacher) to correct before she memorized it. She found herself dreaming and breathing Hindi, studying even as she washed dishes.

A partner with her husband

When they returned to Korba to begin mission work, the Suckaus left. So within a year after arriving in India, they found themselves the only white people at that mission station. Christena took over the dispensary, spending two hours a day there. She was soon called to deliver her first baby. She phoned Dr. Ella Bauman in Champa who gave instructions, and the baby was born without problems.

Christena took note of her firsts: first poisonous snake; first memorization of a verse in Hindi (John 4:9); first opportunity to hear E. Stanley Jones, the famous Methodist missionary; J.R.'s first shot in India by which he felled a deer, improving their diet for several days.

J. R. was preaching, at first using an interpreter. His first laboriously worked out sermon in Hindi was a milestone. During fine weather, he went on tenting tours in the villages. Sometimes she went with him, but often she stayed to attend to the work of the station. She taught Bible courses and Sunday school. Occasionally, she preached.

"The missionary movement was the first step in allowing women to work beyond home and family and to take their place alongside men in the work of the church."[2] Christena was a partner to her husband in the work of disciplining, planning, preaching. She also had her own sphere of work in teaching. Usually, she worked with women and children, and by the end of her long term in India, became known beyond the Mennonite circle and was invited to give demonstrations and write about her methods of teaching.

She seems to have become an authority on the use of flannelgraph material, working out lessons which she took to the villages, setting her material up on the hood of the jeep, and attracting listeners to her drama of the prodigal son or the Easter story. Her article on use of the flannelgraph was published by the National Christian Council of India in 1953.

The Duerksens experienced the usual problems of missionaries: disgruntled servants, discouragements with church members who "fall into sin," mediation of quarrels that villagers brought to them. Letters and reports needed to be written for those 150 people who supported special projects such as the orphans, Bible women, and evangelists.

The best days of our lives

Life was always full. She wrote home, "Time goes so fast and there is always so much I want to do. I wish I were twins. One of me could study and the other of me could work. Triplets would be still better, for then one of me could come home and tell you all about the rest of me—such nonsense."

She didn't know which she had less of, time or money. At a time when they thought they were doing all humanly possible in their work, they were visited by a white couple doing survey maps in the district. Christena realized that the couple had spent a lonely Christmas, and she resolved to try to reach out in the district to those besides the Indians who had needs.

Missionaries spent much time fixing flats, worrying about their cars, and digging them out of the mud. The Duerksens had their share of car trouble. Often they were homebound by high water, poor roads, and washed out bridges.

---

2. Carolyn J. Klingelsmith, "Women in the Mennonite Church, 1900-1930," *Mennonite Quarterly Review*, July 1980, p. 167, quoting Barbara Lamb.

The worst flood came when they were stationed at Mauhadih. The water rose to five inches in the bungalow. All the Christians came to their house, 175 of them, and they put the babies on the table for sleeping. In the Thiessen bungalow nearby, the water rose thirty-three inches.

Of the political problems of India, she makes little mention. She approved of Gandhi's ban on the use of alcohol, but not his program of civil disobedience, which she perceived as stirring up riots and unrest.

The Duerksens were stationed at one time or another at each of the General Conference mission stations in India except Champa. On moving from Mauhadih to Jagdeeshpur, J.R. commented that this new assignment "was so interesting that at the end of seven years it seemed like seven days. . . . The days we spent in Jagdeeshpur were the best days of our lives." This was the new location for the boys' school after the flood in Mauhadih and where the W. F. Unruhs had begun an ingathering of some one thousand Christians.

Gold-bordered sari from the queen of Korba

For vacations, they sought out conventions and conferences with messages for missionaries. "You know, we need to be preached to every once in a while," Christena wrote.

The Duerksens appreciated the kindness of veteran missionary P. A. Penner who "never acts as though all must move about him. He has enough grace to take his hands off of things in order to give the younger missionaries a chance."

Never did they in their letters gossip about other missionaries. They always spoke of their kindness and help, their appreciation for their good examples, and the enjoyment they received from their children. The only exception to this general generosity: when one of the single women who was difficult to live with was assigned to their station, Christena's comment was, "Poor J.R."

Once in a while, Christena was called to have tea with the *rani* (queen) of Korba, a noteworthy event. The *rani* was always interested in the children, and she always gave Christena a parting gift, once a white silk sari with a gold-threaded border. Christena, wishing to identify with Indian women, wore saris at a time when most missionary women did not.

The three Duerksen children were all born in India. The first two, Joe in December 1927 and Christine in January 1930, were born in Champa under the attendance of Dr. Ella Bauman. Lois made a more dramatic appearance. Floods made it impossible to get to Champa, and when she arrived prematurely in August 1933, Augusta Schmidt delivered her.

Joe was five and a half and Christine three and a half. J. R. wrote, "At quarter to five, the children wake up and I tell them that I wanted to show them something. Christine asks immediately, 'Is it a baby?' After they have seen it, Christine dances around the room exclaiming: 'This is the one I prayed for.' After they have seen it, J.J. takes me to the bathroom and asks me why it is not a boy. He cries because God has heard Christine's prayer and not his."

The children were a delight to their parents until the time of parting for school at Woodstock in a North India hill station. They were at home for three months during the winter break and Christena usually spent three months in Landour, taking them out of boarding to make a home for them at Ellengowan, the mission house.

The train trip to Mussoorie took three days and nights. "It almost seems cruel to leave a child of less than six in school a thousand miles from home, and yet that is the only thing to do," Christena told her mother.

Quality time for the family

How did a busy missionary couple make time for the family? For the parents, finding time was difficult since the children's vacations coincided with the time of good weather when missionaries were touring the villages and preaching at tent meetings. Lois remembers that they had family times deliberately set aside, and nobody interrupted that time. Picnicking on the dry riverbed, fudge making on a Petromax burner in the middle of the bedroom floor on a Sunday afternoon—"The times spent at home were quality times that made up for the lack of quantity."

The children seemed to have been good letter writers, but one wonders how encouraged the parents felt after reading this from Joe: "Chrissie is in the hospital with tonsilitus. Duff and I slept out for two nights on a hill. . . . Later we found that a bear was somewhere around there. . . . On Wed. Duff and I attacked a hornet's nest. I got stung on the back of the head. The school is in quarenteen for dyptheria."

Deaths of relatives in America were hard to bear. J.R.'s mother and Christena's oldest brother died, and of course they could not have the comfort of grieving with their own families. Letters took a month to come, although cablegrams were used for such important news as births and deaths.

Later, when Christine was to be married to Harris Waltner, the heartache of not being able to be there was combined with the question of how Chrissie could manage financially to have a nice wedding. When Joe was married to Mary Lou Franz in the United States, they celebrated in India with a party for the missionaries whose children had known their children. Christena baked and decorated a wedding cake.

Standing by the range at home

Christena never owned a home, but the children felt that she made a home wherever she happened to be living. Hers was the task of seeing that there was food and clothing, for making an attractive and comfortable place for her family. She felt it necessary to explain why she employed a cook. His wage was only four dollars a month, so she felt it did not pay for her to peel potatoes, wash dishes, and cook. The Duerksens used their own money to pay for the servants.

Christena showed the Indian women the iron wood-burning stove in her kitchen that didn't smoke but both baked and cooked. The Indian women said, "Poor thing. She has to stand up to cook and we can sit down." She pored over magazines from home, looking for ideas for cooking and sewing, but finding that most suggestions were not adaptable.

Christena became adept at sewing, ripping old things to turn the cloth to make new things, cutting down adult clothes to make children's clothes, improvising, refurbishing, adapting from the boxes sent by friends, relatives, and mission societies. But some things she needed from home. She asked her mother to send baby clothes, enclosing a check: two dozen flannel diapers, woolen bands that tied with tape, and pearl buttons.

She asked her sister Martha "to send pictures of ladies dresses that you think look nice." She was still interested in pretty clothes but they were more difficult to come by. On a rainy Sunday at Woodstock, she walked from church wearing a green dress. As the dress got wet, it began to shrink and by the time she reached home, about four inches of her petticoat was showing, and the dress had become so narrow she could hardly walk.

Too much illness and too little money

Her letters show that illness was a part of life in India. She seemed almost preoccupied with family illnesses and those of other missionary families. One wonders how they could do anything with so much time spent being ill or dragging about with various disabling illnesses. J. R. suffered from boils and then a light case of diphtheria. The children at Woodstock had more than their share of serious childhood illnesses. A cure-all at the mission dispensary was castor oil.

"I wish we could live more like the [Indian] people, but I suppose it would not do because of the health conditions. Even now, fever makes a great deal of trouble for the foreigner." Malaria and typhoid were scourges. They felt threatened with leprosy and cholera.

Once Christena wondered what her itch was, and then her *ayah* found lice while she was brushing her hair. She wondered if she would have to shave her head, as they shaved the heads of the school children, but she solved the problem with kerosene and vinegar. Because of the prickly heat, her little ones dressed "like the children of the land—mostly in sunshine."

There is some mention, but not a great deal, of financial problems. The mission board was having trouble finding money to pay salaries, and sometimes the checks came late. At one time when they were vacationing in Darjeeling, they took a boarding house so that Christena could spend her time writing. They found they did not have enough money for both boarding and the return trip. But then they received an unexpected check for one hundred rupees in back pay and were solvent again.

Once she wrote, "At present we have about 50 cents and the mission has even less. I wanted to make some jelly but can't buy sugar. The mission did not expect any until New Years. We would have had enough if we had not loaned some to the mission. And then the call came that some gift money had come and the board sent half the salaries."

Receiving only half a salary might have seemed a catastrophe, but they knew that the mission board was feeling the effects of a deep world depression. The bright spot in the financial picture was that they could benefit from a favorable exchange rate. (She had money to buy sugar to make jelly, which boiled over while she was writing letters.)

But she found more pleasant things to write about. In India, she found much beauty to praise. The rainy season brought lush parklike growth, and the mountains of Darjeeling and Mussoorie were awe inspiring. "The beauty of it all: if only we could take colored pictures," she wrote.

Furlough time for school and family

Their first furlough was in 1935, after nine years on the field. They lived in Glendale, California, and J. R. preached at Upland and studied Greek at the Bible Institute of Los Angeles. Christena spoke at many women's meetings. Their second furlough was in 1946. She and Christine attended summer school together, Christena taking Philosophy-Science Survey and Journalism.

Their third and last furlough was in 1955. They arrived home to help Joe and Mary Lou pack for India and to attend their ordination in February 1956. Christena wrote, "This is a very important day in the annals of the Jacob R. Duerksen family." She found the service very moving. They were also able to help Lois plan her wedding to Marion Deckert.

Although they had a permit from the Indian government to return to India, the mission board did not ask them to return. There was an unexplained opposition to him by one of his colleagues. The closing of the India door was a disappointment. Christena knew that J. R. was especially suited for mission work. She remarked to a friend after their return, "I no longer hear my lion roar."

However, their work in the churches they served during their last years was appreciated. In 1957, they went to Henderson, Nebraska, where J. R. was interim pastor. Here Christena again taught teacher training classes. After two years, they were called to the Willow Creek Mennonite Church in Paso Robles, California, and then as interim pastor to Dallas, Oregon.

After their return from India, Christena attended a writers' conference. In 1971 her book, *Come with Me*, was published by Faith and Life Press. It was a collection of stories for children based on her experiences in India. She continued her writing of stories and poems for church papers.

"In this day and age, my mother would have been a strong feminist," her daughter Lois said. One can read this interest in women's status between the lines of her letters. Though narrow in experience and travel (she was confined to the missionary experience and the path between home and India), she was in many ways "an all-around person," with interests in writing and teaching as professions, with a love of beauty in nature and music, with an interest in every kind of person, and with a complete dedication to sharing the good news of Jesus.

While she believed in her right to be a person apart from the life of her husband, she was sensitive to feelings about women's place in the church. When they spoke in the Beatrice church, she remarked that although J. R. preached from the pulpit, she took special care to remain below because she understood that women were not supposed to be prominent in that church.

They retired to Reedley, then to North Newton, Kansas, where they could be closer to their children, and finally both went to the Bethesda retirement home at Goessel, Kansas. After a long and debilitating illness, she died on February 7, 1984. J. R. followed shortly after.

She was buried in the white and gold sari that was a gift from the *rani* of Korba, a symbol of the love that flowed to her and from her.

RUTH KREHBIEL JACOBS 1897-1960 Founder, Choristers Guild

Ruth Jacobs: "Juniors like to feel that they are doing something worthwhile. You gain their allegiance by expecting the best they have to give."

22.
Letting the Children Sing

Ruth Krehbiel Jacobs
1897—1960

Few Mennonite women born before 1900 became known as performing musicians or earned a living by practicing the arts in any form. Many women learned to play the piano and organ; a few took singing lessons; in college, they belonged to choirs. A few women turned to music education.

Ruth Jacobs received statewide recognition as a choir director at Bluffton College; and after her marriage, she became well known for her ministry with children's choirs, a nationwide movement that she helped to initiate. She has been called the mother of the children's choir movement.

Singing in the choir in California

Ruth Krehbiel Jacobs was born into a family of church workers. Her Anabaptist ancestors fled from persecution in Switzerland to settle in the Palatinate of South Germany. In 1851, the families emigrated to Lee County, Iowa. Her grandfather, Jacob E. Krehbiel, was the older brother of Christian Krehbiel, one of the founders of the General Conference Mennonite Church. Henry J. Krehbiel, her father, moved with his parents to Summerfield, Illinois, where his uncle was already well established.

Henry attended the Evangelical Synod Seminary at St. Louis and was called to his first pastorate in 1892, at Trenton, Ohio. He married Lydia D. Ruth from Summerfield the next year. Ruth was born on May 30, 1897, the second of five children and the only girl. Her father served the Trenton church for seventeen years. During those years, he helped several smaller congregations resolve their differences so they were able to merge. Eventually, he led the Trenton church into the General Conference.

The call to Reedley, California, to begin a new church was welcome, and he moved his family when Ruth was eleven. During his ministry, the church grew from 34 to 448. Within a family that encouraged intellectual endeavors, within the vigor of a growing church, Ruth grew to adulthood. "I cannot recall ever having heard Reverend Krehbiel preach a sermon in which he did not mention at least a few things about peace."[1]

Ruth took part in the program of her father's church, singing in the choir and attending Christian Endeavor. Anna Eymann remembers her as outgoing, "always willing to play a prank on someone. Her talents were many, but she was never one to belittle anyone less fortunate than she."[2]

Two years of study in Berlin

At Bluffton College, where her father was a founding board member, she majored in music. As the chairperson of the committee that published the first Mennonite English hymnal, her father undoubtedly encouraged her interest in music. After graduation in 1918, she attended the University of California for a year and then taught for two years at the Sanger, California, high school, about ten miles from Reedley.

The highlight of her education came from 1922 to 1924 when she studied voice at the *Hochschule fuer Musik* at the University of Berlin. Lest anyone think of her as a young woman adrift in Europe on her own, it should be noted that she was accompanied by a maiden aunt.[3]

Returning to Bluffton College after her two years abroad, she taught music theory and voice. In 1925, Ruth entertained her parents and twenty of their Bluffton friends at a farewell banquet as the Krehbiels started for the first Mennonite World Conference in Basel, Switzerland. Her father was the only American delegate.[4]

The editor of the Bluffton College yearbook gave Miss Krehbiel high praise for her work with the music clubs. In 1926, this tribute was written: "The Girls Glee Club has this year, no doubt, set a record in the history of clubs. This was due unquestionably to the work of the girls and still greater devotion of its directress, Miss Krehbiel."

In 1928, when she directed the Vesper Choir, the yearbook reported:

1. Winifred Regier, "Biography of Dr. H. J. Krehbiel," research manuscript, undated, Mennonite Library and Archives, North Newton, Kansas.
2. Letter from Anna Eymann, April 1984.
3. "Ruth Krehbiel Jacobs," *The Mennonite*, March 27, 1979, p. 227.
4. H. J. Krehbiel, *A Trip Through Europe* (Newton, Kansas: Herald Publishing Company, 1926), p. 6.

Perhaps no musical organization on the Bluffton Campus has fulfilled its purpose quite as well as has the Vesper Choir. From the time of its entrance up until its departure, a spirit of worship pervaded the entire chapel. . . . And at the close there came the hushed beauty of voices slowly dying in the distance. It left a message in the hearts of listeners, more eloquent than spoken words. . . . Much of the credit goes to the active interest and musical ability of Miss Krehbiel.

To instill that spirit of worship in listeners and in performers was the director's intention. "The emphasis has been not only on excellence but on meaning, on developing persons, on congregational education and appreciation, on worship and personal participation," Cecil E. Lapo wrote in commenting on her later career as a director of children's choirs.[5]

In 1928, the Bluffton College music department also presented the operetta, "Alice in Wonderland." The announcement of Miss Krehbiel's forthcoming marriage to Arthur Leslie Jacobs was made following the performance. She resigned at midterm. At that time, Leslie Jacobs was minister of music at a church in Worcester, Massachusetts. Ruth became director of music at Central Church in the same city.

Turning to children for church music

Her contribution to church music was particularly in the area of the development of children's choirs. Children had taken part in special musical programs of the church at Christmas and on other holidays, but children's choirs were not a part of the educational program of most churches.

Her entry into the area of children's choirs came almost by happenstance. In the Worcester church, the tradition was to have special music provided by a professional mixed quartet. Ruth was committed to provide music with a choir and to build a long-range program of music. When she tried to enlist church members to sing in a choir, they refused. Ruth turned then to the children.

Although she had had no experience in teaching children, she was determined to learn. "The choir was actually something unique at that time, especially in New England, so much so that other churches in an ever widening geographical area requested assistance in starting children's choirs."[6]

---

5. "Looking Back Forwardly," *The Mennonite*, March 27, 1979, p. 227.
6. Federal Lee Whittlesey, quoted in Larry Keith Ball, *Choristers Guild 1949-1980*, University of Southern California, November 1981, p. 36; material on the history of the Choristers Guild comes from Ball's dissertation.

Ruth expressed her faith in the ability and potential of children: "Juniors like to feel that they are doing something worthwhile. You gain their allegiance by expecting the best they have to give."[7]

In 1939, Leslie and Ruth moved to Los Angeles where she worked with the Marlborough School. "During the next ten years, Jacobs came into national prominence, a visionary with the skill to communicate in an exceptionally effective manner."[8] Ruth was invited to lecture and demonstrate her techniques at choir festivals and music seminars in many churches in the country.

Children as ministers of music

Ruth received a flood of requests for help from directors of children's choirs. She began answering them with duplicated letters.

In her first book, *The Successful Children's Choir*, she included her Director's Creed:

> I believe that the children's choir is potentially one of the greatest agencies that the Church possesses for rebuilding its waning strength. No other organization has greater natural opportunity for training in those qualities that characterize a strong Christian faith.
>
> I believe that it offers the opportunity or responsibility for the worship attitudes of the entire congregation. When they enter the chancel as a choir, the children become *ministers* of music.
>
> I believe that what the children absorb unconsciously from their associations with fine music, high ideals, and participation in public worship may have greater value than what we consciously teach them.
>
> I believe that the greatest ultimate purpose of the children's choir is worship, consciousness of the presence of God, and active response to that presence.
>
> I believe that our emphasis must be on the child, not the subject. Great music has no value in itself; only when it penetrates the personality and has its influence there does it really live.
>
> I believe that if the children's choir is to achieve the maximum of its potentialities, it must have thoroughly trained leadership. And it must be recognized by the Church at large as a legitimate and integral part of its education program.[9]

---

7. Norma Lowder, *Choristers Guild Letters*, November 1960, p. 52.
8. Ball, p. 36.
9. (Chicago, Illinois: H. T. Fitz-simons Company, 1948), pp. 7-9; now in its seventh edition.

In her second book, *The Children's Choir*, she deplored the unfriendly situations which had discouraged the formation of children's choirs. Few ministers had recognized their value, and professional church musicians were only superficially trained in their guidance. Religious education directors in general looked on them with distrust. But the children's choir movement steadily increased in numbers and in effectiveness.[10]

The movement becomes the Choristers Guild

Others were associated with the forming of the children's choir movement, but it was Ruth who had the vision for the organization now known as the Choristers Guild. It came into being in 1949 with Ruth as founder and president. It gave the children's choir movement a sense of direction.

"From a very small beginning [the guild] has grown into a non-profit association with an interdenominational and international membership of educators, directors, and clergy concerned that the children's choir should not degenerate into a popular fad."[11] Ruth also edited its periodical, an expansion of her duplicated letters, *Choristers Guild Letters*, and wrote for other professional journals.

Her vision for children's choirs was much broader than that of training performing groups for Sunday worship services. She encouraged the directors to give the children an education in church music, suggesting plans for a "Hymn of the Month" by which the children studied the music, the author, the composer, and its use in the worship service. She printed suggestions from other directors and wrote often of her own philosophy and techniques.

In one issue, she addressed these questions: "Have you lost the enthusiasm that kept you going last Fall? Is the indifference of the choir parents pulling you down? Are the children becoming careless? Is that little trouble maker getting the best of you? Doesn't the church appreciate you? Do you wish you could drop the whole business?" Her responses must surely have rekindled the enthusiasm for the most weary director. The *Letters* also included articles from well-known persons in the field of church music.

In 1951, Ruth launched a program of summer seminars. From these grew local chapters of the Choristers Guild.

Ruth and Leslie Jacobs moved to Memphis, Tennessee, to work at the First Methodist Church. While there, the Choristers Guild was chartered

---

10. Jacobs, *The Successful Choir*.
11. Jacobs, *The Successful Choir*.

as a corporation, with a formal organization of board of directors and members. Ruth became president and her husband secretary-treasurer.

Then came years of evolving the vision for the Guild and with it the necessity to raise money to realize the vision. Membership had grown from 125 to almost 900 by 1954. There was a dream of a Children's Choir Center with a chapel, library, printing press, and dormitory, but first there came the problem of raising enough money to buy a typewriter and pay for occasional secretarial help.

Ruth and Leslie had been doing all the work of editing and mailing the letters, and then absorbing the deficit at year's end. With incorporation, annual donors could become members and have a voice in management. To encourage memberships, she wrote in the September 1954 *Letters*:

> The children's choir represents a tremendous character influence. It works with two of the greatest powers known: religion and music. It works through the strongest moral force known to society—the Christian church.

Ruth's health was affected by the humid climate of Memphis. In the fall of 1954, the Jacobs moved to Santa Barbara, California, where Leslie was called to the First Methodist Church. Ruth spent about three months each year lecturing and conducting seminars and festivals.

In 1956, Leslie resigned his work with the First Methodist Church to become executive director of the Guild. "He was the first full-time, paid employee and the creation of this position was a momentous step in the history of the Guild. With Leslie handling the administrative work, Ruth was left free to do the creative work for the Guild."[12]

In 1958, Ruth launched a program known as The Brotherhood of Song to provide Guild memberships for groups overseas, particularly in the mission fields. Children's choirs in the United States raised money to pay for the memberships. Ruth urged American children to correspond with children in the overseas choirs.

The merits of muslin

John T. Burke, executive director of the Choristers Guild from 1978, was a former colleague of Ruth's in the ministry of music at First Congregational Church, Los Angeles. In the May 1978 *Choristers Guild Letters* he wrote of his regard for her:

> Very early in our association, I was aware of Ruth Jacob's marvelous gifts, not only musically, but personally. Her delightful sense of

---

12. Ball, p. 65.

humor, her quiet yet effective ways, her ingratiating smile, and the warmth of her spirit were infectious. Her dedication to children was all-consuming.[13]

Along with her work in the local churches and her demands from many groups across the country, Ruth managed a home. Her own family appreciated these same qualities that made her loved and respected professionally, and they were aware also of other gifts.

Her sister-in-law, Corrine Krehbiel, wrote of Ruth's role as "auntie" to her seven nieces and nephews. "Ruth loved to sew, and she could have made a career in costumes. In depression time, she was pushing the merits of plain muslin. She was indeed a many talented woman. She was a good mother of [Joan Hardy], an adopted daughter."[14]

On April 30, 1960, just as she was about to conduct a large festival chorus of boys and girls in Shawnee, Oklahoma, Ruth died of a heart attack. Her last words were to the children as she admonished them to "be very quiet deep down inside" as they prepared to sing.[15] She had always taught that performing music should be a worship experience for the performer and the listener. She died while worshiping.

The Choristers Guild is still an active organization. Membership has grown from over 1,800 at the time of her death to nearly 10,000 at present. There are over fifty chapters of the Guild, and the *Letters* are still providing aid and encouragement to choir directors around the world. Clinics and festivals remain professional highlights for church musicians. Another of the purposes of the Choristers Guild has been to make new, good music available. The vision of a Center had not yet materialized, but that, too, could still happen.

Ruth Krehbiel Jacobs was one of the talented people who left the General Conference Mennonite Church to serve in other denominations. Nevertheless, the Mennonite churches have benefited from her wider ministry as choir directors have made use of her talent. The children's choirs that have been developed because of her special skills and encouragement have enhanced the worship experiences in many of our churches.

---

13. *The Mennonite*, p. 7.
14. A letter from Corrine Krehbiel, March 1984.
15. Interview with Janeal Krehbiel, May 1985; she is a member of the national board of directors of the Choristers Guild.

Honora Becker: We remember her warmth and energy, the beauty of her reading voice, the expressiveness of her hands, and the stateliness of her bearing.

23.
Scholar of Life and the Human Spirit

Honora Elizabeth Becker
1899—1982

Honora Becker may have thought that her claim to fame was that as a child she had been admired by an Indian chief. Those who knew her as a Bethel College professor thought of her as an inspired teacher of literature.

English china by way of Russia

Honora cherished an heirloom that had been given as a wedding present to her grandmother in Russia. On the dining room wall in her apartment in North Newton, Honora had hung the Pegasus plate. It was of English china, brown with a gold border showing Pegasus, the Greek flying horse, repeated five times around the border; in the center were a lion and a lioness among the grasses. Honora could not remember a time when her family had not owned the Pegasus plates.

Her parents, Peter J. and Maria Boese Becker, were born in Russia, Maria in the village of Rueckenau in the Molotschna. Maria came with her family to York, Nebraska, in 1878 when she was thirteen. Her mother died during the preparations for emigrating, so Maria, the oldest daughter, mothered the other four children. They brought with them to America a set of plates that had been her mother's wedding dishes. It had been one of the plates that the Boese children set out on Christmas Eve to be filled with goodies by *Naet Klaus*. When Maria and Peter married, her father gave her four of the Pegasus plates, just enough for the four children she was to have.

"I was so proud when Father gave me the plates," Maria said. "They were all we had, so we used them every day. They were so beautiful. Even if there was only simple food in them, the beauty fed our eyes."[1]

Fired with the pioneering spirit, the Beckers had moved from Nebraska to Idaho, but that move proved disappointing. The irrigation scheme promised by the development company failed to materialize, so they moved to a farm near Junction City, Oregon. It was here that Honora was born on December 10, 1899, "an afterthought" to Marie, Agatha Ida, and Martin.

The family prospered in Oregon, but Peter needed a drier climate. They moved to the Oklahoma Territory in 1903. Peter started a hardware, harness, and wagon business in Gotebo.[2]

Braids for an Indian chief

"All you need to do is look at the pictures of Dodge City, and you'll have a pretty good picture of Gotebo," Honora said. Both the settlers and the Indians traded at her father's store. This was a "cowboy and Indian" community, and the Indians were interested particularly in saddles and horses, so her father also became a horse trader. All the children learned to ride. Honora's hometown was named after Kiowa Indian Chief Gotebo.

One of her most treasured memories was her meeting with Chief Gotebo. It was the custom of the community for everyone to go to town on Saturday afternoon. Honora's mother had dressed her three-year-old in a new red-checked gingham dress and braided her dark hair, fastening a red bow on each side of her head and one on the end of each braid. Maria took her down to the store and her father lifted her up to sit on the counter. The old chief had come in, an imposing sight in his sombrero and long braids.

Her father said to Chief Gotebo, "Come see my papoosie."

The old chief stood and looked at Honora. "All at once here he comes, right up to me, picks up one of my braids and holds it out just as long as it will go and he clicks his tongue. I'd been admired by an Indian chief."

The Indians were all around. "People accepted them as necessary, not as evil, but necessary, a part of the life there. But as far as appreciating them particularly, no. It is here where I have such a feeling of appreciation for my parents because my father never exploited an Indian. He just wouldn't. He dealt with them just as honestly and straightforwardly as he did with any white man. And this was not true of all the businessmen."

---

1. From the Honora Becker collection, Box 147-2; a story written by Honora about her mother; in the Mennonite Library and Archives, North Newton, Kansas.
2. Interview with Honora Becker by Keith Sprunger, July 18, 1972, tape 120; in the MLA.

When the Indians came to town, they set up camp in a little natural park across the railroad tracks. The Beckers living three blocks away could hear the tom-toms and dancing during the powwows. There was no rest from the hi-yi-yi-yi, hi-yi-yi-yi. Her mother took the younger children to visit the camp, and they were soon playing with the Indian children while their mother greeted the women in the tepees.

Reading a lot in Gotebo

When the Beckers first moved to Gotebo, they lived in a small shack until they could build a house. A flood came up suddenly and the shack was filled with water. Honora's memory of the flood was seeing her mother's freshly baked *zwieback* floating in the water in the kitchen. Her father advanced his plan to build a substantial house with outbuildings and a corral for horses. The town grew. When it reached a census of over one thousand, the day was properly celebrated at school.

Gotebo had its cultural programs. There was the *chautauqua* with lectures, music, and dramatic readings. There were a motion picture house and a skating rink. The school system provided a high quality education for which she was to be grateful as she learned more about educational systems.

Many families in the town were interested in cultural affairs. Even so, Honora thought that the Beckers were probably the "readingest" family in town. Her father subscribed to *Germania* and another paper, *Hausfrau*, which was passed around among her mother's friends.

Prestige in the Presbyterian church

The Dutch Reformed Church was close by and the pastor and his family became good friends with the Beckers. When the Mennonites started the Ebenezer church, the Beckers joined there. A church was eventually built a few miles out in the country.

Henry Riesen, one of the leaders, earned his living with his grocery store, but he had an interest in the preaching ministry. He started a German school that Honora attended during the summers. Riesen was a graduate of Bethel College, and highly respected by the Beckers. Later, because of her regard for Riesen, Maria asked Honora to promise to spend a year at Bethel College before she finished her college work.

There were other churches in Gotebo.

> Gotebo was churched to death. The elite of Gotebo would go to the Presbyterian. So it did have a kind of prestige over there. I remember one very exciting young minister they had by the name of McClain.

He was a young Scotsman and he had a delightful brogue and it was just a joy to listen to him. At least as a kid I just sat and marveled at him. They had an awful time to keep me being a Mennonite about that time.

Hard to be a Mennonite

Honora was fourteen when World War I came along. Immediately, the community became very patriotic. Being a Mennonite in Oklahoma made one a marked person. She felt persecution in the school, with two strikes against her: she was German and she was Mennonite. Ostracized from the high school play, she felt like an outsider.

Her sister's fiance, Adolph Wagner, although not raised a Mennonite, had joined the church and had been drafted as a conscientious objector. He was sent to a camp where he was cruelly treated.

Because of the breakdown of her father's health, her parents sold the store in Gotebo and moved to Cordell to live on Adolph Wagner's farm. The three other children were living and working in that area, so the family center changed to Cordell. They joined the Sicar Mennonite Church during this period. Honora was encouraged by her high school principal to stay behind in Gotebo to finish school. She took the teacher's exam after graduation and taught in an elementary school near Cordell.

War hysteria against the Mennonites was even more prevalent in Cordell than in Gotebo. She hated to be on the street, and heard often from her former friends, "Oh, Honora, I wish you weren't Mennonite."

But the war ended. "The day I started teaching was the day that we heard the peace whistles from Cordell." Adolph Wagner was released from Fort Leavenworth prison and married her sister Marie. Her brother returned from his noncombatant assignment in the medical corps just before her father died in 1919.

Honora taught in two different schools between 1919 and 1923, taking summer school courses at Western Oklahoma Christian College in Cordell and Southwestern Teachers College in Weatherford.

Going reluctantly to Bethel

By that time Honora had finished three years of college. How could she keep her promise to her mother to attend Bethel College for one year? On exploring the possibility of graduating from Bethel, she was disappointed to find that by the move she would lose credits; the required education courses for Kansas and Oklahoma were different and she would be short senior standing by a few hours.

Reluctantly, she promised her mother she would go to Bethel but she would stay for just one semester. However, before school opened for the second semester, Dr. P. J. Wedel, the registrar, discovered that she could more easily graduate with a history major than with an English major.

"That suited me fine! I loved history, especially the philosophy presented by Professor Moyer."

The only hurdles to be overcome were the education requirements and a few missing hours for graduation. Dr. Thierstein, head of the Education Department, promised to correspond with the State Department of Education concerning her case. Her experience at this small church college had been so positive that she enrolled for the second semester. The embarrassment of eating crow, as she explained why she was not leaving, was alleviated by the welcome she received from her classmates.

Finding a Bethel friend in Colorado

When Professor Moyer became too ill to meet his classes, she took over an academy class and a college class in history for him. This experience convinced her that she did really want to teach at the secondary level and eventually in a college. Also because of this teaching experience, the State Department gave her the missing credits she needed in education, and these gave her enough credits for graduation.

Honora taught for two years at Attica High School, "wonderful two years!" She needed more training to direct high school plays, so she took work at Bethany College. Then Abbyville High School for three years, and a new challenge: she decided to get a graduate degree in English.

Colorado University was the ideal place with its pleasant setting and excellent English department. She attended summers while teaching at Buhler High School. "Also imagine the satisfaction of working [at Colorado University] one summer under a former Bethel English professor, Dr. E. E. Leisy, then an international scholar in American literature."[3]

She received her master's degree in 1938. Dr. J. E. Linscheid, head of the Department of English at Bethel, asked her to teach for him the summer of 1939 while he went to Mayo Clinic for tests. She was glad to help him out, and she welcomed the opportunity to try college teaching. When Dr. Linscheid died suddenly in late August, she was invited to teach at Bethel for the next year. This invitation extended until the close of the school year of 1968, when she retired.

Those twenty-nine years were filled with the activities of a busy campus. She spoke of personal triumphs and defeats. Certainly she must have felt the support of the student community, although she was aware of

---

3. Honora E. Becker, "An Alumna Confesses," *Bethel College Bulletin*, May 1969.

a change in student attitude in general during the late '60s, when many students showed resentment of administrative authority.

Many non-English majors continued to enroll in at least one of Miss Becker's classes; she was well known for her Shakespeare courses. The Shakespeare oak tree was planted near the Administration Building in 1964 by her Shakespeare Comedy class, as much to honor Honora as to honor the Bard's 400th birthday. In 1953, Miss Becker's students and alumni collected funds for her to go to England for the coronation of Queen Elizabeth, and again in 1968 as a retirement gift. She had never had a sabbatical.

Quite a number of her students looked to her as mentor. Tina Block Ediger said, "I majored in English because she was the teacher. Another model for me to emulate. You don't have to be a dried-up person. She made me as an older student feel that I had something to contribute."

Anna Kreider Juhnke wrote, "We remember her warmth and energy, the beauty of her reading voice, the expressiveness of her hands, and the stateliness of her bearing. . . . During her last ten years at Bethel, Miss Becker's English majors received five national fellowships—Woodrow Wilson, Rockefeller, and Danforth. During that decade thirty-two of her students were working on advanced degrees or had completed them."[4]

Clowning and fishing and the lady's dog

Phyllis Bixler, a colleague who accompanied her on the second trip to England, commented on her sense of humor, especially her ability to laugh at herself. For one of the faculty stunt nights, Honora, Phyllis, and Christine Miller, *the* English department, sang Gilbert and Sullivan's "Three Little Maids from School Are We," and convulsed the audience with their performance. There was the tall and stately Honora with her crown of white hair, between her less tall and stately colleagues; most people had not realized that she enjoyed clowning.

There are pictures in Honora's collection that show her in light-hearted moods. There is one of Honora displaying her catch from a fishing party. Another is of Honora dressed as a nun, or perhaps the wife of Bath from Chaucer's *Canterbury Tales*.

Always the reader, for many years she was chairperson of the literature committee of the Bethel College Church. She was active in Delta Kappa Gamma, the honor society for women teachers. Organizations in the area called on her often for talks on Shakespeare or England or for poetry readings.

---

4. The tribute was read at her funeral; in the Honora E. Becker Collection, Box 147, MLA.

In 1942, Honora moved with her mother to Kliewer Home on the college campus. Here she was housemother to eight or ten college women living there when the house was a dormitory. Until her death in 1960 at the age of ninety-five, Maria Becker lived with her daughter, a period of twenty-two years. Mrs. Becker was blind and hard of hearing in her later years and was both a joy and a concern to Honora. Theirs was a shared life of love and helpfulness.

A delight to both women was Mupsie, a little Pekingese, who saw that Honora got her exercise. Honora's nephew said that Mupsie was a woman's dog. He snapped at boys and men.

Kudos and ovations

During Honora's teaching career, she wrote no scholarly articles. All her energy went into her teaching, and she carried heavy teaching loads in literature and sometimes in English composition. She was promoted to full professorship in 1959; on her retirement in 1968, she became Professor Emeritus. The Bethel College Distinguished Alumna award was presented in 1970, an honorary doctorate by Bethel College in 1972.

At a convocation honoring her retirement she said,

> When you've studied literary creativity, you've studied life. It's thinking, feeling, experiencing; it's man's nature and the working of God in the ways of man. It encompasses all the other disciplines. . . . English is always a foundation upon which to build . . . as it is aimed at enriching the human spirit.

Orville Voth, then president of Bethel College, said, "To me you have always represented the highest in scholarship and the personification of what I thought Bethel College ought to be." After she had given her convocation talk, the student body responded with a standing ovation.[5]

Mary and Martha to the faculty

Retirement brought its compensations. She had more time to read and to enjoy the Kliewer flower garden that her mother had nurtured. She learned to play games and spend evenings with friends rather than with student papers. She helped her friend, Edna Ramseyer Kaufman, with the Thursday faculty coffees, playing the Mary-Martha role as she helped in the kitchen and at the same time enjoyed conversations with the faculty. What she missed was the contact with the students who used to come to her office for personal and academic discussions.

---

5. Since then, standing ovations have become more common; this was the first one that I, a long-time teacher at Bethel, had witnessed.

In 1976, she moved from her apartment to a room at the Bethel Home for the Aged. She regretted that she could not walk across the street to the church; she regretted that the residents of the Home did not play her kind of games—she thought dominoes were boring. But in this community, too, she was loved by the people around her. She died April 17, 1982, survived only by a sister-in-law and a number of nephews.

At her memorial service, one of her nephews reminisced about how she came to be called Honora. She had been named Elizabeth, but her brother and the family called her Honey. Of course, she couldn't go through life as Honey, so she chose the name Honora. When her nephews came along, they couldn't pronounce that name, so they called her Tante No. And that was how she was known to her family. Honora seemed a remarkably suitable name.

Honora was shaped by her appreciation for her roots (symbolized by the Pegasus plate), her Oklahoma pioneering youth, her exposure to literature and learning, her work with young people, and her involvement in the church. She emerged as a gracious, honorable, Christian gentlewoman.

24.
Shattered but Not Destroyed

Margarethe Willms Rempel
1901—

Margarethe Rempel told herself that she would write her life story sometime when she was lonely, bored, or unemployed; she hoped that time would never come. Then her husband convinced her that she should tell her children how the Lord had so wonderfully guided her through a life shattered but not destroyed by the tragedy of the Russian Red-White Civil War.

Appropriately, N. N. Driedger had used Psalm 77 as the theme for his sermon celebrating the Rempel's golden wedding. Their lives had gone full circle from "Will the Lord forever discard us, will he never be kind again?" to "Thou wast a God of wonders, thou didst show the world thy strength, rescuing thy people by thy power."[1]

A stubborn child turned friendly

Margarethe Willms was born in Tiegenhagen in the Ukraine to Frank and Anna Rempel Willms. Her arrival on January 1, 1901, according to the Gregorian calendar (January 14 by the Julian reckoning), was an inconvenience to her ten brothers and sisters who had to change their plans for celebrating the day.

Perhaps because of some physical distress, she became a stubborn,

---

1. Margarethe Willms Rempel, *Grandma Reminisces*; in the Mennonite Library and Archives, North Newton, Kansas.

Margarethe Rempel: The girls bid each other tearful good-byes and planned a reunion for ten years later. "It never occurred to us that one of us would not be alive."

willful child. Her father believed in not sparing the rod, to which Margarethe reacted with tears and her mother with heartache. When she was about four, she reports, "I finally outgrew this stubborn stage. On observing my image in the mirror, it dawned on me that a friendly face is more attractive." She did not become a saint, but that lesson stayed with her for life.

She and her brother Peter invented games that they played endlessly. She sewed rags into small sacks that were filled with dirt "grain." Peter rigged up an empty spool for a pulley on a tree branch to haul these up for a game of "miller." They could not go barefoot until after the storks had returned from the south, about March 17.

Each village had one pair of storks whose return was greeted by the youngsters with *Storch, Storch, Bester, bring mir eine Schwester.* ("Stork, stork, dearest, bring me a sister," or brother.) Theirs was a pleasant childhood, with many toys, in a comfortably prosperous family.

Education better than a dowry

In 1911, her parents moved to a new work as houseparents in the home for the aged about ten miles away, hiring a couple to keep house for the younger children in Tiegenhagen. Each Saturday afternoon after school, the younger children packed their suitcases and homework for a weekend with their parents in the *Altenheim.*

For an hour they drove through treeless grain fields, often not meeting another traveler on the road. The love-hungry residents of the Altenheim showered the children with many little deeds and gifts. Old hunchback Jacob shined their shoes; an old lady inquired if she could mend their socks. Altenheim was a place "where so much love was shown me and where I could have passed on more love."

Margarethe completed ten grades of schooling in eight years at a time when girls ordinarily received only six years. Schooling was not thought necessary for a woman's role as homemaker. Brothers might have three more years in the secondary school.

Margarethe spent three years at Ohrloff, a boarding school attended by daughters of the well-to-do. She received her tenth grade diploma in 1916, completing a four-year course in three years. Bidding each other tearful good-byes, she and her friends planned a reunion for 1920, joking that they would leave their husbands and children at home.

> Next to God I thank my parents for these years. My dowry was much leaner and skimpier than that of my sisters because I married at a time when there was little available—all shops and stores were

empty, as were our chests and cupboards in our homes. But the money that my parents gave for schooling is worth more than any dowry of material things. This was a treasure that not even the roughest bandits or thieves could take from me.

Freed from the Reds by the Germans

World War I had begun during her first year at the school. Germany was the enemy. The war brought changes to the comfortable life of the community. Staple foods became scarce, as well as matches, coffee, writing paper, thread, soap, and yard goods. Housewives turned to sugar cane for sugar, *pripps* (roasted rye) for coffee, silkworms for thread, and sheep for wool.

The church conference decided that a medical corps should be organized, but then the Russians became suspicious that the German-speaking Mennonites might be helping the Germans at the front and threatened to evacuate all Mennonite men to Siberia. By the beginning of the third year of the war, Mennonite men, including her brothers and uncles, some as old as forty, were being drafted to serve in the medical corps or to work in the forests.

After her graduation, Margarethe returned to Tiegenhagen. Her sister Lena kept house for the family, and there were good times when they visited with relatives in Halbstadt, four miles away, and the relatives came to help with the harvest.

Margarethe admired her teacher uncle who could talk about many topics other than harvesting. She decided that she did not want to marry a farmer. She wanted more from life than conversation about farming. Still, her brothers and sisters teased, "Margaret, some day you'll be a foolish farmer's wife."

The czar in Petersburg was dethroned in 1917. The Russian army split into two factions, the Whites and the Reds, with the Reds controlling the Ukraine. The Mennonite community was overjoyed when the German army came to the Ukraine to liberate it from the Reds. In some cases, the Mennonites assisted the Germans in arresting Bolshevik sympathizers.[2]

The time for celebration was, however, short. Germany was losing the battle on the French front and had to withdraw from the Ukraine. The Mennonites were to pay dearly for their collaboration. Before the Germans withdrew, brigands organized and robbed various large, isolated estates. The farm owners often left everything to flee to the safety of the villages.

2. Frank H. Epp, *Mennonites in Canada, 1920-1940* (Scottdale, Pennsylvania: Herald Press, 1982), p. 145.

Escape routes blocked

After the czar was dethroned, the men started to return to the villages. Abram Rempel, a school teacher from Paulsheim, returned from forestry service in the Crimea and was given a school in Tiegenhagen. He came to board at the Willms home. He was twenty-two and Margarethe sixteen, and they enjoyed each other's company, reading and doing puzzles together.

But when he became seriously interested in her, she withdrew. "I was simply too young for a serious relationship and wanted to enjoy my youth without any strings attached." Their warm friendship became a strained and aloof tolerance of each other.

Meanwhile, life was becoming more and more uncertain, with robberies and murders being commonplace. "A faction in the Mennonite Brethren Church understood this time of revolution and overthrow of the government as an opportunity to evangelize the Russian populace." They held tent meetings, and when they came to her village, she "decided to make Christ Lord and Master of my life. . . . This decision I have never regretted."

She and two of her brothers joined catechism classes and were baptized in the Halbstadt church in the spring of 1918 by Bishop Klassen (who died in exile in 1941).[3] Other leaders were killed by Nestor Machno's hordes.

By this time, the German military had withdrawn, leaving the village without protection. A vigilante group of younger men was formed, but they were sent to the front, about twenty miles away, to control the bandits. Their defense was ineffective, and the Tiegenhagen villagers prepared to evacuate. One night they all packed the bare essentials into wagons and prepared to flee to other villages. On that night, she and Abram Rempel came to a decision. Over a period of time she had changed her mind about him.

> On a pitch dark February night under open skies, we became engaged and immediately took leave of each other. Without musical fanfare, only the foot soldiers marching and sound of horses' hooves in deep mud, interrupted occasionally by the drivers' commands, marked the occasion. Thus, we went into the unknown—I on foot in one direction and he as driver of the neighbor's wagon in another.

Finding their escape routes blocked, everyone returned the next day, realizing that flight was worse than trying to defend their homes.

---

3. "Halbstadt Mennonite Church," *The Mennonite Encyclopedia*.

Margarethe's Red Sea

Margarethe described the year 1919 as "my red sea." Her parents were still working at the Altenheim and her older brothers and sisters were in their own homes or at the war front. Her brother Jacob and she were the only ones at their home in Tiegenhagen.

The villagers were living in good homes. Politically, they leaned toward the Germans and the White Army. The revolutionary Reds eyed their attractive houses. Some of the Russian peasants had been exploited by the well-to-do Mennonite farmers, so they were ready to join the brigands looting the countryside. The houses had been searched many times for weapons, clothing, and jewelry. The villagers had come to the point where they left the rooms in disarray so that the robbers could see that the place had already been searched thoroughly.

Some time earlier, Margarethe had given small pieces of jewelry to a cousin to keep for her, so when a looter had come demanding jewelry, she had been able to say that she had nothing to give him. "He placed me against the wall, stepped back three paces, aimed his revolver at my forehead and counted. I screamed and covered my eyes with my hands. I was afraid to die in this manner and begged him to spare my life. Having counted to three he lowered his gun and stuck it into his pocket."

Often her brother Jacob was forced to flee as bands of lawless robbers rode through searching for anyone who might be hiding. One day Jacob was caught and driven through the streets. They slashed him badly with their swords, but he was saved by the four shirts he was wearing, all that he owned. Jacob was taken to the hospital at Halbstadt.

Margarethe had been staying with a neighbor, but she decided to go home. She felt safe because she had Russian servants and a cousin staying with her.

> This was the scene at our house when I arrived at home. Just as I entered the house a band of such plunderers turned into our yard, arriving from the neighboring village of Blumenort. Actually, the band consisted of two older and three younger ones. After they had thoroughly searched the house again before our very eyes and while they were having a whispered conference among themselves, my cousin suggested to me in German, that I go hide myself. But how can you go into hiding when five pairs of eyes are focused on you? In the next moment, I was dragged by force into my brother's room and what proceeded to occur there defies all human description! . . . I experienced then that a human being can verily become a beast! How forsaken I was! In the meantime, the Russian servant lady with the

baby entered and upon becoming aware of what was happening she hurriedly made an about-turn, and whimpered, "My God! Lady, what's going on here!" With all the strength I could muster, I defended myself, but what is the strength of an eighteen-year-old girl compared to five manpower?

Finally, she broke loose and ran until she arrived at the schoolhouse where her fiance and another teacher were living. When they asked what happened, she could not speak, and only continued sobbing. "To speak or write about sex at that time was taboo!" They understood and got her to the hospital. She learned later that she was one of many young and older women who had been sexually attacked by Machno's raiders during two successive winters. At least 647 were killed in this civil war.

She concealed from her parents as much as she could the fears she had because she did not want them to give up their work at the Altenheim where they were safer. "The circumstances demanded courage and bravery."

An early engagement

The tenseness eased somewhat when the bands of looters fled from the area, but then thousands of soldiers began coming through the village, authentic soldiers from northern Russia, looking for beds, or even standing space at night, moving on in the morning. They were quiet and mannerly men, worn out from the war. They were hungry, cold, and lice-infested. The lice spread epidemics of typhoid fever, the Spanish grippe, and finally malaria. The village lost more lives from typhus than from the bandits.

Meanwhile, in 1920, a study committee had been sent to Germany and America to find a place willing to accept the Mennonites. "Russia was suddenly very poor. Even in our rich area, nothing was now available. While my brothers were still in the Crimea, most of our land was taken from us. Horses were scarce and the machinery was old." The government demanded more of the grain, so seed, too, was scarce. The people had grown tired, longing for happy times again.

Margarethe and Abram decided to announce their engagement early, partly to save her from the attention of the soldiers who were billeted in the village. Her parents came from the Altenheim and a simple announcement was made. Her father offered a short prayer and they were engaged.

When Abram came to visit her on the following Sunday, "We looked at each other rather shyly, because we hadn't expected to be engaged so suddenly." They waited a year to be married because she was not yet twenty.

The aforementioned school reunion took place in 1920. Times had changed drastically since the happy time of graduation. One girl had died. "We thought of everything in our plans, but it had never occurred to us that perhaps one of us would not be alive." They had a wonderful day at Margarethe's house, and she announced her engagement and received their congratulations. Everybody tried on the gold ring that Abram had somehow saved for the occasion.

They were married in May 1921. Abram wore his good navy blue suit, only three years old, his best white shirt out of five he owned, and his polished shoes. Margarethe wore a dress made from lace remnants, white stockings knit by a lady from the Altenheim, white shoes made by a German soldier and a borrowed wedding veil. The young people decorated the barns with garlands from the Altenheim, but only flowers were in abundance. Her wedding gifts were items people could spare from what they had: a few plates from a set, a tablecloth or a towel. "We felt very rich, because the couples that married before and after us didn't receive any wedding gifts at all."

The happy day closed with sadness. Three armed soldiers arrived to arrest her uncle and three of her husband's friends. They were not released until weeks later.

Margarethe and Abram moved into a room in her parents' home. She and Rosa, the Russian maid, cooked for her three brothers, Abram, and a German soldier. (Her parents were still managing the Altenheim.) Margarethe had a note of praise for Rosa, who received only room and board for her work.

Fateful hospitality to a general

The year of her marriage was also the year of her father's death. In January 1920, Franz and Anna Willms had given lodging at the Altenheim to General Akimow, a general of the White Army. The general and his wife were hiding out until the White Army could topple the Red. That spring when the Whites again dispersed the Reds, Akimow donned his general's uniform and reported to the White Army. He escaped from Russia, never to be seen again.

When the Reds returned, the fact that her father had given shelter to their enemy had fateful consequences. The Red Army took over the administration of the Altenheim, and the Willms returned to Tiegenhagen. In October 1921, Franz Willms was arrested and taken away to be tried for hiding General Akimow. He and four others were shot near the Halbstadt graveyard. The details are cloudy, but probably other Russians in the community were afraid that if he were interrogated further, he might reveal their names as those who had also associated with General Akimow.

"When first the news of her husband's fate was broken to [my mother], she uttered a terrible cry of anguish and in her grief implored: 'O, God, why this way,' but from then on she accepted her lot." Anna Willms was to be a widow for almost nineteen years.

Years of hunger and cold

During the first year of Margarethe and Abram's marriage, there was no harvest. This was the first of the "hunger years." They tried grinding corn to make some kind of bread, and they tried eating barley with the hulls left on. "Whenever two or three people gathered, we talked of having nice white bread or even a piece of meat, but we had nothing."

The Russians were willing to eat cats, but the Mennonites, no! They were glad to eat horse meat, and when one came into the village for sale, they purchased it and made it into sausage. The Mennonites wrote for help to anyone they knew in America. "We found an old photo and an address from Hillsboro, Kansas. We wrote to them and in three months time received a package of flour, sugar, rice, and lard. It tasted real good at Easter with the horse meat."

In the fall, help came from Mennonite Central Committee, but it was for people worse off than her family. For the starving, there was one meal a day from the American kitchen. "But we cooked borscht from a rhubarb-like plant. We ate this for days, no, not days, but months."

Fuel was as scarce as food. "But God provided for us as he did for Elijah. Nothing had grown any better than a sort of tumbleweed that the wind blew into the hedges. This was hauled home. It burnt good, but was not the best of heat. But thank God, we got through with it."

In August of 1922, the first baby, Marianne, was born. A bedspread was cut up for baby blankets and diapers were made from another spread. Margarethe traded the skirt of her wedding gown for a petticoat and made nighties out of it. The following year, parcels came from America. Everyone in the village received some article of clothing. They didn't even want to wear these clothes because they were brand new and they wanted to save them for Sunday, but they didn't have anything else to wear.

Shaving clean in Ontario

In 1922, Lenin ordered all teachers who were ministers to be laid off. Because of this edict, a vacancy occurred at Paulsheim and Abram Rempel was offered the position at his old school. Life was a bit easier there when fruit became available from the orchards.

Many people were leaving for Canada. Margarethe and Abram waited a long time for their passports, but finally their turn to leave came in 1925. They held an auction sale to dispose of the few possessions they could not take along. She baked and toasted *zwieback* for the journey.

They traveled with her sister Lena and husband Jacob Epp, Abram's sister Lena and husband Gerhard Neufeld, Margarethe's three brothers, and her mother. David Toews in Canada arranged credit financing with the Canadian Pacific Railroad, enabling them to be admitted to Canada. In Russia, B. B. Janz, taking great personal risk, had arranged for their passports.

Their group left in November 1925 and arrived in Ontario in December, to be greeted by friends and relatives who had emigrated before. Margarethe was impressed first of all by the new look of the men. "It astonished us to see these formerly bearded men, now clean shaven.... However, we soon got accustomed to the clean-shaven Canadians and all our men soon followed their example."

They were eager to adapt to their new country. The Rempels were among the 3,772 Russian Mennonites who entered Canada in 1925. After 1926 very few were allowed to leave Russia.[4]

Thirteen of the group were allowed to stay in Waterloo, while the others proceeded to Manitoba. " 'Have you work?' was the first English sentence we learned from our friends, who themselves had had a hard time finding work. We also learned to 'spell' our names, which was new to us."

The first job for the two former teachers was shoveling coal at a railway station. Later Abram was able to find better work at a furniture factory for good wages for those times. When scarlet fever hit the children, that was the end of job hunting for the still unemployed. The town provided them with free groceries sent to their home during this time. "What a compassionate government to take such good care of its new arrivals."

Spring came, and the men still waited for work. "Even though playing crokinole had been a good pastime, they realized they could not make their living at it," she commented wryly. Abram's sister Lena and her husband Gerhard had found a job with a farmer, Tillman Martin, and he dropped off fruit and milk weekly. "O God, forgive us for not having been thankful enough for that either. How our children ate apples."

4. Epp, p. 178.

Learning English while drying dishes

The Epps and Rempels were offered a farm on Pelee Island, out in the middle of Lake Erie just south of Leamington. They moved there with her mother and brother Peter. The crops failed that first year, but they stayed on for six years. A few other Mennonite families were living on Pelee Island when they arrived and others joined them until there were twenty families.

In 1932, her husband was chosen and ordained for the ministry. Rudy, Helen, and Arthur were born there. All of the women had to help their farmer husbands in the fields. "Many a tear flowed silently in the tobacco field. One of our friends later said, 'I not only cried, but screamed.' "

In 1931, the Rempels decided to move to Wheatley to take over a small dairy farm. Ernest was born there, and Margarethe's mother came to live with them to help out and to spend her last years. During World War II, they again learned to be thrifty, or more so. The Mennonites experienced some difficulty with the community, such as attempts to ban the German worship services and vandalism to the church. Toward the end of the war, they found a farm of their own and moved in shortly before Harry was born. She was forty-two.

"We accepted every child with love. And how could it have been otherwise because each time a new baby arrived its father would say, 'Another beautiful baby.' "

She continued her struggle to learn English. When young Helen protested about drying dishes, Margarethe said, "Come, while we do dishes, I'll spell some words that you dictate to me." And so they both learned English.

Abram, although trained to be a teacher, enjoyed being a farmer. He accepted his call to the ministry with enthusiasm and devoted as much time as he could to serving the congregation. "He thrived on visiting and taking active part in church conferences. The United Mennonite Education Institute is largely the result of his foresight and drive."

They sold the farm to Ernie and moved to a house in Leamington about 1967. Abram suffered from heart trouble and had a pacemaker installed in 1971. He died in May 1972. As a widow, she learned to rely on her seven children and her twenty-three grandchildren.

At this writing, Margarethe continues to live in the Pickwick Apartments adjacent to the Leamington Mennonite Home. Alert and articulate, she goes to the Home to read to those her age or younger. Her grandson says that she is very independent. Rather than ask her daughter who lives nearby to drive her downtown, she takes public transportation to go to the bank.

She is still more comfortable with the German language, but because her grandchildren understand English better, she writes to them in English. Margarethe is very interested in keeping in touch with her grandchildren, writing to them and helping out with unexpected gifts. Besides *Grandma Remembers*, she had written an article earlier about life on Pelee Island for *Der Herald*, and recently "A Day in the Pickwick Apartments" for *Der Bote*:[5]

> Old age has arrived, my walk is getting more unsteady, my memory is failing, my face is wrinkled with folds. But I am not ashamed of these folds for they are symptoms of an honest fight. . . . My life has had many difficult moments, but this one thing I do, forgetting those things which are behind and reaching forth unto those things which are before.

---

5. An interview with Larry Cornies, July 1984.

25.
Saying Yes to Need

Caroline Banwar Theodore
1901—1952

When Dr. Caroline was practicing medicine in her private clinic in Champa, India, a patient came from Korba, twenty-five miles to the north, with an ulcer on his left cheek that was already gangrenous. Although fully certified in nursing and midwifery, Caroline hardly had the qualifications to perform the surgery needed to save the man's life. But she could not say no to a need.

So Caroline, assisted by her doctor husband, decided to take the risk of removing the cheek and lower jaw. The patient survived.

This dramatic success opened doors for Dr. Caroline in Korba. The *rani* (queen) of Korba State often invited her family to stay in the palace guest house. In lieu of fees, the *rani* gave her the village of Banjari. Whatever the villagers owed to the queen in taxes was to go to Dr. Caroline. However, she did not take advantage of this largess. Helping when called on was in character for "Dr. Caro." Profiting from a situation was not.

Making a home in jungle country

Caroline Banwar was born on February 13, 1901, in Purulia in Old Bengal, part of which is now in the state of Bihar. Her parents, Joseph and Trophenia Bai, were evangelistic workers for the German Baptists.

When Caroline was two years old, Missionary P. A. Penner asked her mother and father to come to Champa to be house parents for the healthy

Caroline Theodore: She was the typical Indian woman both by look and by nature: simple, shy, soft-spoken, and serene.

children of patients being treated for leprosy (or Hansen's disease, as it is now known) and to help build a Christian community among the people with leprosy. Her mother became a Bible woman (working as an evangelist among the women), and both parents were to become respected mission workers. This was jungle country at the time, and the Banwars had to clear land for their home on the edge of Champa.

Caroline was the oldest with two sisters and five brothers. Her brother Puran and his wife Lili became church leaders in Sarguji; her sister Shanti became a doctor and her sister Rachel a headmistress at Funk Memorial School in Janjgir.[1]

First doctor in Champa dispensary

Caroline attended the mission primary school at Champa through fourth grade and then she was sent to the school for girls at Janjgir where Annie Funk was principal.[2] Her first schoolroom was a mud hut, but soon she was to move with her classmates to the new brick building. After completing her elementary education, Caroline attended the Bardsley Girls High School at Katni.

As the first secondary school matriculate from Champa, Caroline was encouraged by the Penners to become a doctor. The mission made it possible for her to attend the Christian Medical College for Women at Ludhiana. Immediately after graduation in 1924, Caroline came back to Champa to be the first doctor in the Champa dispensary. This was a year before Doctors Harvey and Ella Bauman arrived. The Baumans came to India as the first General Conference Mennonite medical missionaries.[3]

"There were no [doctors for people] nor hospitals when we arrived in Champa in November 1925. There were, however, two cow hospitals," Dr. Ella wrote, alluding to a fact of Hindu life at the time: the health of a sacred cow was more important than the health of a person.

The new mission hospital was opened about eight months after the arrival of the Baumans. They lived next door to the Banwars, and Dr. Ella became Caroline's friend and model. Caroline went to their home almost every evening after work. She became attached to their infant son Kenneth and taught him Hindi before he learned English.

---

1. Much information comes from her son, S. K. Theodore, chief medical officer at the Bharat Aluminium Co., Korba; from Dr. Ella Bauman, March 1984; William Walter, whose mother was raised in the Banwar and Penner households.
2. Annie Funk was to lose her life in the sinking of the *Titanic* in 1912; the school was then named for her.
3. "Dr. Caroline Banwar S. Theodore," *Missionary News and Notes*, June 1952, p. 2.

Wedding delayed an hour

Caroline's son Joe remembers her as a happy person, always smiling. She was a short woman, only four feet, ten inches tall, of dark complexion with *adivasi* or tribal features. William Walter thought of her as the typical Indian woman "both by look and by nature: simple, shy, soft-spoken, and serene. These qualities endeared her to all. She was 'Caro Didi' (sister) to those close to her whether Christian or non-Christian. At times, chiding, too. Even in anger, she always had a soft corner in her heart."

When Caroline was in her late twenties, she met Harold Theodore at a missionary conference. He came from a well-known Christian family and at the time was a teacher at Sagar. In June 1930, they were married in Champa before a large gathering of Christian and non-Christian friends. On the morning of her wedding day, she made an emergency call in the village. Because of a flash cloudburst, she could not return in time for the wedding and it was delayed by an hour.

End of the mission relationship

Dr. Caroline continued working on the staff of the Champa Christian Hospital while her husband was a salesman for a medical company. Their first child Sharat, to be known as Joe, was born in April 1931. Three other children were born later, but they did not survive infancy. The reason given for the deaths of the children was that she did not get enough rest during her pregnancies.

She stopped working for six months to be with her husband in Calcutta. In 1935, they returned to Champa and, persuaded by her husband, she left the mission to go into private practice. In 1937, Harold took a degree from King Edward's Medical School and the two worked together in Champa. The marriage was not always happy. Theodore was not a friend of the mission, and she, the obedient wife, felt that she must follow his wishes.

Her son Joe speaks of a happy childhood and of closeness to the Bauman children. He attended school at Jabalpur, a journey by train of a day and a night away from Champa. He played soccer two or three evenings a week and as a devoted mother who also enjoyed fun, Caroline traveled several times to see him play. When his father was in the army from 1942 to 1945, she never let him feel "that there was something missing."

Caroline wanted her son to become a doctor. She asked him to help her with her work and he assisted her from secondary school on. She did not know during her lifetime that he would eventually be able to attend the same medical college at Ludhiana from which she had graduated. When he started practicing, he found that because of her reputation, doors in Korba were open to him as they had been to her.

Underpaid and overworked

More should be said of Caroline's career as a doctor. As the only Indian doctor in the area during the early years, she was overworked. Her ten years on the staff of the mission hospital had been years of mutual appreciation. She had great respect for the doctors she worked with and a sense of satisfaction from working in a mission hospital, even though remuneration was not nearly equal to what she could earn privately.

"Work at the mission hospital was not well paid," says Joe. "Our family was considered upper middle class, but I remember that I received my first wrist watch and my first woolen coat when I went off to college."

Caroline Banwar and Ella Bauman were probably the first General Conference Mennonite women to receive medical degrees, and Caroline was the first Indian person in the mission to do so. In the beginning of her practice, she treated only women, but when she went into private practice, both men and women came to the clinic.

She was a doctor always on call. Traveling by bicycle and bullock cart, she went to remote villages for weekly outdoor clinics.

An employer of "clean" patients

Her compassion for the poor extended beyond the doctor's office. She was always willing to treat people with leprosy, showing a concern not only for their present treatment but also for their rehabilitation.

"Clean" patients had difficulty finding employment; employers were afraid of contamination. She helped these patients to find work, even hiring them as her personal help in the house and yard. She arranged for a Fair Price shop to be opened for the poor so that they could buy commodities at minimum prices determined by the government.

Nurtured in the faith by her devout parents, Dr. Caroline had joined the church at an early age. As an adult, she participated in the activities of the church. Even after leaving the mission hospital staff, she and her family continued regular attendance at the Champa Mennonite Church. Twice she served as treasurer. She began the day at her own clinic with worship.

End of her medical practice

Ill health forced her to discontinue her practice in 1942. In 1951, just two days after she and Harold had celebrated their twenty-first anniversary, she suffered from a cerebral stroke and became bedridden.

During her last months she moved to Jagdeeshpur to be nursed by her sister, Dr. Shanti Banwar. She died there from complications of heart trouble and diabetes on April 1, 1952. Memorial services were held the next day in Champa at three different places: first at the Nursing Home where she had her private practice, then at the Bethesda Leprosy Home church, and finally at the Champa Mennonite Church where she was a member.

William Walter wrote: "Her death came too soon and too cruelly. It is tragic that one so dedicated to alleviation of suffering should suffer so much pain in her last days. But she endured this part of her life with surprising patience and valor. She remained undaunted and calm on her death bed, after comforting those attending her."

The writer of India mission history said in 1928, "Dr. Caroline Banwar represents the highest attainment in training and service of our Indian helpers."[4]

Dr. Caroline tried to live up to the responsibilities that came to her in her role as a Christian doctor. Clearly, her faith enhanced her professional skills. As a second-generation Christian, she carried on a tradition of a family committed to extending the kingdom of God through a service of word and deed.

---

4. *Twenty-five Years with God in India* (Berne, Indiana: Mennonite Book Concern, 1929), p. 140.

26.
Serving Where Needed

Wilhelmina Kuyf
1901—1967

Born in Antwerp, Belgium, on March 29, 1901, Wilhelmina Kuyf's comparatively short life of sixty-six years was to take her to Philadelphia; three times to China; to the Mennonite Central Committee office in Pennsylvania; to India; and finally to the conference offices in Newton, Kansas. She used her skills in typing, office administration, nursing, counseling, and Bible teaching to serve the church.

Growing up Dutch

Her parents were Petrus Jacobus and Cornelia Desramaut Kuyf, Dutch citizens. Peter had run away from an orphanage to go to sea, and he worked as a sailor until about 1902 when he, Cornelia, and eight-month-old Wilhelmina came to Philadelphia from Belgium.[1]

There they became the owners of a small grocery store. Another daughter Theresa completed the family until the Kuyfs adopted Jane when they were already in their sixties. Peter and Cornelia also took in foster children.

The family enjoyed contact with many friends, particularly those from First Mennonite Church in Philadelphia. Part of the pleasure of growing up came from leaving the city to drive east of Philadelphia to the

---

1. *Seventy-fifth Anniversary of the First Mennonite Church of Philadelphia, The Diamond Jubilee, 1865-1940*, p. 40.

262 | ENCIRCLED

Wilhelmina Kuyf: Life with Willa was easy. They did not need to spend their time smoothing things out but could put their emotional energy into their work.

town of Browns Mills in South Jersey where the Kuyfs owned a cottage on Mirror Lake. Later, a group of her classmates from Hartford Seminary set up a small camp next to the Kuyf property.[2] These friends were to be a moral support for Willa (as she came to be known to her friends) when she went to China.

Years later when she was sitting out bomb threats in a dark cellar with other missionaries, they would talk about childhood experiences. Willa wrote:

> Perhaps you should have scolded and licked me more, I wouldn't hold it against you, but I can't help but be glad that we always were such good pals, even if Papa did have to say often to me, "Have a little style about you, girl," or "Use a little elbow grease." Or you often had to get mad and start setting the table yourself, Mama, 'cause my nose was always in a book.
>
> You remember, too, Papa's old refrain, "Are you going to get up, or do I have to drag you out like a dog?" and Theresa's and my delighted answer, "Come drag us out like dogs."[3]

After graduating from William Penn High School for Girls in 1919, Willa worked until 1931 as a secretary to earn money for college. However, most of those savings were lost when the bank closed in the crash of 1929. She attended Bluffton College in Ohio for two years where she waited tables and typed her way through.

In 1935, after two years, she received her bachelor's degree from Hartford School of Religious Education. A friend from the church had loaned her money for her schooling, which she repaid from her next earnings. During one college summer and for a year after graduation, she was a social worker at Pennsylvania Hospital in Philadelphia.[4] Some of her earnings were used to help Theresa through nursing school.

First Mennonite of Philadelphia

Willa's mother had been a member of the Mennonite church in Holland, so it was natural for the family to become members of the First Mennonite Church of Philadelphia. Willa joined the church when she was twelve. Her sister Theresa said: "Every phase of her life was always directed toward her goal of going to the mission field." Nathaniel B. Grubb, her

---

2. A letter from Theresa Hunsberger, April 1984.
3. From the Wilhelmina Kuyf Collection, Mennonite Library and Archives, North Newton, Kansas, Box 130-1, Folder 3; letter of January 2, 1939.
4. Wilhelmina Kuyf Collection, Personnel File.

pastor from the time she entered the doors of the church until she left for China, had a profound influence on her.

Willa is listed among sixteen persons from this church who had entered the ministry by 1940. Another was Ann Allebach, the first ordained woman in the General Conference Mennonite Church.

Her appointment deplored

Willa was ordained in 1935. Early in 1936, mission board member Howard Nyce suggested that she apply to the board for an assignment. She did and was accepted at its February meeting.

Her appointment was not without opposition, however. In March, C. H. Suckau wrote for the deacons of the Berne, Indiana, church: "I am informed that Miss Kuyf has been solely trained as a social worker, having attended Bluffton College and Hartford Seminary. The only biblical training which she has being what little could be gotten at Bluffton College. . . . Her appointment is deplorable."

P. H. Richert's answer on March 30, 1936, informed the deacons that Willa had had thirteen Bible courses, in addition to courses in Chinese culture and religions, and that the mission board had been impressed during the interview that "she has a passion for lost souls and a consciousness that the Crucified and Risen Christ is their only hope."

The board suggested that her background in social work would be to her advantage. She had impressed even the most conservative person on the board with her promise to make the personal effort to lead souls to Christ as the chief feature of her work.

Willa left Philadelphia in early April, surely one of the shortest periods of preparation for a foreign missionary. She stopped in Newton, Kansas, for visits with the members of the mission board. As a Pennsylvanian, she took a sly poke at Kansas topography: on a drive to Moundridge, the weather was fine, "and I could see all of Kansas at once."

First assignment in China

Sailing from Vancouver, Willa arrived in a very modern China. When no one met her in Peiping, she telephoned the language school, "and within ten minutes someone in a nice car came and my worries were again over."

At the school she found a comfortable room overlooking the garden. She made friends in abundance and found acquaintances from Philadelphia, Hartford Seminary, and Bluffton; friends of friends were kind to her.

Letters home were filled with longing to hear from her family and the gang from Hartford Seminary. "Don't forget to let me know Jane's (and other people's) wisecracks." She wanted church bulletins, "because although I am far away, First Mennonite is still *my* church." She gave instructions for things she needed, with admonitions that they were to take the cost from her account: "If Kerson's has a sale of cotton dresses around the end of the summer, buy me a darkish voile, *smart*, with almost elbow length sleeves. Only one, however, and the original price must not be more than $1.99."

"Mama, if you saw all these cute little naked children, you would probably want to sit down and make clothes for them all, bless your heart.

"Papa, yesterday I had a sudden hard wish that I might talk current events and world politics with you for just an hour."

She enjoyed her language study, and she appreciated her Chinese teachers most when they told jokes. "Chinese interests me so much that the four hours in the morning go by like a streak." One of the new missionaries had said that the Chinese language was too difficult even to be interesting. "We don't agree on that, but we do agree on wishing we knew more of it."

War came in July 1937, and it was impossible to go the mission station at Taming (pronounced dah ming') in Hopei Province when she was ready. The Japanese were in control of the mission field and for a time traveling was impossible. She settled in at the YWCA in Peiping teaching Bible and English.

Finally, in April 1938 she was able join the missionary community at Taming. She soon became deeply involved in the work of the station. In spite of the war, she was able to go out by bicycle to surrounding villages where churches had been established, going with a Chinese nurse and a Bible woman. She worked mostly with women and children.

They learned to tell the difference between the sounds of rifles, revolvers, shells, and trench-mortars. Although they took refuge in cellars a few nights, the war made little difference in their work except to limit the distance that they could travel.[5] It was a good time for the mission; people had an amazing interest in the Christian story.

A battle with pneumonia

In January 1939, her life was threatened by a bout with pneumonia. A telegram went to her parents. Dr. Lloyd Pannabecker and Elizabeth Goertz came from the hospital in Kai-chow to attend her at the Taming hospital; the Taming missionaries, William and Matilda Voth and Agane-

---

5. Letter to the First Mennonite Church of Philadelphia, April 21, 1959, in the Wilhelmina Kuyf Collection, Box 130-1, Folder 8.

tha Fast, cared for her; and the Chinese congregation prayed for her every evening for an hour.

Gradually she eased back into the work, making herself useful with secretarial work for Matilda Voth and cooking for Aganetha and the Chinese servant as they went out for evangelistic work. But she was impatient to get on with real mission work. Cooking was not her favorite thing, and she deplored her lack of skill. Later in the year on the same subject, she said, "While I realize that women's field is in the kitchen, it always bothers me some, because I would so much rather be out in the country."

When she was able to go about, she became more and more involved in the clinic and nursing work. As an opening wedge into the homes, they used little packages of navel cord dressings for the birth of a new baby. "This thrills me how this work goes on."

The Japanese conquerors

The Japanese were in the city, but they were not oppressive. They gave the missionaries questionnaires by the yard to fill out and wanted to be informed of every move. Two hundred refugees slept at the house one night. In August 1939, she wrote, "Don't worry about me, personally. It doesn't seem to be a matter of personal safety, most of the time, and anyway, at a time like this, one realizes that the whole cause is so much bigger than any one person in it."

The church was burgeoning. She hoped to gather up the youngsters for Sunday school during the church service so that more grown-ups could get into the building.

Marie Regier and Willa became good friends when they worked together in 1941. Marie wrote to Willa's mother that life with Willa was easy. They did not need to spend their time smoothing things out but could put their emotional energy into their work. They had so much to talk about, catching up on the forty years when they had not known each other.

Willa wrote of Marie: "She is experimenting with the power of prayer in a fine way. . . . She is progressive and forward looking in her plans for our work in the country, and I find again that my role is that of a follower. I'm just not a leader, but God uses us all." Willa was forty years old that year and taking stock of her life.

The winters were to be endured. Her winter ensemble to attend church consisted of three pairs of socks, three pairs of trousers, a Chinese garment over a woolen dress, then a winter coat. Willa quoted a Chinese saying: "In summertime everyone is hot, but in wintertime only the poor suffer from the cold."

She described a bike ride in her father's terms: eighty hurricanes lashed together. The wind pushed them home and all they did was steer. "This is not a tall story," she told her father who had a penchant for tall stories.

By October 1940, rumors were flying that the mission's days in China were numbered. The United States consul urged them to go home. "As for me, until God shows me different, I'm acting as though we were to stay a long time."

By February 1941, the missionaries had a plan to evacuate mothers and children, those of impaired health, and those whose furloughs were soon due. Willa wanted to see her term through, and she felt the Lord's will for her was to stay.

In June, P. H. Richert wrote that the board advised everyone to come home, but it did not mean that the board did not appreciate the decision of some of the missionaries to stay on a while. But in July, a letter from the board urged them all to come home. "It made me so mad I cried. They did say at the end of the letter that it was not a command."

Internment in Taming

Until December 8, 1941, the missionaries had been allowed to go through the city gates unmolested, but the day after Pearl Harbor, they were put under house arrest. Maria and H. J. Brown, Willa, and five Nazarene missionaries were confined to the Taming house. They were not allowed to work at all; for three months they could not even step into the street. The Chinese Christians ministered to them with visits, bringing food that they should have eaten themselves.

One Christian woman said, "Take these things, eat them. If missionaries hadn't come, would we be walking on the road to heaven now?"

Willa wrote, "We found ourselves over and over again praying that our friends might truly 'stand fast in the faith.'" Regular instruction classes were held during the six months before Willa left, and "seventy new Christians joined the body of Christ which we call the church."

Willa was interned in the Taming house until June 1942, when she was allowed to begin her journey home, finally sailing on the *Gripsholm*, a neutral Swedish ship. Because her furlough had come due in April, she returned home, but the other four Mennonite missionaries chose to stay in China.[6]

Willa reached Philadelphia in August 1942. Churches in the United

---

6. *Missionary News and Notes*, September 1942, p. 5; in a letter to P. H. Richert, August 5, 1942.

States and Canada called on her for reports, and she told them of her hopes and prayers for the Christian church in China. She waited impatiently to go back.

To India with MCC

In 1944, Willa went to Akron, Pennsylvania, to work for the Mennonite Central Committee. Therefore, she was close at hand when MCC decided to send a relief team to China.[7] She left in March 1945. After tedious layovers in Lisbon and Alexandria, she arrived in steaming Calcutta in August. Willa was given half a room in the Calcutta Girls School. She commented on the old-fashioned fan that hung from the middle of the ceiling, "the kind they used to have in ice-cream parlors." Three baths a day in the galvanized iron tub were not unusual.

For five months Willa typed and filed and organized for the MCC relief unit in Calcutta. The stopover in India was an interesting experience, but her heart was not in it. She longed to get back to China and real work. The food was good but not as good as Chinese. The babies were cute but not as cute as Chinese. The country, just after the rains, was beautiful but. . .

Back to China

Finally, finally, came the news in December that she would be flying by troop carrier to China on the last day of the year. Since passengers could take only a small amount of baggage on the plane, she hung as much as she could on her person by sewing a towel inside her coat. She carried her typewriter and took some teasing when she weighed in. She was in Chungking on January 1, 1946.

A stop at Hankow, Hupeh, at the Lutheran Home, showed the destruction from Japanese bombs in 1937 and from American bombs in 1944. At church services in Chungking, she sat behind General Marshall and noted that he followed the Scripture passages in his Bible.

She, Clayton Beyler, and Lawrence Burkholder, along with two Friends Ambulance Unit members, were assigned to accompany six tons of medicine to Chengchow, traveling by box car, a six-day camping-out experience.

The men partitioned off space for her at the end of the car where she quickly set up her typewriter and got to the business of writing letters. Along the way, they ordered a good meal every day and then bought more tea in which to wash the dishes. As the only person in the group who knew

---

7. Letter written to her church.

Chinese, she was helpful with the language. They were traveling over ruined track, with some fear of bandits.

Unit headquarters at Chengchow, Honan, was the Southern Baptist Hospital, which had been bombed in 1937 while the Pannabecker brothers had been working there. The Friends were to get it going again, directing an international unit of twenty-five people. The unit was delighted to have Willa as secretary, and she worked for anyone who needed her.

The living quarters were poorly equipped, since the Japanese had removed many of the furnishings. Bit by bit, Chinese servants brought back what they had concealed, to the amazement of those who had worked in India. They would not have expected any of it back.

"There is plenty of work ahead for us all, except that mine looks mostly like office work, and the thought recurs, were my four years in college necessary? However, as I've heard all along the way, someone has to do it." In March, she wrote that she had typed like crazy on the big machine that would make twelve copies if she hit hard enough. The current typing job then was an appeal for funds to go out to about ten different distributing groups.

Sharing Christmas

Everyone in the unit shared their Christmas packages, from salted peanuts to books, Lifesavers, and chewing gum. It was a "swell crowd." Willa always found good people to work with, and wrote about how much she appreciated them. She wished that her seventy-eight-year-old father could be in China with his tool kit; he could do so much fixing up. Willa continued writing weekly, loving letters to her family, telling them how much she depended on their letters for her peace of mind.

The Chinese church was well filled, even though there were no foreign missionaries around. A young man who needed someone to talk to came along home from church with the Mennonite workers. "You know, that's a real advantage of being older; the young people, men and women, need an older friend and sometimes I'm it."

She was assigned to work that was more exciting than typing when she supervised the storing of forty bales of clothing from the Brethren Service Committee. She went with Pannabecker and Burkholder to see the work of 5,000 Chinese who were putting the Yellow River back in its old channel.

The flooding had been "caused when the dikes holding back the river were destroyed by Chinese armies in 1938 in order to stop the rapid advance of the Japanese armies. Hundreds of thousands of productive farmland were turned into wasteland by this desperate gesture."[8]

Once needing transportation to go to a village to arrange a loan, they borrowed a railroad handcar. "Now sometime I'd like to get a ride on a submarine. I've never had that experience." This was the kind of activity to write home about, and she reported her experiences in a three-paged, single-spaced, no-margins letter. "With all this going on, you can see how much joy there is in life for me."

We need more workers

In May, she moved with the unit to quarters loaned by the Canadian Church Mission at Kaifeng, Honan, closer to the the Mennonite mission field. The area was considered particularly needy because of the refugees pouring in.

There was a constant coming and going of visitors: members of international relief committees, young men to teach tractor use to the Chinese, and Miss Goertz to open a medical unit in a nearby town. No one had time to teach the new cook. "WE NEED MORE WORKERS," Willa wrote.

During 1946, thirty-two men and women were in the MCC unit, involved in fifteen projects. Dale Nebel took over as director from Clayton Beyler. Beyler in his farewell speech said, "Wilhelmina says, 'Men may come and men may go, but I go on forever.' "

A suitcase full of money

Money became a problem as inflation rose to crazy heights. MCC continued using the bank exchange rates even though everyone else went to the black market. Rates of inflation were quoted not in years or months, but in days. It took a suitcase full of money to buy a meal, and it was cheaper to burn the lower denominations for fuel than to use the money to buy coal.[9] Willa went to the bank on her bicycle with 15 million Chinese dollars, and the whole lot was so heavy that when she carried it on her handlebars and shifted weight, she fell off.

By April 1947, the unit was more and more conscious of the war, but the daily work was little affected. The worst was the sound of shooting and the uncertainty of how long they could go on; their communication with Shanghai was cut off. But the work seemed so worthwhile and was so exhilarating that no one suggested leaving China. One researcher speaks of the overabundance of optimism present in the work in China.

---

8. Tim E. Schrag, "The Mennonites Confront the Revolution: The Rise and Fall of MCC in China, 1945—1950," research paper, Bethel College, April 1976, p. 7, in the MLA.
9. Schrag, p. 12.

In December 1947, the decision was made to end the work in Kaifeng and move to Shanghai. Willa was upset that the decision had been made so hastily. The Communists identified the Mennonites as Americans, thus the enemies who were supplying arms and ammunition. Mennonite Central Committee had, in fact, identified with the Nationalists, and the Nationalists were running out of territory.

Mennonite leaders investigated other possibilities for projects, but when Shanghai was taken by the Communists in May 1949, the unit was disbanded. By October, most of the workers had left the country.

When Willa's MCC term was over in February 1948, she left China. After a short furlough, she returned to the mission field that fall.

In and out of China

Back in China, Willa worked in the Far West, in Chengtu, Szechuan province, with students from the large universities in this town. Her coworkers were the Voths, the Boehrs, Elizabeth Goertz, and Aganetha Fast. But by the end of 1950, the Communists had come into the Far West.

The day after Christmas, Willa and Elizabeth Goertz asked for their exit permits. "The time had come when all foreigners were an embarrassment to our Chinese friends." They received the permits and began the long journey home by way of Hong Kong.

Shortly after her arrival home on April 11, 1951, Willa received one letter from a Chinese friend that said, "Temporarily, don't write me." She heard from no one else, but she never ceased to pray for the church in China.

On North America assignment

By mid October, Willa was established in Newton, Kansas, as an administrative assistant to John Thiessen, executive secretary of the Board of Missions. And so began her fourth and last term of work with the church. There is no more correspondence except Willa's letter to her church in which she expressed her satisfaction with work that kept her in touch with Mennonite missions all over the world.

Tina Block Ediger, who came to work in the mission office, found an unmarried woman, dedicated to her job, but different from the single women she had known. "Here was this sparkling woman. I think she had been in love with a young man and then this call to missions was stronger than her feeling for him, and she made her choice in favor of missions. She accepted her role of singleness. She was not a sad sack or an old maid. She enjoyed life."[10]

10. Interview with Tina Block Ediger, March 1984.

When Tina had applied for work with the Board of Missions, Willa had replied: "If for only one year, don't bother to come. It would be worthwhile to train you only if you stay two years." Tina had never worked for a woman before, but she did not think of Willa as a woman boss. They became great friends.

Sometimes when she was dictating letters, Willa would get off on a China tangent. "She had enjoyed that part of her life and spoke kindly of it."

Willa exhibited a strong sense of humor, especially with Eleanor Camp, who was the coordinator for Women's Missionary Association (now Women in Mission). They bandied words, and they savored and studied and played with words. Eleanor would say, "Willa, you're the cream in my coffee," and Willa would respond, "Eleanor, you're the sour cream in my borscht."

For questions of grammar, Willa went to Eleanor. Once they doctored up John Thiessen's report, and he asked who wrote it. Willa learned that one does not change the boss's creation.

Living simply in Newton

For a time, Willa lived with Sam and Pauline Goering, former China missionaries. In 1955, her parents bought a little house in Newton and she went to live with them. Her friends came to appreciate her joking sailor father and her kind little knitting mother. Peter liked to tell tall tales, and Willa would remonstrate. Her mother's sweaters were distributed to mission causes at home and abroad. They had company every Sunday, with a chicken dinner prepared by Willa's mother, for Willa never learned to enjoy cooking. All three Kuyfs joined the Bethel College Mennonite Church.

The family lived very simply. One lamp was enough for a house; it could be moved from place to place as they needed it. The lifestyle suited Willa, who had learned to be thrifty from her China experience. She rescued carbon paper from the wastebasket, saying, "I hit so hard, I can use it"; but the file copies would be too faint to read.

Willa worked at the conference office from 1951 to 1963. Unfortunately, she could not enjoy her retirement. During her last year or so of work she suffered from loss of memory and mental confusion. Some of her China experiences haunted her. At one time she said she wanted to become so thin she could go through a crack.

The mission board arranged for Willa and her parents to go to the Bethel Home for the Aged in Newton. Her mother died in 1961 and her father in 1962. Willa lived on until March 6, 1967.

Willa would undoubtedly have been embarrassed to know that she became dependent on her friends and relatives during her last years. She had spent her life giving: to her church, her family, and her friends.

When she was deprived of the life of giving that she found most challenging, telling the Chinese of the love of Christ, she turned to other areas where she was needed. She applied the same spirit of zealous giving to supporting missionaries as she had to being one. Well prepared for her vocation of preaching Christ, she was not too proud to work for him in other ways, but she preferred not to have to cook.

Katharina Epp: The decision to marry may have been impulsive, but the marriage that followed was stable, loving, and enduring.

27.
Strong Woman in the Chaco

Katharina Ratzlaff Epp
1902—1984

"My mother was a strong woman. I remember how we always called her when a wagon did not budge. When she pushed, the wagon always moved," Gerhard wrote in describing the physical strength of his mother.

Toward the end of her life, when she experienced a draining illness and her physical strength was disappearing, Katharina relied on faith and trust in God, the habit of a lifetime: "There is little strength left in my body! From day to day I feel how my energy seeps away, in everything, in my speaking, in thinking, in my whole body. How good that I still can read the Bible everyday: more important grows the Word of God for me."[1]

Tests of strength and memory

Katharina was born August 16, 1902, in Steinfeld, Zagradovka, South Russia, the second child of Abram and Katharina Fast Ratzlaff. When she was seven, her family moved to Slavgorod in West Siberia.

Early on, Katharina earned a reputation as a strong and healthy child, and one with a prodigious memory. She enjoyed games that tested her strength. Along with the young men in her village, she raised and rode horses. The school she attended offered only the basic courses, which

---

1. Most of this information was given by the family, especially by her son Hans and his wife Ingrid, her daughter Kaethe and son Gerhard, and her husband in a tribute written at the time of her death. Myrtle Unruh, a longtime mission worker in Fernheim Colony, translated material from the German.

were not enough to challenge her inquiring mind. Although she read what was available, books were few.

A favorite pastime was to make a game of memorizing. Whenever she heard a recitation in church, or when the choir sang a new song, she listened so intently that when she got home she could repeat the poem or song without a mistake, astonishing her family and friends.

At fourteen, she was baptized and joined the Mennonite Brethren Church. Her faith was childlike and heartfelt. She knew that it must be expressed in deeds as well as words. Some years later she loved and was loved by a young man in her village, but because he was not interested in Christianity, they did not become engaged.

Katharina had no opportunity to attend secondary school. She yearned for further education, but the prevailing opinion was "Why should girls study?"

No diploma from the school of medicine

The settlement had no hospital or medical help, so Katharina decided that the study of medicine would be challenging for herself and helpful for others. Her father died in 1920, and when her mother remarried, Katharina was free to go to her grandparents, the Fasts at Zagradovka, to study *Tracktmoaki* (chiropractic) with the famous Frau Wiens.

Her teacher could not read or write, and her knowledge was limited, so Katharina soon learned what there was to learn. After a year she decided to return to Slavgorod. She took a course in obstetrics and began to practice midwifery.

Called to a difficult case where the baby was not positioned properly for delivery, Katharina had to decide whether she should save the mother or let both mother and child die. She decided to try to save the mother, who did survive. A troublemaker in the neighborhood notified the administrators that Katharina was a child murderer, and Katharina was called to the Russian court, which had a reputation for being unpredictable.

She decided to go into hiding and went to the Molotschna Colony where she took the name of Katharina Friesen. She found work in a "nerve healing center," or mental hospital. There she used all opportunities for further study: a course in psychiatric nursing, then a job as chemist's assistant in a women's clinic; she studied psychotherapy and bonesetting.

In 1926, although she did not have the required prerequisites, Katharina was allowed to enter the new school of medicine at Halbstadt, recommended by her wide experience and reputation as a stable and indomitable person. The medical course consisted of two periods of three years each, with a year between for practical experience. One of her fellow students was Anna Epp. They began a friendship which was to last a lifetime.

Collectivization of farms was affecting the Mennonites, and by this time the Communist government was also beginning to invade the Mennonite schools. After three years at Halbstadt, both Anna and Katharina realized that they would never receive their diplomas because they did not intend to join the atheist circle or become Communists. In 1929, Katharina found herself adrift without school, employment, or home.

Newlyweds in East Siberia

Katharina had known Anna's brother, Johann Epp, and they decided rather suddenly to be married. They took Anna and Katharina's schoolmates to a cafe for coffee and there announced the engagement. Johann writes that "in one strike there had been many changes in my life. Knowing nothing about this I had arrived in the morning and there we were coming back, the three of us."

Two weeks later on November 22, 1929, Johann and Katharina were married in the Epp home with only a few friends and family attending. The decision may have been impulsive, but the marriage that followed was stable, loving, and enduring.

The newlyweds packed their suitcases to go to Moscow to obtain papers for emigrating, but learned that the doors were already closed. Relatives in the Amur region in southern Siberia urged them to come there, since collectivism had not yet affected the remote area farms, so Johann and Katharina joined her parents at Schumanowka.

In 1927, four Mennonite colonies had been established in East Siberia about sixty kilometers from the Amur River. The villages had prospered, and the villagers hoped that they were far enough away from Moscow not to be bothered by the Bolshevik terror. This hope was shattered shortly after, and the villagers began to emigrate, a few at a time, usually small groups of single young men hoping to get to relatives in North America. Attempting escape was risky; a few were captured by the secret police and executed. But the ones who succeeded reported back with advice on how to make the crossing.[2]

Across the Amur River on sixty sleds

On arriving in Siberia, Johann found work, but after four months he was invited to become a Communist and change to a better job. When he said

2. Walter Quiring, "Russian Mennonites in the Chaco," *Mennonite Quarterly Review*, April 1934, p. 70.

no, he was threatened by the authorities. He went into hiding in the home of Katharina's oldest sister. On December 17, 1930, Johann and Katharina, together with all of the Mennonites of Schumanowka and Pribreshnoje, fled on sixty sleds across the ice of the Amur River to China. The plan was to go to Harbin, a Russian-Chinese center, rest for a week, then make their way to Canada.

Disasters began with the bus trip from the border to Tsitsikar, where they were to entrain for Harbin. The 510-kilometer bus ride, says one writer, "was more frightful than the flight by night across the Amur. Birth and death in the over-filled buses, hunger and freezing, murder and plunder were their lot; they escaped nothing."[3]

Harassed in Harbin by the Chinese authorities and threatened with being returned to Russia, the refugees tried to make a living while they waited for permission to go to Canada or the United States. Times were hard in China, work was scarce and they were underpaid. Strenuous work might pay a dollar a day. The menu consisted of rice, fish, and tea. The German Consulate attempted to relieve conditions by building refugee homes.

"The constant endeavors of the Mennonite relief committees in Europe and North America were directed to the goal of transporting the refugees as soon as possible from Harbin to America," Walter Quiring wrote. There were over 700 destitute German refugees in Harbin during this time, most of them Mennonite. Two hundred of them reached the United States before both the United States and Canada closed their doors to further immigration. These countries were suffering their own economic depression.

Community and church life went on during this waiting period, and Johann was elected minister in the General Conference Mennonite Church.

To an adobe brick home in Paraguay

In May 1932, the Epps, with help from Mennonite Central Committee and the Protestant Aid Office, sailed for Paraguay in a group of 373. Johann wrote that the military freighter had few conveniences. As the only person with medical training, Katharina attended to the emigrees, although she did not feel well herself.

The Chaco had been opened by an earlier settlement of Mennonites from Canada in 1926 and a group from Germany in 1930. The Harbin Mennonites settled in four villages to the north and east of the Fernheim

---

3. Quiring, "Russian Mennonites."

villages. The area was called the *Harbinerecke*, the Harbin corner. Pioneering in the Chaco promised to be rigorous, but the emigrees were thankful to have found a home, knowing that any place would be easier to live in than China. And this was a place to feel at home, where others also spoke German, Low German, and Russian.

The Epps settled with their relatives in Karlsruhe 16. They lived there for thirty-three years, raising a family of six children, building a farm, providing leadership in the church and medical help in the community. They began with no earthly goods, and they had to rely on their own robust health, the skill of their hands, and their faith that this was God's will for them. The children arrived close together: Kaethe in 1932, followed by Gerhard, Hans, Heinz, Anita, and Hillegonde at approximately two-year intervals.

The Epps built an adobe brick home of two buildings: one house was for the kitchen and dining room and the other the bedrooms. Most of the visiting was done outside in the yard. As in Russia, the homes were built along a street, and the farm plots were usually outside the village. A cooperative store in a neighboring village provided the basic needs: cloth, thread, buckets, a few dishes, a few canned goods, flour, and sugar. Eventually the Epps were to have a good orchard with lemons, guavas, and dates from November to February, and oranges, grapefruit (a Chaco specialty), tangerines, and papaya from March to October.

Becoming Doctor Epp

Katharina performed a number of roles at Karlsruhe that tested her physical and mental strength. This community had no certified doctor. Because Katharina had more experience and training than anyone else, she soon received many calls for midwifery and nursing, bonesetting, physical therapy, and counseling. Unlike some practitioners who lacked medical degrees, Katharina knew her limitations.

Ingrid, her daughter-in-law, wrote, "She depended deeply on God's help. Her children say that on many occasions when severely sick people came for help, the mother first went into another room to pray for guidance and then she did all she knew for the patient."

Kaethe wrote that Katharina believed in the power of intercession of children. When Katharina was called to the home of a very sick person, she would say, "Children, you will pray diligently for these sick people, that they shall get well again, and also that I might do the right thing to help them."

Katharina had a special concern for the Indians who lived near the village and worked for the Mennonite farmers. She gave smallpox vaccinations and treated their sick. During a measles and pneumonia epidemic, Katharina improvised a hospital in a workshed for sick children and nursed them to health without medicines. She formed a lasting friendship with one of the Indian women who often came to visit and, during Katharina's last illness, to pray at her bedside.

Johann and Katharina were called "the Dr. Epps," although Katharina was the one who cared for the sick. Her vocation as doctor created a tension felt both by Katharina and her family. The time allotted to church and community conflicted with time demanded by her home and children. The tension came from not knowing which came first, home or community. Sometimes she felt that the needs were greater than her strength.

Gerhard wrote:

> We come home from school at noon. Again there are people on our yard. When will we eat our lunch? I count the wagons and buggies; there are twenty. Usually there are five or six. After a while, Mother comes and takes the food from the woodburning stove. Quite often the food is either burnt or cold. We eat. That food never hurt us. Without resting, she attends the rest of the people. Then there are the dishes and time for our troubles.
>
> I don't know where she found the time to sing with us or tell us stories. She could tell such interesting stories from the Bible and about Indians that the other children from the village often joined us to listen.

Katharina, though a midwife, feared pregnancies, which were difficult for her, as were the births of the children. But once they arrived, she loved them dearly. She told her children that she had never felt close to her own parents, but she had appreciated the fact that her mother, during her own personal crises, had cared for her lovingly. Hans wrote that his mother loved children very much. Her arms were never too tired to hold her children and she could drive the horses with a child on her arm.

Learning from the Indians

Katharina said her knowledge of child care came from practicing on her own children. She also learned from the Indians. "For instance, in this hot weather not to put a baby into a warm bed, not to overdress a child, let the children play a lot in the sun, let them eat freshly cooked beans with their fingers, let them play in sand and water."

Like many mothers, she believed that her grown children should be free to live their own lives. Hans said, "The message she gave to us was:

'You may go your way. The eternal hand of the Father will not leave you.' "

On the other hand, she expected them to be self-disciplined, even perfect. She expected them to show their love for her in ways that she had taught them. She found it difficult to loosen the ties.

Although Katharina enjoyed her role as mother, she found little pleasure in that of housewife, performing those tasks with self-discipline, accepting them as her responsibility. Her days were often long and her nights short.

Learning to farm in the Chaco

Katharina's work as a doctor might have brought in a little pocket money, but most people could not pay a fee. Income was from the land. Katharina shared with her minister-farmer husband the work of clearing the fields of bush and then plowing and planting.

The Mennonites found farming different from their experience in Russia. Wheat and potatoes did not do well in the tropical climate, they learned. They turned to kaffir corn, sweet potatoes, beans, peanuts, and manioc, with cotton for a cash crop. One of the crops that the Epps learned to produce was dates. Katharina considered dates a good source of iron for her sick people. Considerable work was involved in picking and drying the fruit, for each date had to be handled several times. After being dried in the intense Chaco sun, the dates were packaged for sale locally.

Cornelius W. Friesen wrote in a tribute in the *Mennoblatt* that if callers who came for help could not find Dr. Epp at home, very likely she would be at the acreage outside the village.

> As you followed the winding pathway, you finally came to the clearing and you would see how rapidly Mr. Epp would walk behind the plow which was drawn by well-cared for horses. And what was Mrs. Epp doing? She, an able housewife, was right there, barefoot, placing peanut seeds in the freshly plowed moist soil, and immediately covering them with her feet.
>
> In order to help the patient, the driver of the patient's horse and buggy took over Mrs. Epp's job and she drove the patient to her house to provide the help needed.

Katharina did not always appreciate the help of the substitute, who might not plant the seeds as carefully as she required. One day when she returned to the field, she found that the helper had planted the rows too close together. She knew the plants would not have room to grow properly. She marked the ones he had planted to show him how poorly the plants had done. Later, to her chagrin, "She found the plants all standing in the row, smiling and saying, 'We are all here.' "[4]

At the center of their lives, the church

The church in Karlsruhe included three groups: Mennonite Brethren, Evangelical Mennonite Brethren, and General Conference Mennonite, in which Johann was an ordained minister. The three congregations met together in the village three Sundays a month and in Filadelfia as separate denominations the fourth Sunday.

Part of Katharina's strength was evident in her role of leadership to the women of the church. She had been active in starting a *Frauenverein* in the General Conference church that she joined in the Chaco. She had a special feeling for hurts and needs of people, probably from her own experience of hurt and need. She had been close to death five times. She had suffered from depression.

Hans wrote, "Mama was a believer, had faith that God moves mountains, but she also had depressions and had to fight battles of her own faith." These battles she also had the strength to overcome.

Katharina was known as a good hostess. Anyone visiting the community or working with the mission or Mennonite Central Committee was made to feel at home, for the Epps were interested in building the fellowship of the church and community. Kaethe remembered that many a traveling preacher stayed at the Epps, and her mother gave them the best she had, including a special jam which was served only to guests. "When her church demanded her counsel or time, she was always willing to help."

In 1965, the Epps moved from Karlsruhe to Filadelfia where life was easier. Johann had less farm work but could still have a yard and garden. He still took turns preaching, and the church was the center for their lives. For her, the move meant that she could take part in the women's mission society and be more active doing spiritual counseling and helping the sick. But by that time, qualified doctors were available, as was a hospital.

Katharina had dreaded becoming old and dependent. However, a dependent old age was in store. For that burden, too, she called up strength to accept. Paralyzed, confined to a wheelchair, she was cared for by her husband and daughter Kaethe. Though she suffered loss of speech, Katharina kept a clear mind and was at peace with life even as she looked forward to "going home." She watched with satisfaction as her children

---

4. July 16, 1980, p. 5, in *Mennoblatt*, Fernheim's bimonthly paper.

and grandchildren became doctors, nurses, teachers, preachers, and farmers.

She died on October 15, 1984. One of her last jottings was, "As [Christian] in *Pilgrim's Progress* at the end looks up to heaven and calls out, 'I see that I am at the destination of my pilgrimage,' so—I!"

Anna Epp: She found her family repeating the pioneering efforts she had experienced in Russia.

28.
Singing the Lord's Song in Foreign Lands

Anna Enns Epp
1902—1958

The story of Anna Epp is the story of many of the Mennonite women who grew up in Russia and moved with their families to North or South America. Some of them, after pioneering in new settlements in Russia, went on to begin again with their husbands in such places as Manitoba, British Columbia, Kansas, and the Paraguayan Chaco.

Anna speaks for those women who as wives of church leaders quietly supported their husbands with prayers and hard work and kept the farm or business going while husbands preached and traveled to extend the kingdom of God. She speaks for those women with large families who knew the pain and pleasure of loving, directing, teaching, and correcting according to the needs of each child.

Anna along with Heinrich had a special vision for her family: she wanted them to have a Christian education. Her oldest son Henry wrote, "Anna's vision was not just education; it was education that would help us decide to be Christians and follow them and their parents in Christian ways and services. She believed that a Christian faith and a Christian education would make us a better people and give us a better life."[1]

Life in Russia was satisfying in the early years, but later difficult and sometimes frightening. Life in Canada was often physically demanding

---

1. Most of the material for this biography came from a number of Anna's children: Henry, Bruno, Frank, Anna Ens, Menno, Martin, Susan Froese, Lydia Friesen, Linda Sawatzky, Viola Loewen, and Rudi.

and financially uncertain. The family depended on faith and prayer. But through the years, her children remembered her as a singing mother. She never asked, "How shall we sing the Lord's song in a foreign land?" They remember her laughing brown eyes and her long dark hair arranged in a braided bun at the nape of her neck.

The good life in Talma in the Terek

Anna's father, Frank F. Enns, had grown up in Alexanderthal in the Molotschna. From his own experience, he could sing a well-known folk song with the theme "wonderful is youth." He married Anna Duerksen in 1893. Because the Molotschna area was becoming overpopulated, they moved in 1901 with their two daughters, Helena and Elizabeth, to the village of Talma in the Terek.[2]

A week's wagon journey from the Molotschna, the Terek is just north of the Caucasus Mountains and west of the Caspian Sea. A newly established settlement then, it was to grow to fifteen villages.

Anna was born there on October 24, 1902. She was to have two younger brothers, Gerhard and Frank.

The climate was mild, with rare snowfalls in winter. The tamarisk with it lovely blossom and fragrance was used for fuel. Water from the Terek River was used for irrigation, and many kinds of fruit could be grown. The Tartars in the surrounding villages were good customers, and dried fruit was in demand back in the home village of Alexanderthal. Fruit drying was the work of women and girls, as was stacking hay. Even as a child, Anna helped by riding one of the horses hitched to the threshing stone.

During bad years, the villagers suffered from floods, locusts, malaria, or mosquitoes. Their Tartar neighbors, with their primitive standards of farming, remained friendly; but the Caucasus Mountain tribes, who swooped down to plunder from time to time, threatened the peace of the community.

This was Anna's life for sixteen years. Well educated for her day, she had attended the village school and for one year the Fortbildungschule, perhaps the equal of a ninth-grade education today. Her grandparents and her parents were well-read, eager for their children to advance in their schoolwork. Anna was well-trained in German, and wrote in a beautiful Gothic script.

---

2. F. F. Enns, *Elder Enns: "Ohm Franz"* (Winnipeg, 1979), translated by Margaret Enns Frederickson, p. 23. Information about the years in Russia comes from this source.

Chorales to last a lifetime

In 1903, Anna's father was elected to the ministry of his congregation. As a minister, he was expected to lead the singing. He and his wife practiced the hymns at home until he was confident of the melody. As the girls grew older, they joined in and learned chorales to last a lifetime.

In 1906, "Ohm Franz" was ordained as elder and charged with serving neighboring colonies. His home congregation acquired a chest of homeopathic medicines which they gave to their elder along with manuals for him to study. This kind of service was to make "Dr. Enns" welcome in other communities on his later pilgrimages.

The Enns sisters attended choir twice a week in winter, once in summer. Song festivals were popular. Almost every person played an instrument and Anna learned to play the guitar.

"Mild summer evenings were hauntingly beautiful when the village youth gathered under the trees in an orchard. . . . At that time, people were still aware of what the concept of leisure really meant and the young ones sang,

Far in the south the beautiful Terek,
Terek is my native land
Where the shady willow trees
Rustle at the Talma's strand."

Orderly structure fell apart

In 1917, as World War I took its toll by weakening law and order, the Mennonite villagers became aware of the decline of Russia. When Russia lost to Germany and the Red and White armies began battling, even the distant provinces felt the loss of civil control. Just at the time when the Enns family had paid off its farm debt and was beginning to look forward to a time of prosperity, the structure of an orderly life fell apart.

The Chechenzen mountain people, who had always been an irritation, now became a menace. The once friendly Tartars joined them in raids that led to murders and robberies.

In February 1918, Elder Enns was told that the family should leave in one day's time. But not even that much time was allowed. The Tartars knew that the Chechenzen would get what the Mennonites left, so they came during the night to start loading their own wagons without asking the Mennonites what they planned to take with them.

The Tartars came to the Enns' house as the family was having its last evening worship. The family grabbed what it could and fled. The Ennses joined the two-mile wagon train headed for the railroad station at Chassaw-Jurt, leaving behind their farm equipment and all their animals.

Eventually, they were able to reach relatives in the Ssuvorovka area. The Ennses wanted to get back to the Molotschna, but the battle line of the civil war lay across their path. In the village of Nickolaifeld, they were taken in by the Janzen family who gave the family of seven the use of the living room.

Ssuvorovka was a water-poor region. "So the water in the kitchen had to be used twice for dish-washing and then given to the pigs." Food was scarce. The older girls worked on neighboring farms and were paid in food. For his medical skills, their father might be paid in onions that the family was glad to add to its black bread and *pripps* for breakfast.

Six orphans taken in

When the war came to Nickolaifeld, the soldiers were billeted with the villagers. Anna and her sisters were harassed by the soldiers who demanded to be catered to by the young women. One night, the soldiers stole all the belongings that the Ennses had stored in the attic, including their good clothes.

The soldiers' parting gifts to the village were lice and typhus. In an effort to get rid of the lice, the girls burned the straw bedding and ironed their underwear every night. Having already had typhus, Elder Enns was immune and was able to help the stricken. Until they, too, became ill, the girls nursed other families. Mrs. Janzen, their hostess, died. Across the street, Aunt Thiessen and her husband died, leaving six children who for a time became part of the Enns family.

When the Red army left the village, the Ennses joined other families to rent the railroad boxcars to return to Alexanderthal. The trip that should have taken two days took two full weeks because the locomotive was often diverted, leaving the refugee cars stranded. During those stops, Anna helped the women make brush fires over which they made *borscht* with burdock leaves.

At Alexanderthal, the girls and the older Thiessen children were at once given work by their Duerksen grandparents. Elder Enns again treated the sick, as the dreaded typhus broke out there, too. Anna and her sisters, now more or less immune, nursed the victims. Added to these burdens came the Machno bands with their reign of terror.

In 1920, when Anna was eighteen, her father was asked to move to Memrik. Two family weddings took place during this period. Lena married Johann Neufeld from Memrik and Liese married Johann Dueck (or Dyck) from the Molotschna.

After three years, Elder Enns was able to ordain a young man as elder for the Memrik congregation, leaving him free to accept a call to the Ssuvorovka, an area closer to the Terek. The dream of Elder and Anna Enns was to return to the settlement where the good life of the past might be restored. With Anna, Gerhard, and Frank, the parents moved back to the village of Nickolaifeld.

Anna meets a teacher

The love story of Anna Enns and Heinrich Epp began in Nickolaifeld. Heinrich, the son of Martin and Susanna Epp, was born in the Molotschna, but the Epp family had lived briefly in the Ssuvorovka. Heinrich had returned to Halbstadt for teacher education, but the civil war and famine interrupted his schooling. In 1922, enroute to North America with a cousin, he was forced to detour through Ssuvorovka, where he was nursed through a serious illness by relatives.[3]

Anna and Heinrich were married in May 1924. If her father had a vision of returning to the Terek, Anna and Heinrich had a vision of their own: to escape the perils of Russia and start a family in Canada. Having been refused a passport, Heinrich's hope was that he and Anna could emigrate with other Mennonites under a group passport.

The 200 people in the group sent him to Moscow to make application, but he returned to Nickolaifeld under the impression that the passport would be refused. When he arrived back at the settlement, he found that the group had already sold their possessions, intent on emigrating. They firmly believed that God would make it possible for them to leave Russia. And God did. Four months after their marriage, Heinrich and Anna emigrated with a large number of other families.[4]

Arriving in Canada in October 1924, the Epps, after a brief stay in Drake, Saskatchewan, made their first home in Winkler, Manitoba, with Anna's aunt, Kornelia Regehr. Heinrich worked as clerk in the Kroeker Brothers Store, earning twenty and then fifty dollars a month. Unlike a number of the immigrants, they took seriously the repayment of their travel debt. At the end of the second year, the $320 was paid.[5] Their first child, Henry, was born in Winkler.

Four families on a farm in Manitoba

Back in Nickolaifeld, the new government became more and more repres-

---

3. Anna Epp Ens, *The House of Heinrich* (Winnipeg, Manitoba: Epp Book Committee, 1980), p. 183.
4. Larry Kehler, "Portrait of a Pioneer," *Canadian Mennonite*, October 22, 1954, pp. 4-5. Anna was almost twenty-two and her husband only twenty.
5. Kehler, p. 5.

sive. Mennonites were being forced to teach Communism in their schools. Elder Enns gave up his dream of returning to the Terek and started thinking of emigrating. In April 1926, he and his wife Anna, their two sons, the families of the two older daughters, and a niece joined Anna and Heinrich in Tante Regehr's small house. Now the four families, joyfully but snugly, were reunited. Elder Enns was assigned by the General Conference mission board to visit the scattered Mennonites in the prairie provinces.

By 1927, the four families had moved to a large farm three miles south of Lena and two miles north of the U.S.-Canada border. For a time, all of them lived in a single family house, cooking together and working the farm. Bruno and Frank were born there in 1927 and 1929. The next year, the Epps moved to their own farm where they barely made enough to pay the rent and make a living for their growing family. Annie, Menno, Martin, George, and Susan were born there between 1931 and 1937. Before they left for British Columbia in 1945, Lydia, Linda, Alvin, and Viola had been born.

Children organized for evening chores

Most of the years at Lena were the Great Depression years, and Anna found her family repeating the pioneering efforts that she had experienced in Russia, but in a climate less kind and a soil less productive. She enjoyed farm work. Even when pregnant, she helped with the farm chores and field work, putting up hay in the way she had learned in Russia.

She took part in every aspect of farming and organized the children for doing evening chores. They were also responsible for running the milk separator, churning butter, and washing clothes. Every one took turns washing dishes. Father Heinrich might either be out in the field or attending to church duties.

Lessons learned in Russia during the hard years were applied to the Lena life. Necessity forced Anna to make do with what was available. Their Catholic landlord brought used clothing by the boxful and Anna became adept at ripping up adult clothing to make things for the children. Woolen items were unraveled to be knit into mittens, scarves, and stockings. "Mother would often explain our situation but I never heard her complain," says Menno.

Anna's father was elder of the Lena church, a branch of the Whitewater Mennonite Church. When Elder Enns moved to Whitewater in 1931, Heinrich, who had been ordained in 1929, became the leading minister at Lena. It was the custom for visitors to the church to stay with the minister's family. Anna hosted itinerant clergy, visiting missionaries, and other church workers. Annie remembers the woman who came for two weeks to teach summer Bible school and endeared herself by sewing identical dresses for Susie, Lydia, and Linda.

Without a refrigerator and deep freeze, canning of garden produce, butchering, and butter churning were major tasks. In the warm months, butter and milk were cooled in buckets hung in the well; later an ice cellar was built behind the house and food could be cooled there during the summer.

Still, in spite of the austerity at Lena, the children remember their mother as a happy person. "Mom was known to be a real tease," Annie wrote, especially to her brother Frank. Back in Nickolaifeld, Frank's pig had been sacrificed for Anna's wedding meal. "This precipitated a family crisis." When he was grown and already a teacher, he came back to visit his sister. As Heinrich put a half-grown pig into the trunk of Frank's car, Anna said, "There, you have the pig back which you had to give up for my wedding." Menno wrote: "I remember her chuckles. Didn't her body bounce with laughter at times?"

Henry wrote:

> I can confirm that in the earliest years of their family life Mom laughed much. Keep in mind, there was little to laugh about. The home was a granary on a totally neglected and rotted yard in the prairies. The quarter section surrounding this yard was a low-production soil, had many water holes and countless stones, every year a new crop to be gathered and piled into the fences.
>
> The two-room home received a shed. The basement was a hole in the ground infested with rats and ants. The ants got into sealed jam-jars and gave jam a uniquely distasteful odor and taste. We walked down into the cellar with lanterns and accepted the fact that rats would scamper over our toes and assumed that this was life. Never a complaint that I know of.

The Lena farm was close to the highway. This nearness was a convenience, but it also brought strangers to their door and some degree of insecurity. Henry commented on one of the incidents at Lena:

> In the middle of a violent Manitoba blizzard a man walked into the unlocked home and called for help till Mom woke Dad, and after contacting the Neufelds, near neighbors, all returned to go to find a car in the ditch and a lady friend freezing. She (drunk and incoherent) lay in our guest room through the night and then died. A police investigation followed and this was conducted in our home. And

Anna accommodated all who came and went even as she ministered to the dying woman until a doctor could reach our isolated farm. This respect for all human beings was a legacy demonstrated to us in our childhood.

Youngsters singing with their mothers

In the early years at Lena, Anna and her sisters sang as a trio at *Jugendverein*, funerals, and other community functions. Henry remembered the pleasure of singing with his mother in an intergenerational choir. The occasion was a song festival, held in a hayloft, organized by Anna's brother-in-law. "We youngsters stood beside our mothers and sang alto or soprano. All of us memorized all the anthems."

The community expressed its unity in another way. The colonists believed that to survive, they needed unity in language. The Enns-related families agreed to nurture the reading and writing of High German. English classes were taught during winter evenings for the older men so that they could talk to their English neighbors and transact business in town. Such classes were not considered necessary for women because women, always accompanied to town by their husbands, didn't need English. Anna never became fluent in English.

Heinrich and Anna counted each child as a gift from God. Still, she must have been somewhat self-conscious about the size of her family. Her sisters had smaller families, but others in the Lena congregation had ten to thirteen children. Anna confided to one of these women during a Sunday afternoon visit: "I enjoy much more going to families with many children; they understand us better."

Susan wrote that soon after they moved to British Columbia, she and Lydia, then eight and seven, worked for a neighbor picking raspberries. "In a family like ours anything could happen, I guess, and Lydia and I tried to convince the [woman they worked for] that we were born twenty days apart. Even if our mother was good at having children, this was beyond her comprehension. She was just as firm in her disbelief as we were in our belief." The girls, born twenty days and one year apart, were young and innocent enough to disregard the prerequisite year.

The concern for a Christian education for their children was ever present. To quote Henry: " 'That all their children receive church school education no matter the cost, because it was an investment in the life beyond death' was how my parents put it then." They determined that their children must attend a high school, an unusual goal in that community.

Henry completed grade nine by correspondence and attended Mennonite Collegiate Institute at Gretna, a boarding school, one day's travel from Lena. "I am still remembered as the one wearing one jacket for three years, the sleeves getting shorter and shorter and the elbow patches larger and larger." His parents saved money for him to come home once a year, but they could not provide pocket money. When he graduated in 1942, his brother Bruno followed him at MCI.

At the time, some families in the Lena congregation thought that education was a waste of money, but the Enns family from which Anna came, set a pattern that others were to follow. "Today the price paid by the poorest pioneers of Lena has paid off as dozens of descendants of Lena families serve God and man professionally in many vocations and in many countries."

To a new home in British Columbia

The Epps had purchased the farm they had been renting, to be paid with one-third of the annual crop. In 1945, realizing they had only a slim hope of paying for the farm, Heinrich and Anna decided to move to British Columbia which held more promise of work for their family. And Mennonite Educational Institute at Clearbrook was close enough for the children to attend and still live at home.

They left the church they had served so long, the home they had built, and their friends in the community where they had lived for nearly twenty years. (Anna's mother had died in 1938 and her father in 1940.) The Epps held a sale that left them with a ten-year-old Chevrolet, a train ticket to British Columbia, and a modest down payment on a farm there. The leave-taking must have reminded them of an earlier departure when they left Russia for an unknown place. This time they were a middle-aged couple uprooting their family to start again on the pioneer road.

Setting up the new home at Mt. Lehman was not easy, but here Anna had new conveniences she could enjoy: running water, electricity, a separate bathroom with a tub, and a pantry with a sink. The house itself was somewhat dilapidated and the boys had to sleep in another building. The dairy and berry farm demanded intensive labor. The land had to be cleared and more berries planted. Although the children were in school, they worked evenings and weekends. Rudi, the last of the children, was born in 1948. Later that year, Anna had a successful operation for cancer.

Never tired of praying

Heinrich soon became elder of the 140-member congregation of the West Abbotsford church. Eventually, he was elected to serve on the provincial and conference mission and relief committees. Anna was concerned about his frequent absences from farm and family and about his health. But she quietly accepted his decisions regarding his ministry.

She went with him on his visitations in the community and was involved in marriage counseling sessions held in their home. She was willing to sacrifice for her husband as well as for her children. On one occasion, she helped him pay a traffic fine of twelve dollars by returning a dress she had just purchased for that amount.

Anna was always a faithful member of the Women's Auxiliary. She attended the monthly meetings and enjoyed them as special times of inspiration and encouragement. Particularly in the last years, she brought home material to sew for mission projects.

In one of her last letters she wrote, "I don't want to tire of praying." Annie wrote, "We were getting ready for church one Sunday morning. Her bedroom door was closed. But I needed something from her room. I opened the door quietly and slipped in. There was mother on her knees. Probably praying for Dad who would be preaching. Or maybe for her sons (preachers in distant places) or for me (a Sunday school teacher)."

After World War II, relatives came as refugees. Space was found for Katja Klassen and her three boys. Katja worked in the berry patch and received farm produce as well as wages. Anna became her sister, mother, and friend.

According to Viola, "She was a soft touch for peddlers, and she cooked and supplied clothes for refugees." Susan wrote: "In spite of the fact that our table was already always full, at Christmas or other festive occasions, invitations would be given to friends who were not in a position to be with their families."

Her family remembers her housewifely gifts. She was clever with her hands at sewing and making patchwork blankets for the family and for Mennonite Central Committee. Susan wrote, "And often when she was busy at knitting or crocheting in the evenings, she had the *Rundschau* or *Der Bote* on her lap, reading the stories to us if we would listen."

A mother to her children

Gradually life became easier. A new house was built in 1953. Here again a guest recognized a need and met it. Annie tells of the visit of J. J. Esau, the blind evangelist, for a series of meetings. Of course, he stayed with the Epps during that time. He asked Anna to show him around the kitchen.

"After feeling the cabinets, sink, fridge area where there was no fridge, he came to this eastern wall. What was this empty place for, he wanted to know. Eventually for the electric range, she said. Where was she cooking now? In the basement on the wood-fed cookstove." Esau appealed to the congregation for an offering to provide an electric range for Anna for her birthday.

To her thirteen children, Anna was probably thirteen different mothers, but they have some memories in common. She was a quiet, contemplating woman, a pillar in the home, easygoing in bad times as well as good. She could be firm, but the older ones thought she was too lenient with the younger ones. Anna's response was, *"Ich bin dochwohl schon zu muede.'* (Perhaps, I am already too tired.) The younger ones thought she was strict enough.

Anna interceded for her children with their father about such things as the girls cutting their long hair. They knew that their parents loved each other. "It used to make me giggle the way she would straighten Dad's tie and give him a kiss before he went on his daily trip to the post office," Viola wrote.

Her children speak of her insights into what life was all about. Martin appreciated the way she let him learn by making mistakes. When he asked for a sharp kitchen knife for carving, she told him that he would cut himself, and he said he would not, but if he did he would not cry. They were both right: he cut himself but he did not cry. Later his mother encouraged him to go into teaching, giving him confidence when he needed it.

She cultivated the special interests and gifts of all her children. For Frank, "She was about the only member of the family that commented on my poetry." She also "was one of the first donors to the radio program I was involved in" with a sacrificial contribution.

Her oldest knew that she cared for him just as much as for those that followed. Her first trip out of the house after the birth of a baby was to church, "presenting her child to Jesus in the temple." Henry said, "Whenever I left home, her last word to me was 'remain faithful.' "

Anna and Heinrich's desire to provide Christian education for their children had gratifying results. Frank wrote:

> Thirteen times she prepared her children for a Christian high school, first in Manitoba, then in British Columbia, and beyond that for Bible school, Bible college, biblical seminary, teachers' college, and university. The thirteen alone spent more than seventy years in church schools.
>
> [With spouses] they have devoted over five hundred person-years to various forms of ministry in five Canadian provinces, several American states, and seven foreign countries.

Her support for her children extended to their spouses. Menno wrote: "One reason for going to weddings of her children, particularly those in the distant places, was that Mother might learn something of the context, relationship of the other parent and child, so that she might better learn to accept, understand, and relate to the new in-law in her life." She was faithful in writing letters to her children away from home.

Her children recognized that Anna would have enjoyed more formal training, but opportunities were limited. She told Linda that she had once wanted to be a teacher. Anna had always liked to read, and when life eased a bit, she found time even for fiction.

The loss of Heinrich

In April 1958, Heinrich died of a brain hemorrhage. When Anna returned from the hospital the night of his death, Linda heard her moan, *"Kinder, ihr wisst nicht wie es ist, nach 35 Jahren, als ob ein Teil von mir gerissen ist."* (Children, you don't know what it's like; as if after thirty-five years a part of me has been torn off.) "Those were the only words of grief I heard from her."

Six of the children were still living at home. Rudi was only ten years old. Anna was frustrated as she tried to counsel her children without the help of Heinrich.

Added to this was the loneliness of the "forgotten widow." Three months after the funeral she said to Henry, "I knew that the widows were very lonely, but I did not think that the people could forget their *Aeltesten*'s widow in three months. . . . I was with him among the people so often, and now I am another church member who knows not what goes on."

But in October she wrote to the children: "The Ladies Auxiliary has not forgotten me." They came to celebrate her fifty-sixth birthday with devotions, gifts, and *Plauderstunde* (chatterboxing).

Low income was a problem. She considered it a miracle when the family was finally able to sell the Mt. Lehman farm and with volunteer help build a house for her in Clearbrook.

In October, on a visit to Menno's family, she mentioned that she felt something was happening to her speech. Not long after, she began to have severe headaches. Finally, the diagnosis was that she had an inoperable brain tumor. For a number of weeks she lay semi-comatose, moving in and out of consciousness. Every day some of the family were with her, praying, singing, visiting. And one day, "Three of us were singing, tenor, bass, and soprano. Suddenly we hear the alto tune hummed and note that it can come only from Mom."

She died December 16, 1958. Susan counted her blessings for her: Anna would probably have listed them as the opportunity to immigrate to Canada, the move to British Columbia to settle on their own farm, the support of a church community, and the love received from Heinrich and her children. Henry, speaking for them all, felt that her prayers would always influence their lives.

Pauline Raid: She actively promoted the products of the slaw cutter company.

29.
Her Husband's Partner

Pauline Krehbiel Raid
1907—1984

In an age and a world that often seems obsessed with the job, Pauline is a healthy reminder to us that a personal sense of worthiness does not need to be linked to a job. Her sense of worth was deeply engrained in what she considered her most worthy task: to be herself and to plumb deeply the wellspring of life and to share her joyous discoveries with others.[1]

Although she taught school before her marriage, she did not work outside her home afterward. However, she was thoroughly involved in her husband's activities as he served as pastor, college professor, and executive for mutual aid organizations. To his many-faceted career, she made herself a partner. Only she could answer the question: Did she feel that she was overshadowed by her husband, and if she did, did she resent it? The answer seems to be no.[2]

Pauline had written in her diary when she was seventy, "There are still plenty of good tunes left in an old violin. . . . We want to keep on contributing to humankind in whatever paths the Lord leads us." Her death at seventy-six seemed premature. She had not had time to play all her tunes.

Pauline Krehbiel was born November 4, 1907, to August and Laura

---

1. Melvin Schmidt at the memorial service for Pauline Raid.
2. From interviews with Howard Raid, Alison Hiebert, Mary Holtkamp, and Phyllis Friesen in April 1984; excerpts from her journal selected by Elaine Rich; and tributes written and spoken at the time of her death.

Krebill Krehbiel in Donnellson, Iowa, one of eight children. Her parents, of Swiss background, had come from South Germany by way of Ohio. Her father worked in Donnellson as an upholsterer. The family brought a piano into their home as soon as one became available, so Pauline received an early start on what might be considered a career of music.

Support for meaningful activities

After graduating from Donnellson High School in 1926, Pauline attended Bluffton College for one year and then went to Iowa State Teachers College to receive her teaching certificate and then her degree in 1938. In the meantime, she taught for seven years in her home high school where Howard Raid taught literature, history, and science. Besides directing high school choral groups and coaching soloists for music contests, she gave private piano lessons.

Howard, too, had grown up in Donnellson. They had known each other for most of their lives. (His great-great-grandfather and her great-great-grandmother came from the village of Freidelsheim in South Germany.) When Howard was senior superintendent in the Zion Mennonite Church, she was junior superintendent. The Zion church is the surviving congregation of the three that met together at West Point, Iowa, to organize the General Conference Mennonite Church in 1860. Howard had attended Parsons College.

Although registered as a conscientious objector at the beginning of World War II, Howard did not pass his physical examination and so was exempted from any service. He volunteered for administrative duty, but was not needed.

Howard and Pauline were married in 1940. He held administrative positions in Iowa schools until 1943 when they were called to the Bethel Church at Fortuna, Missouri. Their only child, Elizabeth Ann, was born there. Pauline was an active minister's wife. For a time she was president of the Middle District women's conference.

In 1945, Howard began graduate work at the university at Ames, Iowa, where the Raids became friends of Kenneth and Elise Boulding, Quaker peace activists. Both families were involved in the Fellowship of Reconciliation.

In 1947, while at Ames, the Raids received a call to Bluffton College. Bluffton was to be Pauline's home for the remainder of her life. Howard was called to teach economics, but he found that what was needed was a business teacher.

While teaching, he worked summers on his graduate degree and after six years was awarded a Ph. D. in economics from Ohio State. During this time, like typical graduate students, they lived simply and pinched pennies. Pauline made her own clothes and gardened.

One of the tributes written to Howard after her death said, "I know full well that you could not have been involved in so many very meaningful activities without the support and loyalty of Mrs. Raid." Those "meaningful activities" included teaching full time, directing the Bluffton Slaw Cutter Company and mutual aid societies, as well as "minor" activities such as the family tour guide business one summer in Europe.

Nurturing mutual aid societies

As a college professor's wife, Pauline entertained his students with coffees once or twice a year. His students were her students so she shared his involvement with them. While he was gone on business, she took care of his classes. Her friends remember Howard and Pauline as they walked across campus, her arm through his, on their way to campus activities.

The Bluffton Slaw Cutter Company grew out of his college business class. Owned mostly by the Raids, it provided a laboratory for the students. She actively promoted its products, and many people around Bluffton are loyal slaw-cutter fans. In 1954, the Rapid Salad Set was selected for an award in good design by the New York Museum of Modern Art.

Howard's activities with mutual aid societies became a long-time and deeper involvement for her than his others, for here she took over responsibility for the book work. He was instrumental in bringing all the known mutual aid groups together, and out of this in 1954 grew the Association of Mennonite Aid Societies. He was chairman for ten years and secretary for nineteen.

They also were active in the local Mennonite Mutual Aid Society. They helped organize Mennonite Indemnity, a reinsurance plan that could support other mutual aid groups in times of disasters. The societies were organized to insure property, the insuree paying in proportion to the losses of the company. Early on, they loaned money to young men in Civilian Public Service. The Mennonite Brotherhood Aid Association loaned money to people who could not get funds from second mortgages.

Pauline was secretary of this group, a local property insurance society, for twelve years. She prepared all the policies and policy changes and signed all legal papers as the chief executive officer. She was in charge of the minutes and the minute book. This organization had about $60 million of insurance in force.

Together, the Raids attended annual meetings of mutual aid societies in the United States and Canada. In 1957, they traveled for two months visiting organizations west of Ohio; in 1959, they took in those in the

East, Pauline making all arrangements for the travel. She met many new people, and she felt that her ministry was to talk to members of the companies, hear what they were doing, and encourage them. In her future business correspondence, she included personal notes to the people she had met.

Pauline rode a camel

Together the Raids organized the Swiss community's historical society. People came to the campus to tell stories in Swiss and sing High German songs. The Raids developed a community burial society. She supported Howard as a member of the first Bluffton city planning commission.

In the summer of 1966, they worked with Mennonite Travel Service in Akron, and then took a leave of absence the next January to work from Amsterdam, setting up tours. Earlier, in 1964, as leaders of a Swiss tour group, all three family members had participated, daughter Elizabeth being given the responsibility for counting the suitcases. Someone, remembering, wrote to Howard, "Pauline rode a camel. What a good sport she is."

Together they went to Freeman Junior College in South Dakota in 1967. Howard served as president for two years during a period of transition. Always interested in books and reading, Pauline became active in the bookstore and started a reading club. She kept a record of the books she read, and the list was long and varied.

Living with bricks and sawdust

Together they built their home after several years of drawing house plans. When the bricks were delivered, Pauline and Elizabeth sorted them by color so that the lighter could be mixed with the darker. For a year and a half they lived in the house as they worked on it, putting up with the saws and the sawdust but enjoying the experience.

Pauline supported Howard in all those things she understood. Some projects she did not support, although she did not oppose them. She considered his limestone business too risky, but she was to enjoy its benefits in later years.

What kind of woman is it who works so closely with her husband that at first glance she would seem to be his alter ego?

As it happened, she did have a profession of her own in which he could not participate, or to only a limited extent. Although she stopped teaching school when she and Howard were married, she continued to be involved in many musical activities. Howard said he could not share her musical interests, for he couldn't carry a tune. Nevertheless, he appreciated her talent and encouraged her participation in musical organizations.

Being uniquely Pauline

For twenty-five years she directed or accompanied the junior choir at the First Mennonite Church in Bluffton. For thirty-six years she sang in or played for the *Messiah*. She sang in the Bluffton College Choral Society. Elizabeth received piano lessons from her mother until she entered college. The Raids were justifiably proud when Elizabeth won first place in the state contest.

Pauline had the ability to memorize easily. She could play and sing hundreds of songs from memory and could identify the numbers she heard at programs. Howard believed that she had perfect pitch. Pauline did not use music as a background for other activities, for she wanted to pay attention to every note. "Not only that, but it seemed she would see it in her mind in some manner so that she could not do any other activity."

So she did have a career that was uniquely her own; her personality, too, was uniquely Pauline. Her journal entries give a clue to her thoughts and aspirations. The tribute to her sister-in-law who died in 1971 reveals some of her own ideals:

> I liked so much to be in Helen's presence. I always felt good, worthwhile, important, and glad to be with her. I enjoyed talking with her. Her conversations were not filled with chatter, they were about things that mattered and were important to her and to me. She had a good and positive attitude on life. She always tried to see the good in each person and in each experience. She seemed to have a special sensitivity to the feelings, the hurts, and pains of other people. Helen was a disciplined person. She believed in the church and its activities.

A quotation by William Fox had appealed to her: "She always seemed unusually serene, but in a thoughtful way, as if she had weighed everything and was resolved to be at peace."

Her friends saw her as a calm person, and perhaps she willed calmness for herself. Howard knew that she did not like to argue, that she wanted to get things straightened out quietly, and he felt that she appeared to be more calm than she really was.

Her neighbors saw her as a rather reserved woman, but on the other hand quite outspoken. "She had more interest and concern about people than they realized," one of them said. Another observed that she never said anything negative about anybody.

Howard said, "My wife's mission to people other than her family was to speak and visit with everyone she met. She was good in drawing people out, where I was shorter in speech." College graduates remember her as the one who always spoke to them on campus and had an interest in their lives. Dean Donald Pannabecker said, "She spoke to each the word she thought each needed."

Living the simple life

Pauline, having been raised during the Depression, espoused the simple life even after it was no longer necessary. "She saved absolutely everything, and used food to the last bit." On the other hand, she bought things of good quality. She was a good bargainer, according to her husband. Pauline kept her own account book and managed their personal finances. She rode her bicycle around the campus but did not drive a car.

She liked routine. Dinner was at twelve and supper at five-thirty, and she wanted to serve them on time so that she was freed for other activities.

Howard pondered the question of what made her human rather than saintly. "She had difficulty making decisions, but perhaps this was a family trait. She was slow in accepting new ideas (some of mine). And she was not mechanical. When I was standing on a chair and had asked for a screwdriver, she would just as likely hand me the pliers."

Pauline had a special feeling for the neighbor children. She let each child know that he or she was important. Every day she went to the window to watch them go to and from school. Only one of the children was her own. Once she said that it was "remarkable that she had had that one." She kept close to her three grandchildren with letters, riddles, and scrapbooks.

With her neighbors she had a close relationship. They shared garden produce and baked goods, books, and magazines. These things along with notes and quotations were left and picked up on the back steps by the Raid kitchen door.

Pauline was recognized as a leader. As a minister's wife, and even before, she was active in church groups, president of the first Middle District Conference of Young People and of the Middle District Women's Conference, a member of the local Women in Mission. She taught a Sunday school class for forty years. Although she was not a joiner of many clubs, she did belong to the Alice Freeman Club, a group that promoted strong community service; a reading group; and the college Faculty Club. She enjoyed being a leader. "She was often involved in preparing the programs for these organizations. She spoke easily in public," Howard said.

Starting young to face old age

In her journal, Pauline had written several thoughts on growing old: "Old age is like everything else; to make a success of it, you have to start young." Her last entry was, "Growing old takes lots of time."

An entry on work was prophetic: "The really important task has two ingredients: a definite plan and not quite enough time to finish it. . . . I find each day too short for all that I really want to do, for all the thoughts I want to think, all the walks I want to take, all the books I want to read, all the friends I want to see."

When she felt a hard lump below the shoulder, Pauline and Howard both had the premonition that it indicated serious trouble.[3] But they proceeded with their plan to visit their daughter and family, the Steve Pankratzes in Minnesota, and other relatives in Iowa, never mentioning the threat that was in their minds.

When they returned home, she checked into the hospital for tests. The Raids shared their concern about the tests with the Sunday school class and their relatives. "After all, being ill is a part of living. Sometimes we are well, and sometimes ill. Many people were supportive in this period of waiting. After all, they can only be supportive if they know what one faces ahead. Therefore, we felt it was important to share our concern."

The tests showed that she had lung cancer, far advanced. The doctor in answer to their question of "How long?" said, "Maybe weeks. Maybe months."

Neither she nor Howard had had a serious illness before; they had spent less than $100 a year on medical bills. Her only problem had been a cough caused by a postnasal drip, and x-rays four years earlier had not indicated any real problem.

Pauline thought about the possibility of using chemotherapy or radiation treatments, but she decided that she would not try them. The chance of improvement or retarding the cancer was limited. She elected to go home and live out her life as normally as possible.

Having always felt that her life was in partnership with God first of all and then with her husband, she felt that her preparation for death would be accomplished within that partnership. She went about her usual tasks as well as she could, wanting to feel as much in control of her life as possible. She worried about Howard's being able to take care of himself.

Howard went through a period of blaming himself. Had he been the cause of stress for her? "Finally I had to realize that it was useless to waste my energies trying to determine the cause of lung cancer. . . . We soon

---

3. *Bluffton News*, March 8, 22, 29; Howard wrote a series of articles on her illness and death.

decided that our task was to find meaning for those days we had together. Our relationship deepened. My wife and I realized that we were in this experience together. . . . I found peace in the struggle with the *why* question when I dwelt on the rich full life that we had had over the many years."

Days never lived before

Some friends suggested that the Raids should pray for a miracle. Pauline rejected this idea. They prayed instead "for strength from God to deal with the cancer in a Christian manner."

Pauline died at home on February 12, 1984, surrounded by her family, her pastor, and her nurse. She was buried in the Zion Mennonite Cemetery at Donnellson.

At the memorial service in Bluffton, this prayer from her journal was read:

Thank you for death which sets a limit to pride
    of nation, religion, or position,
That in the face of death I may see the fragile beauty of life.
Thank you for life which offers me days never lived before
That I may spend and not hoard my life
    And choose joy over pleasure,
    peace before ease,
    trust instead of safety,
    and Love above all.

Also appropriate was the quotation from *Pilgrim's Progress* read by Dean Pannabecker:

> Pilgrim with his two companions, Christian and Hopeful, reached the river separating this world from the Celestial City beyond. And, in a dream, Pilgrim watches Christian and Hopeful, conquering their fears, cross the river and emerge triumphant on the other side.
> As they approach the gates, all the trumpets sound.
> As they pass through the gates and are transfigured, the sound of harps is heard.
> And as the gates close behind them, all the bells play.

Surely, Pauline, musician, would be pleased with such a reception to the Celestial City.

30.
Breaking Through Her Prison of Pain

Amanda Dahlenburg Friesen
1909—1982

by Helen Friesen

In some of her writing, Amanda Friesen said that, as a child, she had always associated the word *sad* with someone who had a physical deformity.

But during her school days, she met a boy whose leg was partially paralyzed. The impression stayed with her of how happy the boy seemed even though it was difficult for him to compete in games. His brace gave him an awkward gait but he always tried. She watched in amazement as he mounted his slippery little pony and rode to and from school, hugging his mount with his knees and dangling his dinner pail as he rode.

Later, during times of her own pain and stress, she recalled that boy's cheerful example and also the verse from the Bible: "No temptation has overtaken you that is not common to man. God is faithful, and he will not let you be tempted beyond your strength, but with the temptation will also provide the way of escape, that you may be able to endure it" (1 Cor. 10:13). And so she accepted the challenge of her affliction.[1]

In her childhood, Amanda, who loved to romp and play on the family farm near Avon, South Dakota, was always pained to hear of someone who was handicapped. One afternoon her sister hobbled about the yard, pretending to be a cripple. Not seeing any humor in the play, Amanda begged

---

1. This material comes from interviews with Jacob Friesen and from Amanda Friesen's own writings.

308 | ENCIRCLED

Amanda Friesen: When she inherited twenty-five dollars, she gave it to help dig a well in India.

her to stop, feeling that being crippled would be tragic. She did not dream that in her late twenties she would be glad to use crutches. Nor did she realize how much strength and comfort she would find in a wall motto: "I can do all things through Christ, who strengtheneth me" (Phil. 4:13).

Amanda was the third of six children born to William and Delia (Paul) Dahlenburg near Springfield, South Dakota, on December 3, 1909. Her grandparents on both sides of her family had emigrated from Germany, the Dahlenburgs in 1874 from Mecklenburg.

During her childhood years she enjoyed activities common to many farm children: picking mulberries, helping bring home the cows, riding the big white sow, picking bushels of corncobs for the hungry kitchen stove, helping her father skin jackrabbits, wading in the ditches after a rain, and digging worms to go fishing.

Legacy for a well in India

After four girls, the family had a baby boy, a great delight to his sisters. They took charge of him when their mother did the laundry. Amanda nestled close to her mother's rocking chair when the baby was fed and listened to her sing lullabies.

Her parents were of Lutheran background. The Dahlenburg children had attended a Presbyterian Sunday school held in a country school near their farm, but Amanda was confirmed in the Lutheran faith. During her teen years, J. A. Schmidt, originally from Avon, held evangelistic services in the community. He visited in the Dahlenburg home and asked them whether they had accepted Christ. Amanda's mother had done so earlier, probably before her marriage, but her father made his commitment to Christ at that time.

After this experience, they wanted to join the Friedensburg Mennonite Church at Avon. The church was willing to accept them without rebaptism, but Amanda decided that she wanted to be immersed. Pastor David Schultz baptized her in the river at Avon in the early 1930s, although the Friedensburg church did not ordinarily practice immersion.

When her grandparents died, Amanda inherited twenty-five dollars. About this time, she heard a missionary speak about the need for a well in India. Although she told no one at the time, she gave all of her inheritance to help dig that well. Later Amanda met one of the missionaries from that field and learned to her pleasure that the well was still serving the people of the area.

Amanda did not receive much formal education. She went to elementary school in the Avon area but did not go to high school. Later, she attended Freeman Junior College for Bible courses taught by P. R.

Schroeder and P. P. Tschetter. In 1932 and 1933, she attended Northwestern Bible School in Minneapolis for two years. While going to school in Minneapolis, she worked as a household helper. She met Jacob Friesen during those years.

Pastor and teacher's wife

Amanda and Jacob were married in June 1936. Jacob served as pastor of churches in the Doland and Huron, South Dakota, areas. He also taught school in Avon and other small towns, teaching for about twenty-five years.

There was happiness in the Friesen household when their first child, Lois Joy, was born in August 1937. The women of the community held a baby shower for Amanda, and the baby received many pretty little dresses and other gifts. Although Lois was a healthy baby at birth, she lived only eleven days. Amanda chose a simple white dress for Lois to wear for the funeral and packed away the rest of the lovely clothes, hoping that some day another baby might be able to use them.

Years later, when poverty and suffering stalked Europe, Amanda made a decision about the baby clothes. One night, unable to sleep because of pain, she prayed for the unfortunate children who were victims of this tragedy, wishing she could do something for them. A voice out of the darkness seemed to say, "How about the baby clothes you've been hoarding all these years?" She responded to the call and sent those lovely things meant for her daughter to someone who needed them.

Well acquainted with pain

When she was about thirty, she was diagnosed as having rheumatoid arthritis. This misfortune shaped the rest of her life. Beginning in 1939, and for the next forty years, she was unable to sit in a chair because of the stiffness in her spine caused by the disease. She became well acquainted with pain, especially in the early years. For a period of ten years, she was bedfast, but with the help of her inventive husband she was able to become more mobile.

Padded footwear, a smooth floor, and a walker helped her so that she could get to the kitchen sink to do the dishes that Jacob placed within her limited reach. Her stiff body gave her just two choices: she could be either vertical or horizontal. Jacob designed and built a bed that could be placed at any angle between horizontal and vertical. The children dubbed it her "up and down" bed.

Once she was in a vertical position she used crutches to get about to do a number of activities around the house. She could eat with the family by standing with a crutch under each arm. When she wanted to lie down, she backed up to her bed, pushed the button, and was able to stop at any angle.

She enjoyed her garden as well as cooking and sewing for her family. Unable to bend, she developed ingenious ways of solving problems. Things on the floor might as well have been in China. One time while her family was at church, she took her crutches and headed for the kitchen to prepare fried fish for dinner. She got the package of fish fillets from the refrigerator, but before she reached the stove, she dropped the package on the floor. Ordinarily, she could have called one of the children to give her a helping hand. Now she was alone, helpless. She wondered why bending had to be so important. Perhaps she should just use her head to solve the problem. Something clicked. She went for the long-handled dustpan and her broom. Into the dustpan went the fish. She was pleased to have landed the fish, for now she could join the ranks of fish-story tellers without even leaving home.

Her husband fixed the car so that they could travel together. She would lie down and with the help of prismatic glasses could see the sights through the rear window of the car. Those prism glasses also made it possible for Amanda to write and read while lying down.

Her last three children were born by cesarean section after she had developed arthritis. Philip was born in November 1943, Gerald in June 1945, and Jewell in April 1947.

Caring for the children

How does a handicapped mother take care of her brood? Love and resourcefulness made it possible. She remembered how her own mother had rocked her brother and the warmth of that love.

Since she couldn't use a rocking chair when the babies were small, she rocked them by running the bed up and down. She also learned to diaper the babies while they lay on her tummy when she was in bed. She used an adjustable table to give her baby a sponge bath. A rolling table helped her transport Jewell to the playpen, which was kept on top of the dining room table. Without bending, Amanda could change the baby's diapers while she was in the playpen. This was Jewell's kingdom, where she ate her first meals and took her first steps.

Amanda disciplined with love. Out of necessity, she developed a unique system for calling them when they were needed. She arranged a code of rings on a whistle for each child. One ring meant that all three were to report to her.

One day her small son dropped a jar of cream. When she heard the crash and saw him standing in a lake of cream, she scolded him sharply and told him he should have been more careful.

"Mamma," he sobbed, "I didn't mean to. You drop things, too, don't you?"

She apologized quickly and he forgave her, but she remembered how ashamed she felt that she had placed a higher value on the quart of cream than on the feelings of her son.

The Tinker Toy Christmas tree

Before her arthritis put an end to it, Amanda played the piano. Her talents were inherited by her children. She gave her oldest son his first music lesson from her bed. When the children were practicing, her musical ear helped her to tell from her prone position when they struck wrong notes. She also sang with them.

When they were older, they had to practice their instruments for band lessons. The children complained one day of being tired. If they had to practice, they wanted to be comfortable. So Jewell seated herself in a chair with her saxophone. The boys took off their shoes and lay down on the floor. The one with the trombone put a pillow under his head and put his feet on a chair. The one with the French horn hooked both heels over the edge of the table. Amanda watched in amazement, sure that they couldn't play that way; yet they went through the entire march. She could only laugh at their antics. "Better than a bottle of pills," she said.

One year, when the children were asking for a Christmas tree, she told them that this year they would use their money to provide milk for some hungry baby because of all the hunger in the world. The children seemed to understand. A few days before Christmas the boys called for her to hurry and come see because now they had a tree. With her crutches under her arms, she made her way to their side. From their set of Tinker Toys, they had designed a tree. She rejoiced with them and told them to put it on the table and decorate it with tinsel and angel hair. The family never forgot the year of the Tinker Toy tree.

She enjoyed company. Some came with the mistaken notion of bringing her cheer, but she was one person whose joyous spirit infected everyone who came in contact with her. Her upbeat nature refused to give in to discouragement. Her friends enjoyed getting letters sharing how a passage from the Bible had spoken to her. She kept in touch with people by phone to encourage them. Sometimes she mentioned to them insights on something she had read.

Victory over discouragement

Amanda devoted many hours to prayer, surrounding her family and friends with her intercession. Since she spent many hours a day on her back, this occupation became an innate part of her.

She had needed faith and courage when their first daughter had died as an infant, and then again when their son Gerald died in 1961 at the age of fifteen from a blood clot.

During the early years of her battle with arthritis, her husband Jacob worked with the local Easter seals drive. He was asked to bring Amanda along to a meeting of the Crippled Children's Association in a Methodist Church at Pierre, South Dakota. She was to give the talk. As she visited with the group informally, she stood with her back against the wall and with a crutch under each arm, resting one hand on the chair in front of her for support. The audience smiled when after testing the chair and finding that it moved too easily on the slick floor, she asked her husband to sit on the chair.

She recalled for her listeners how she had overheard the words of the doctor spoken in low tones outside her hospital room: "She may get some good out of a wheelchair, but that is all we can expect."

The gloomy specter of discouragement hung over her shoulder as she contemplated her future. She fancied she heard it mock her with "Cripple! You're a cripple! Admit it. Say it out loud! Are you afraid to?"

As she stirred uneasily, the battle continued. "You are chained. Bound. Try to move. You can't! Cripple!"

As the specter was speaking, Amanda's eyes filled with tears. With her crippled hand she tried to brush away the tears. With a clear voice, she pushed back her enemy. "No, I won't be discouraged yet. I still remember clearly those words of Job which I read years before this affliction came. They speak to me now."

In triumph, she said, "Thou shalt come to thy grave in a good age, like as a shock of corn cometh in his season. . . . Unto God would I commit my cause, who doeth great things . . . unsearchable things . . . without number."

She reached for her black leather-bound Bible and opened it to read, "Paul, a prisoner of the Lord."

These six words seemed to satisfy her and she closed the Bible and laid it aside. She recalled that Paul had written letters which had been a blessing to many people through the years. He, too, was bound and chained, not permitted to come and go as he wished, but he did a great work. If Paul could be a prisoner of the Lord and still rejoice, then surely she could be a patient of the Lord and somehow do something worthwhile with her life.

Even though she had had her share of frustrations because of her condition, she found that some of them came when she forgot to remember the promises of God. If Paul and Silas could rejoice when their feet were in stocks, then surely she could also rejoice in her prison. If Paul didn't waste a lot of time grumbling, then neither would she. She would not let her immobilized body cripple her spirit or faith in God.

That was her message to her listeners at the meeting.

This major victory over discouragement helped her through the minor skirmishes that were yet to come, such as when a well-meaning visitor mentioned, "It must take a great deal of money for doctor bills."

Using the pen in her hand

After the visitor left, Amanda felt keenly her inability to earn a penny. Once again she reached for her Bible and read the story of Moses. She pictured this lonely shepherd turning aside for the burning bush and read again God's question to Moses: "What hast thou in thy hand?"

For Moses, the answer had been a rod. As a child she had thrilled to the miracles that Moses and his rod had performed with the help of God. Now, this story gave hope to her spirit.

"What is in your hand?" She glanced down and saw she had a pen in her hand. Since God had used Moses and his rod, God could do the same for her with her pen. She received encouragement from her husband.

Although crippled in body, Amanda left no doubt that she was not crippled in mind or spirit. She developed the gifts she had. She enjoyed poetry, and poetry suited her style. Since she did not have advanced training, she used various methods to learn how to write poetry. She relied on her contacts with editors who helped her develop her style. She found books that explained how it should be done and collected books of synonyms to suggest rhymes.

Her humor is reflected in much of her poetry, of which about 300 have been published. The family decided to use her legacy of poetry as a tribute to her. Following her death, they published about 400 of her poems in a book called *Verse From Twisted Fingers*.

Whatever she observed drew a response from her in poetry. It could be in nature as she saw it from her window or in incidents involving her family. She made poems for special events and shared them with those for whom they were intended. For example, even though she couldn't sit in a rocking chair when her last three children were born, she could sing for them. She composed a poem about a creaking rocking chair that delighted them.

One time she looked out of her window after a night when frost had painted the otherwise bare and frozen yard to resemble a fairyland. Even a lone Russian thistle sparkled with tiny diamonds. The ugly weed had become a shining object.

She glanced at her own body, twisted and bent by her disease, and thought, "Someday God will change my body into a glorious resurrection body."

She recorded some of the incidents of her life in comments under the title "Why Worry?" which were published as a newsletter called *Handicapped Hobbyists*.

Here is one of her short poems called *Little Things*:

> Light will shine through narrow windows
> If the panes are clean.
>
> Night will seem a friend the moment
> The first star is seen.
>
> Narrow strips of crooked lightning
> Brighten ink dark sky.
>
> Poems live on blessing many
> Though the poets die.

Amanda was always involved in the church. Teaching was natural for her. Bible school and Sunday school were always part of her life, no matter where they lived. During her husband's days as a pastor, she always taught wherever his church might be.

She developed her talents as storyteller quite early by making up stories for her children. Even when flat on her back, she would gather them around her bed and tell them stories. She encouraged and helped them memorize Bible verses and told them Bible stories. She even found time to write little plays and songs. The music she composed found its way into *Junior Messenger*, now known as *On the Line*.

She continued attending church services even after she lost the ability to bend. This meant she had to stand during the entire service. In later years, when she could no longer go to church, she listened to religious radio programs for spiritual sustenance.

Stronger than a giant

The state of South Dakota observes a special day called Shut-in Day. On one of these occasions, a father and his son called on Amanda Friesen.

She was quite frail at the time and bedfast from a struggle with rheumatoid arthritis.

As they left the house, the son heard his father say, "Stronger than a giant. Yes, stronger than a giant."

"Did my ears hear right?" asked the boy. "What can you mean? You could push that skinny old lady over with a toothpick."

"Did you hear one word of complaint from her lips all the time we were visiting? Anyone who can live cheerfully in spite of handicaps, in my book, is stronger than a giant."

The boy recalled how earlier he had chafed while he waited for his broken arm to heal and understood what his father meant.

Amanda died on April 20, 1982, in Mountain Lake, Minnesota, where she and Jacob were living in retirement. Her son Philip and his wife Kim were working in Taiwan under the Commission on Overseas Missions and returned in time to attend the funeral. Jewell and her husband Richard Breneman came from Pennsylvania. Amanda was buried in the Emmanuel Mennonite cemetery at Doland.

Amanda lived with personal tragedy for the greater part of her adult life. Her response to adversity was a positive attitude, by which she deliberately sought ways of living a fulfilled life. She found support from her husband and children. She was grateful for their assistance with those family chores which she could not do.

One of her quotations, "A good wife backs her husband up when he is right and helps him back down when he is wrong," speaks of the support she gave him. For his part, her husband said, "I wouldn't be the man I am today it it wasn't for her."

For real support, she looked to her faith. She understood the promises of God to Job, of Christ to Paul, and she took them to apply to her own condition. As a "prisoner of the Lord" she was free to be sensitive to the needs of others.

31.
Reader of the Cheyenne Scriptures

Julia Yellow Horse Shoulderblade
1913—1973

The ministry of Julia Shoulderblade bridged two cultures, the Indian and the white; and in her lifetime, she saw her Cheyenne people adopting more and more the white world's customs, even as the white culture changed during her lifetime. The Cheyennes could not remain isolated from United States history in the 1900s. Their young men took part in World War II and their young women found jobs in the towns.

Julia's funeral service illustrates a blending of cultures. A group from the Petter Memorial Church at Lame Deer, Montana, sang hymns in Cheyenne, and a quartet of Cheyenne women from the Birney Mennonite Church sang hymns in English. Although the service followed some traditional aspects, Julia had asked that the Cheyenne custom of burying the deceased's belongings with the body not be observed, as she would not need them in her next life.

The prestige of the Coal Bears

The Yellow Horse family was well known on the Northern Cheyenne Reservation in southeastern Montana. Her mother's name was Rose Coal Bear (in Cheyenne, *Moheno'e*, meaning Sitting with the Gathered). Her relatives had for generations been Keepers of the Sacred Hat, an office that demanded a good-natured and honest man. The Hat was a bundle of sacred objects that had meaning in the religious ceremonies of the North-

Julia Shoulderblade: She sang the old missionary hymns as well as Cheyenne spiritual songs.

ern Cheyenne. Because of this position, the Coal Bear family had some prestige.[1]

Julia's father was John Yellow Horse (in Cheyenne, *Heovo'hame*, meaning Has Yellow Horse). Julia was born May 1, 1913, and named *Maheonehoehne'e*, meaning Woman Coming Out Holy. Her mother was from Lame Deer and her father from Birney, Indian towns about twenty miles apart.[2]

When Julia was three, her father died. Later Rose married Milton Whiteman who was to become one of the two ministers that Missionary Rodolphe Petter ordained among the Northern Cheyennes. Milton was from Lame Deer. For a time, he was chief of police, so the family moved around on the reservation to wherever he was stationed. Milton was also well-known as a singer at Cheyenne social functions. His Indian name was *Meshoko'e*, meaning Bushy-faced Person.

The faith of her parents

Julia received what would be considered a good education for her time. She attended government boarding schools at Busby, Montana, and Salem, Oregon; and while her stepfather was stationed in Ashland, she attended St. Labre Indian School, a private school. She finished eighth grade and probably a year or two of secondary school. Rose, her mother, did not read or speak English, but she could read Cheyenne. Milton could read, write, and speak English well.

Bertha Petter mentioned in her letters that Julia was sending a buckskin dress to the Kauffman Museum at Bethel College. It is a young girl's ceremonial dress, the color of pecan shell. The yoke and skirt are trimmed with small cowrie shells and tiny metal bells. The sleeves and hem are fringed. Julia wore it on festival occasions.

As the stepdaughter of Milton Whiteman, who was active in the Mennonite church, she joined the church and was always a part of the Christian community. Julia must have received some of the strength of her faith from her mother and stepfather. Milton was firm in his belief that he was right in his relationship with God.

Twice in his life, he had something of an experience like Job. Once, while preaching, he was struck with a paralysis in his face, and another time his horse was killed by lightning while Milton was riding. His

---

1. John Stands In Timber, *Cheyenne Memories* (New Haven, Connecticut: Yale University Press, 1967), p. 74.
2. Much information comes from an article by Malcolm Wenger, "Julia Shoulderblade," *Missions Today*, August 1973; from interviews with Malcolm and Esther Wenger, and Willis Busenitz; from the diary of Bertha Petter.

congregation interpreted these incidents as signs from God, that Milton was being punished. He and his family felt alone, always under pressure, and they learned to stand firmly in their faith.

Grieved by her elopement

Julia's courtship and marriage were not according to tradition.

Marriageable Cheyenne girls were well protected by their families. Cheyenne women had a reputation for chastity, and girls were strictly obedient and careful of appearances. A young man was expected to court a girl for one to five years, during which time he might give presents, including horses, to the father or brother of the girl.

The traditional way of arranging a marriage was for a friend to do the negotiating for the young man. He applied to her parents for their consent when he felt that the girl would have him. The parents might talk the matter over with the other relatives. Gifts were sent to help the parents decide. The young man might ask the girl to elope with him, but she would usually put him off, for an elopement was considered disgraceful. The girl presumably had the last word on whom she wished to marry, but her parents might use verbal persuasion. Many presents were exchanged between the young man and his family and her family.

Julia disappointed her Indian family and her Christian missionary friends by eloping with James Shoulderblade. During World War II, a number of the Cheyenne young men were drafted. The Mennonite church tried to keep in touch with them, and Julia was one who wrote to a number of the soldiers. One of them was James Shoulderblade, who fought through Africa and Europe.

When James returned from his three years in the war, it was evident that he had experienced situations which would have caused some men to break down physically and emotionally. He would not talk about those horrors. James considered himself tough. He carried a gun constantly, "just waiting for some white man to push me around," he said. James, who had roots in Ashland, was like a son to Mrs. Laura Petter, the widowed missionary in charge of the work there.

When the friendship between James and Julia developed into a romance, the Christian community was disturbed because James was not a committed Christian. Since the pastors would not marry them, James and Julia eloped to Forsyth and were married on March 19, 1946.

Bertha Petter, the missionary at Lame Deer, reported the event in her diary: "Moheno'e [Julia's mother] came to say Julia had gone to see Beatrice and there James got her, took her to Ashland and Forsyth to be married. We were grieved." Julia was a favorite of the Petters, and they felt that they had lost her from the faith.

Deathbed commission for ministry

Julia was accepted back into the church after the marriage, and James attended occasionally. About two years later, James was converted after a preaching service by John Suderman from Oraibi, Arizona. "Toughness and bitterness melted away," Wenger wrote, and James was a new person in Christ. He was baptized the following Sunday.

James and Julia Shoulderblade together served their people in a significant ministry that was to last for twenty-seven years. Both became active in the Lame Deer Mennonite Church, where they began home cottage prayer meetings. They started a summer camp meeting up in the hills at Crazyhead Springs in 1949 which is still being carried on today. After a brief ministry to the Busby congregation, they were called to the church at Birney. They accepted and served from 1966 to 1973, although they kept their home in Lame Deer.

James' call to the ministry is described by Malcolm Wenger:

> When Milton Whiteman was on his deathbed, he called James to his bedside and told him that he wanted to pass on to him the sacred responsibility of the Christian ministry that had been committed to him in ordination. As James knelt beside the bed, Milton laid on his hands and prayed. He then gave James his copy of the *Minister's Manual*. For a long time after Milton died, James did not share this experience with anyone. However, when other Christians began to ask him to assume pastoral leadership, he told them of this experience.

The Northern District Committee on the Ministry recognized this ordination officially in May 1970.

Singing the Cheyenne spiritual songs

Julia and James were among the first in Montana to openly sing the indigenous Cheyenne spiritual songs. In the early years, the use of these songs was forbidden by the missionaries because they used Cheyenne tunes with words composed by the Cheyenne Christians. Today their use is widely accepted. The hymns were introduced by visiting Cheyennes from Oklahoma.

The Shoulderblades started using them at wakes and then at prayer meetings. They would not sing these Cheyenne spiritual songs at the beginning of the worship services. They would sing the Petter songs, those he had translated from the old hymns, but toward the end of the service James would lead out and Julia would follow with Cheyenne spiritual songs. This was their way of saying what God meant to them.

About 1960, the Shoulderblades asked Missionary Wenger to make recordings of their singing. They envisioned a time when the Cheyenne could have a hymnbook with these spiritual songs along with hymns translated from non-Indian sources. The final result was *Tsese-Ma-'heone'Nemeototse*, edited by David Graber, a book of songs with music, in both English and Cheyenne. Included in the volume is a handbook with notes on the words and music of many of the hymns. James Shoulderblade was on the editorial committee, but Julia died before it was published in 1982.

A fluent reader of the Cheyenne Bible

Julia's gifts lay in her formal and informal participation in the work of the church. Especially appreciated by the Lame Deer and the Birney congregations was her ability to read Scripture in Cheyenne. She was one of the few Cheyenne Christians who could read Petter's translations fluently. She would explain and make comments with perception.

In 1954, when Bertha Petter gave up teaching her Cheyenne Sunday school class for the older people, Julia took it over. Esther Wenger said, "She preached, but not from behind the pulpit." For years Julia was active in the home Bible study groups, gathering women in her home even until the last days when she was crippled with arthritis.

Going to the homes was an important part of Julia's ministry. She was welcome in homes of people who never attended church. The Wengers estimated that she must have visited in half the homes in Lame Deer.

The Cheyenne have a tradition of gift giving as a way of honoring people. Class distinction means little among the Cheyenne. People are honored for what they give away rather than for what they keep. You share with people who need and when you need, they will share with you. Gift giving is always part of a celebration.

Julia brought together the idea of caring for God's family within the Christian community and the old Cheyenne way of gift giving. She used it as she organized meetings for women both in the church circles and on the outer edge. She and the church women arranged showers for young mothers and young brides, always including devotions. The events were well planned with nice refreshments and lovely gifts, drawing women into the circle.

She brought the women together to make blankets or comforters. They would make one for themselves and another to be given away to those who were sick or cold, or to a child whose parent had died.

Julia was a good home manager. She baked her own bread and "her fry bread was just tops," according to Esther Wenger.

Home and family caught between cultures

The Shoulderblades had one daughter and three sons: Timothy, Wendaline Valdo (obviously named after Laura Petter's husband), Mary Magdaline, and Titus. They were often a cause of concern and heartache. Here Julia was caught between her cultures.

The Cheyenne were once noted for good discipline. According to tradition, parents did not discipline children; uncles and aunts were given that responsibility. But Julia had no brothers and sisters to rely on as disciplinarians. In the transition when parents were to become responsible for the training of children, the boarding school took over and eliminated the original safeguards. Julia and James were overprotective of their children and did not know how to discipline them.

Perhaps another of Julia's weaknesses was listed above as one of her strengths. Her gift giving went to what whites would consider unacceptable lengths. Even James became frustrated when she would have to go into debt for it. Saving for a rainy day is not part of the Cheyenne tradition.

Julia was a strong person, perhaps too much so. Things couldn't be done in any other way but her way, and changes could not be made in the church until she was gone. And when she was gone, the church seemed not to know how to carry on, and James missed her direction.

Ill health plagued her for much of her life. Diabetes and arthritis sapped her energy. She had a bout with cancer three years before she died. But even during the times she was bedridden, her daughter said she had an active prayer life, calling people by name, including women of other churches who had sent materials for sewing. She prepared tapes of her reading of the Scriptures, with explanations. She asked her daughter Magdaline to impress on the Christian women that they must take up the responsibility of praying for others and witnessing to them.

Two months before her death, she had a heart attack. She asked to be buried at Birney, her mother's home community, where the cottonwoods grow along the Tongue River and the hills rise steeply to the south. She died May 16, 1973. Julia bridged the two cultures, her Cheyenne past with its tradition of the spirit of the Sacred Hat, and the Christian present with its faith in God.

Margreet Stubbe: The church ought to fulfill a service role in the neighborhood and not just provide pastoral care for its members.

32.
Finding New Forms for Christian Witness

Margreet Stubbe
1926—

by Lydia Penner

Ten years ago the fishing village forming the old core of the city of Ijmuiden in The Netherlands was sanitated—that is, the old and run-down houses were demolished. The Mennonite church was left standing alone on an empty plain. New houses came, and today a community of worker families has formed. Most of the residents are not churchgoers, and there are several Turkish immigrant families who hold to the religion of Islam.

For Margreet Stubbe, pastor of the Mennonite church since 1972, this situation focuses the issue of the church's role in society. Margreet's view of a church adapted to the needs of the times has been shaped by nearly thirty years in various forms of ministry and religious education.

Minister in a melancholy community

Born in Amsterdam in 1926, Margreet lived there all her life until she became a minister. Her father was a civil engineer and taught at an electrotechnical school. Her mother had studied music but had never made a career of it, even part time. Margreet was one of three children. A brother died in a flying accident in 1952. Margreet lives with her younger sister Rina, a teacher.

Margreet graduated from high school in 1947 and went on to study theology at the Mennonite seminary in Amsterdam, from which she graduated in 1954.[1]

Margreet's parents were Mennonite, but she was the only one in her family who went to church regularly. She was greatly inspired by the woman who gave instruction in the faith when she was in her teens. The teacher knew the Bible well and was enthusiastic about Francis of Assisi.

From childhood, Margreet was known as friendly by nature, as someone who could get along with everyone. It was always difficult for her to accept the conflict model of dealing with situations, that is, confronting people, though she came to see that it is sometimes a good thing to stand up for an unpopular notion, even if a heated, unpleasant discussion ensues.

For instance, she raised hackles in Ijmuiden by saying that "Jesus didn't come for pastoral care, but for the neighborhood and for minimum wages for Dutch and Turkish families." And yet, typically, she asked herself whether it was fair to upset people not in a position to respond to her challenge.

She considers her absentmindedness as a great weakness. It is a family trait. But knowing this about herself has made her careful, and she has seldom forgotten appointments. When there is something to be organized, she usually calls upon people who are good at it because she herself is not.

Margreet first served three small congregations part time while teaching religion, also part time, in an elementary school. In this area, the residents were known for their melancholy temperament. Sometimes there was a suicide. When believers of her own congregations took their own lives, she would agonize, asking herself what she might have done to prevent it.

Learning about suicide

In 1963, she felt that she could no longer handle the work, although she had had many good experiences with the members. (She particularly appreciated the good experience of preparing a work camp to renovate the church.) She felt she lacked adequate knowledge of the Bible and of pastoral psychology. Back she went to studying.

She earned the Dutch equivalent of a master's degree in New Testament in 1968. A three-month course in pastoral clinical training (derived

---

1. "In no other country have the Mennonites had a theological seminary of such long standing nor have the ministers received such uniform and thorough theological training as is the case in Holland" (*Mennonite Encyclopedia*, Vol. I, p. 110).

from the Menninger Foundation in Kansas) and a course in psychotherapy helped her understand the reasons for the suicides she had known and taught her to notice early warning signs of depression in the people under her pastoral care.

As part of her master's degree she had a two-hour oral examination on pastoral theology in which she had to advise the examining professor what he should say to someone who had attempted suicide. During this exam, which she regards as a momentous experience, she learned that a suicide attempt is a result of weighing negatives and positives.

Margreet returned to pastoral work in 1969, accepting a call to Monnickendam, North Holland. In addition, she taught at two schools, one a high school for university entrance and another for business administration students. Although she had earlier enjoyed teaching, she found it hard work because of the necessity of keeping order, and she preferred one-to-one conversation.

She became pastor of the Ijmuiden congregation in 1972. Later that year, she gave up teaching and accepted a half-time job at the Menno Simons House in Amsterdam, a senior citizens' residence with semi-independent apartments attached. There she provides pastoral care for 285 residents.

Margreet has written a book, *Thuis in een tehuis?* (At Home in a Home?) It is about her experiences in ministering to old people.

Including children in communion

Gentle-voiced, gray-haired Margreet lives quietly and simply with her sister on a residential street in Amsterdam. Outwardly, she does not seem like a revolutionary.

Because church going is no longer a custom of the majority of the Dutch population and the rituals of church life are far removed from people's experience, she came to believe that new forms have to be found which are suited to the needs of the times.

She has tried to find these new forms in the Ijmuiden Mennonite Church. Three couples from the community got a children's club going which grew in three years from five to twenty-five children.

In the monthly family services, when children and adults have church together (in The Netherlands children and adults usually have separate services), the activities are not structured as in the traditional service, which usually has a pattern of call to worship, song, Scripture reading, song, Scripture reading, song, prayer, sermon, organ number, prayer, song, blessing. Her family services include *bibliodrama*, puppet shows, and games as well as a time of formal meditation and prayer in a circle.

Margreet agreed to the parents' request to have the children take part in the communion service, though this decision was later criticized by some church council members. Her critics said that unbaptized children could not understand communion and what it means; communion is for baptized members of the church who have made a conscious, adult decision for the community of faith.

But Margreet found this communion service with the children a particularly moving experience. "When I was explaining the meaning of it, and the bread and wine were given out, the children were deeply silent. They were learning something they will never forget."

Margreet's view of life and the church is reflected in the theme she chose for one of the family services in Ijmuiden: "God permits laughter." One part of the service had the children act out stiff-necked, tight-lipped, frowning people to depict the attitude of the Pharisees. This contrasted to the view that God can be worshiped in festive, playful ways.

Margreet faced the fact that the children coming to the club were unlikely to be baptized and become members of the church later. It had been her experience that few people take this step. The best one could expect was that they would learn something of what God and Jesus mean.

Turning away the Muslims

She believed that the church ought to fulfill a service role in the neighborhood and not just provide pastoral care for its own members. She was disappointed when the church council decided against renting the meeting room to the Turkish Muslims for use as a Koran school. She felt the church had thereby lost an opportunity for communication with these immigrants. No other church welcomed them either.

In her view, the church should go even further: there should be a sign on the church door announcing its availability to meet spiritual and material needs. But such an ambition is difficult to realize in Ijmuiden—or anywhere—for there are few people under forty actively involved in the congregation, and old people haven't the energy.

Margreet's keen awareness that "we are in a transitional period" is rather unusual even in a Mennonite conference used to adapting to the times. In most congregations, the Mennonite church service and congregational structure hasn't changed in decades, even centuries, and the primary concern of church councils is the inner life of the congregation. Community service by individuals or groups is respected and supported but is not a priority.

In her pastoral work, Margreet has always tried for reconciliation between estranged people. But she has learned to accept that people can be spiritually destroyed sometimes if pressed into a reconciliation they're not ready for. This applies especially to old people and their children. Social workers nowadays are taught that if children do not want to visit their elderly parents—because of past experiences—they should not be pressured to do so. Margreet feels that she tends to try longer to achieve reconciliation than other professional helpers do.

Her experience in pastoral care encouraged her natural tendency to take the broader view of faith. With old people, she has learned not to talk about preparation for death, but about what life has meant. "It's not necessary always to come with open Bible. The conversation itself can sometimes be a confession of guilt. Prayer also occurs without the folding of hands. You can't ask people whether they're saved or freed; you notice it in their life if it's so."

Margreet never married. Being single meant carrying alone the burden of things in her pastoral work which she couldn't tell anyone. But she always felt supported by the congregation; when she called upon people, they were willing to help. "We have to appeal to the belief in the priesthood of all believers," she says.

The woman minister issue

Performing all the functions of minister as a woman was never an issue in her years of service with the Dutch Mennonites. They have accepted female ministers since shortly after the turn of the century, and women participate in the church without any restrictions on principle.

The point about female role restrictions came up only once—at a meeting of a European Mennonite mission organization when a Dutch brother suggested that she and another woman minister not join the other ministers at the communion table, out of consideration for the attitude of the foreign brothers who did not approve of women in that role. When she and her female colleague protested, they were called feminists, a label Margreet dislikes because it stereotypes her. She thinks the wives of ministers have more problems than female ministers because their function is less clearly defined.

Margreet's openness to new forms in church life and expressions of faith is encouraged by the hopefulness of her disposition. Rejoicing means to go and do something celebrative and enjoyable when things are getting to you; to see hope in a sunrise; to rest in retreat when you can't handle it any more. She sees rejoicing as an imperative, but not something you put on; it has to come from within. She sums up her view of life by quoting Philippians 4:4: "Rejoice in the Lord always."

Sara Hartzler: She never gave a lecture that wasn't a sermon, and all of her sermons were lectures writ large.

Epp, Hillegonde 279
Epp, Ingrid 279
Epp, Jacob 252
Epp, Johann 277
Epp, Linda 290, 291
Epp, Lydia 290, 291, 292
Epp, Kaethe 279
Epp, Katharina Ratzlaff 275-83
Epp, Lena Willms 252
Epp, Martin 289, 290, 295
Epp, Menno H. 290, 291, 296
Epp, Rudi 293
Epp, Sister Ida 77
Epp, Susan 290, 291, 292, 294, 297
Epp, Susanna 289
Epp, Viola 290, 294
Esau, J. J. 294
Europe 142
Europe, Alsace-Lorraine 86
Evangelical Mennonite Brethen 63, 67
Evangelical Synod Seminary 227
Ewert, August 70
Eymann, Anna 228
Eymann, Clara 125

faith 339
Faith and Life Press 145, 225
Fast, Aganetha 266, 271
feminism 141
Fenton, Carroll 172
flannelgraph 220
Fluck, Florence White 195-204
Fluck, Victor 198, 202
foster children 31
Fox, William 303
Francis of Assisi 326
Franz, Mary Lou 222
Frederick III 15
Freeman Academy 208, 209
Freeman Junior College 110, 111, 302, 309
Frei, Ruth 200
Frey, Aganetha 163
Frey, J. B. 163, 171
Frey, John 168
Friesen, Amanda Dahlenburg 307-16
Friesen, Cornelius W. 281
Friesen, Gerald 311
Friesen, Helen 307, 351
Friesen, Jacob 310
Friesen, Jewell 311
Friesen, Katie 143
Friesen, Kim 316
Friesen, Lois Joy 310
Friesen, Philip 311, 316
Fry, Elisabeth 18

Full Circle 1
Funk, A. E. 20
Funk, Annie 257
Funk, Herta 6
Funk Memorial School 257

Gaeddert, Jessie Brown 80
Gandhi, Mahatma 221
Garrett Biblical Institute 182
General Conference office building 146
Gerber, Samuel 44
German Baptists 255
Germany 99, 137, 143, 246
Germany, Altenau 56
Germany, Altona 17, 18
Germany, Baden 73
Germany, Bavaria 125
Germany, Berlin 129
Germany, Danzig 33, 35
Germany, Eichstock 125
Germany, Erlangen 17
Germany, Freidelsheim 300
Germany, Galicia 137
Germany, Hamburg 21, 137
Germany, Kaiserwerth 22
Germany, Marienburg 33
Germany, Mecklenburg 309
Germany, Palatinate 227
Germany, Westphalia 17
Goering, Pauline 272
Goering, Sam 272
Goertz, Elizabeth 183, 265, 270, 271
Goerz, David 74, 75, 82, 137
Goerz, Katie 75
Goldwater, Barry 173
Goshen Academy 97, 188
Goshen College 97, 188, 189, 332, 334
Gotebo, Kiowa Chief 236
Gottschall, W. S. 105
Graber, David 322
Grace Bible Institute 70
Grandma Remembers 254
Greencroft Retirement Center 184, 193
Grubb, Nathaniel B. 263
Gundy, Clara Louise Struhbar 4, 85-93
Gundy, Donald 89
Gundy, George 88
Gundy, Gerdon 89, 93
Gundy, Jacob 88
Gundy, John 91
Gundy, Lena Kinzinger 88
Gundy, Ralph 89, 90
Guth, John 88

Habegger, Alfred 48, 51
Habegger, Barbara 51

Habegger, Carl 151
Habegger, Jules 154
Habegger, Martha Lena Baumgartner 38, 40, 149-62
Habegger, Martin 152
Habegger, Ruth 154
Hamm, Emelie Siemens. *See* Mosiman, Emelie Siemens Hamm.
Hamm, Emily Siemens 33
Hamm, Peter 33
Hamm, William 35
Hansen's disease 257
happiness 338
Harder, Abram 213
Harder, Bobby 216
Harder, Christena. *See* Duerksen, Christena Harder.
Harder, Ethel 128
Harder, Harry 216
Harder, Joe 215
Harder, Martha 215
Harder, William 215
Hardy, Joan 233
Hartford Seminary 263, 264
Hartzler, Emma 335
Hartzler, Erin 334
Hartzler, Gregory A. 332, 334
Hartzler, Kelly 334
Hartzler, Sara Kathryn Kreider 331-39
Hartzler, Shannon 334
Harvard University 140
Hauck, Pegi 143
Haury, R. S. 78
Haury, Samuel S. 23
Hausfrau 237
Heffelbower, Clare Ann Ruth 128, 129, 134
Hege, Jacob 57
Heinlein, Robert 335
Hemingway, Ernest 173
Herald Press 334
Hesston College 189
Hiebert, Anna 129
Hiebert, D. G. 79
Hiebert, Evangeline 174
Hiebert, J. N. C. 129
Hill, LaVera 121, 124
Hillary, Sir Edmund 132
Holt, Greta 161
Holy Land 209
Home Mission Board 107
Hong Kong 182
Hopi culture 169, 174
Hopi Mennonite Church 171
Hopi people 163
Hopi push war 166
Hopi, Kachina clan 165
Horny, Elisabeth 19, 21
humor 336

Huntington's disease 71

Ickes, Mrs. Harold 170
Idaho 129
Illinois, Bloomington 142
Illinois, Congerville 87, 89
Illinois, Danvers 86, 87
Illinois, East Washington Church 88
Illinois, Evanston 188
Illinois, Meadows 85, 90
Illinois, Meadows Home 90
Illinois, Peoria 89
Illinois, Rock Creek 88
Illinois, Science Ridge Church 188
Illinois, Stephenson County 187
Illinois, Sterling 95, 188
Illinois, Summerfield 21, 75, 125, 137, 227
Illinois, Urbana 141
Illinois, Washington 86, 87
Illinois Wesleyan University 142
India 22, 75, 105, 108, 112, 128, 129, 178, 187, 218, 261
India, Bethesda Leprosy Home Church 260
India, Bihar 255
India, Cape Comorin 132
India, Champa 221, 255
India, Champa Church 259
India, Darjeeling 132, 224
India, Delhi 133
India, Golden Jubilee 132
India, Himalayas 133
India, Jabalpur 258
India, Jagdeeshpur 221
India, Janjgir 257
India, Katni 257
India, Kodaikanal School 129
India, Korba 219, 255, 259
India, Landour 219
India, Ludhiana 257, 259
India, Madras 130
India, Mauhadih 221
India, Mussoorie 222, 224
India, Old Bengal 255
India, Sagar 258
India, Sarguji 257
India, Vellore Medical College 132
India, Woodstock School 133, 222, 223
Indian Americans 13, 22
Indiana, Adams County 29, 149
Indiana, Berne 10, 13, 30, 32, 41, 49, 107, 110, 149
Indiana, Berne First Church 152, 264
Indiana, Elkhart 183

Indiana, Elkhart Hively Avenue Church 184
Indiana, Goshen 184, 191
Indiana, Goshen Eighth Street Church 192, 332, 335
Indiana, Linn Grove Mennonites 149
Indiana University 332
Indiana, Woodburn 92
Indianapolis 161
Interdenominational Deaconess Home and Hospital 75
In the Service of the King 81
Iowa 137
Iowa, Ames 300
Iowa, Donnellson 300, 306
Iowa, Donnellson Zion Church 300
Iowa, Lee County 227
Iowa, Pulaski 24
Iowa State Teachers College 300
Iowa State University 300
Iowa, West Point 125, 300
Iraq 143
Italy, Rome 129

Jacobs, Arthur Leslie 229
Jacobs, Ruth Krehbiel 227-33
Jantzen, Albert 58
Jantzen, Anna 59
Jantzen, Anna Wiebe 55-60
Jantzen, Aron 130
Jantzen, Daniel 57
Jantzen, Frank F. 57
Jantzen, Kathryn 130
Jantzen, Lubin 59
Jantzen, Mary 58
Jantzen, Minna 58
Jantzen, Oswald 58
Jantzen, Ruth 59
Janzen, George P., Sr. 70
Janzen, Helene 60
Janzen, Pete 104
Janzen, Susanna 101
Japan, Yokohama 130
Juhnke, Anna Kreider 240, 331
Junior Messenger 315

Kansas, Burrton 139
Kansas, Fort Leavenworth 141
Kansas, Garden Township Church 127, 218
Kansas, Goessel 23, 74, 76, 225
Kansas, Halstead 74, 127, 137
Kansas, Halstead Krehbieltown 139

Kansas, Harvey County 139
Kansas, Hesston 127
Kansas, Hillsboro 57, 114, 251
Kansas, Moundridge 140, 264
Kansas, Newton 23, 51, 57, 76, 139, 142, 219, 261, 264, 271, 331
Kansas, Newton First Church 24, 81, 139, 144
Kansas, North Newton 225, 235
Kansas, North Newton Bethel College Church 144, 147, 211, 240, 272
Kauffman Museum 50, 319
Kaufman, Edmund G. 141, 192
Kaufman, Edna Ramseyer 241
Kaufman, Frieda Marie 4, 23, 45, 73-83
Kaufman, John 73, 74
Kaufman, Marie Egle 73
Kaufmann, Maurice 120, 124
Keepers of the Sacred Hat 317
Kentucky 119
kindergarten 137
King Edward's Medical School 258
King, Joe 87
Kings School of Oratory 97
Kingsview Mental Hospital 113
Kinsinger, Bertha Elise. *See* Petter, Bertha Elise Kinsinger.
Kinsinger, Helen Kennel 43
Kinsinger, Joseph 43
Kinsinger, Mike 88
Klassen, Katja 294
Kliewer, Emma Ruth 32
Kliewer, J. W. 32, 107, 140, 152
Koontz, Bessie 114
Koontz, Elbert 113
Koontz, Esther Ruth Schroeder 113, 114
Koontz, Louise Schroeder 113
Kope, Ruth Dettweiler 128
Krehbiel, August 299
Krehbiel, Christian 74, 137, 139, 145
Krehbiel, Corrine 233
Krehbiel, Elva Agnes. *See* Leisy, Elva Agnes Krehbiel.
Krehbiel, H. P. 135, 143
Krehbiel, Henry J. 35, 138, 227
Krehbiel, Jacob E. 227